DANCE AND ACTIVISM

DANCE AND ACTIVISM

A Century of Radical Dance Across the World

Dana Mills

BLOOMSBURY ACADEMIC
LONDON • NEW YORK • OXFORD • NEW DELHI • SYDNEY

BLOOMSBURY ACADEMIC
Bloomsbury Publishing Plc
50 Bedford Square, London, WC1B 3DP, UK
1385 Broadway, New York, NY 10018, USA
29 Earlsfort Terrace, Dublin 2, Ireland

BLOOMSBURY, BLOOMSBURY ACADEMIC and the Diana logo are
trademarks of Bloomsbury Publishing Plc

First published in Great Britain 2021
Paperback edition published 2022
Reprinted 2023

Copyright © Dana Mills, 2021, 2022

Dana Mills has asserted her right under the Copyright, Designs and Patents
Act, 1988, to be identified as Author of this work.

For legal purposes the Acknowledgments on pp. x–xvi constitute an
extension of this copyright page.

Cover design by Jade Barnett
Cover image © Henrik Sorensen / Getty Images

All rights reserved. No part of this publication may be reproduced or transmitted in any form or by
any means, electronic or mechanical, including photocopying, recording, or any information storage
or retrieval system, without prior permission in writing from the publishers.

Bloomsbury Publishing Plc does not have any control over, or responsibility for, any third-party
websites referred to or in this book. All internet addresses
given in this book were correct at the time of going to press. The author
and publisher regret any inconvenience caused if addresses have
changed or sites have ceased to exist, but can accept no
responsibility for any such changes.

A catalogue record for this book is available from the British Library.

Library of Congress Cataloging-in-Publication Data

Names: Mills, Dana, 1981– author.

Title: Dance and activism : a century of radical dance across the world / Dana Mills.
Description: London, UK ; New York, NY : Bloomsbury Academic, 2021. | Includes bibliographical
references and index. | Summary: "This study focuses on dance as an activist practice in and of
itself, across geographical locations and over the course of a century, from 1920 to 2020. Through
doing so, it considers how dance has been an empowering agent for political action throughout
civilisation. Dance and Activism offers a glimpse of different strategies of mobilizing the human
body for good and justice for all, and captures the increasing political activism epitomized by bodies
moving on the streets in some of the most turbulent political situations. This has, most recently,
undoubtedly been partly owing to the rise of the far-right internationally, which has marked an
increase in direct action on the streets. Offering a survey of key events across the century, such as
the fall of President Zuma in South Africa; pro-reproductive rights action in Poland and Argentina;
and the recent women's marches against Donald Trump's presidency, you will see how dance has
become an urgent field of study. Key geographical locations are explored as sites of radical dance
– the Lower East Side of New York; Gaza; Syria; Cairo; Iran; Iraq; Johannesburg – to name but a few
– and get insights into some of the major figures in the history of dance, including Pearl Primus,
Martha Graham, Anna Sokolow and Ahmad Joudah. Crucially, lesser or unknown dancers, who have
in some way influenced politics, all over the world are brought into the limelight (the Syrian
ballerinas and Hussein Smko, for example). Dance and Activism troubles the boundary between
theory and practice, while presenting concrete case studies as a site for robust theoretical
analysis"—Provided by publisher.
Identifiers: LCCN 2020045161 (print) | LCCN 2020045162 (ebook) |
ISBN 9781350137011 (hardback) | ISBN 9781350137028 (epub) | ISBN 9781350137035 (epub)
Subjects: LCSH: Dance—Political aspects. | Dance and globalization. |
Human body—Political aspects. | Political art.
Classification: LCC GV1588.45 .M55 2021 (print) | LCC GV1588.45 (ebook) | DDC 792.8—dc23
LC record available at https://lccn.loc.gov/2020045161
LC ebook record available at https://lccn.loc.gov/2020045162

ISBN:	HB:	978-1-3501-3701-1
	PB:	978-1-3503-2169-4
	ePDF:	978-1-3501-3702-8
	eBook:	978-1-3501-3703-5

Typeset by RefineCatch Limited, Bungay, Suffolk
Printed and bound in Great Britain

To find out more about our authors and books visit www.bloomsbury.com
and sign up for our newsletters.

This book was written for all dancers who work to make the world a better place.

And especially my friends, Leah Cox and Blakeley White-McGuire.

Dedicated to the memory of my father, Harold Mills.

This is not the end but only the beginning of the struggle ... We must not be like some Christians who sin for six days and go to church on the seventh, but we must speak for the cause daily, and make the men, and especially the women that we meet, come into the ranks to help us.

ELEANOR MARX, 1890

CONTENTS

List of Illustrations   ix

Preface and Acknowledgments   x

**1   IF WE CAN'T DANCE, WE DON'T WANT TO BE
PART OF YOUR REVOLUTION**   1

Alienation   7

Solidarity   10

Method   19

2   PRELUDE TO ACTION   27

Martha Graham: Embodied Chronicle   28

"Go Ahead and be a Bastard": Anna Sokolow   42

"Through Dance I Have Experienced the Wordless Joy of
Freedom": Pearl Primus   53

Dance as Intervention, Dance as Action   64

3   BALLET BEYOND BORDERS   65

"No One is Born Hating Another Person Because of the Color of
his Skin"   68

"Going around the House Like a Butterfly"   72

Ballet, Home, Syria   75

The Canon Must be Fired! Ballet and the Long Arc of
History   80

There is Only Now: Radical Ballet Going Forward   86

4   ERBIL/NEW YORK CITY: BREAK/DANCE   89

The Body in Battle   89

Those Who Leave and Those Who Stay   92

Not Just for You, But for the Rest of the Earth   96

Ballade of Belonging   98

At the Still Point of the Turning World 101
Break/Dance: Echoing Further: Erbil 106

5 STEPS IN THE STREET: REVOLUTION DJ 109

Dance on the March 109
The People (Dancing) United Can Never be Defeated 110
Dancing Onwards! 126

6 DANCE AS A HOME 129

Transitions 131
Home, Exile, Words, Movement 135
Arriving 140
Storytelling 142
Unraveling 145
Homelessness–Devastation–Exile 148

7 SPECTRE, HAUNTING 151

Notes 169
Bibliography 189
Index 195

LIST OF ILLUSTRATIONS

Martha Graham in "Spectre—1914" from "Chronicle"	23
Emma Goldman addressing a rally in support of birth control at Union Square, 1916	28
Concert program for the Martha Graham Dance Company at the Guild Theatre, December 20, 1936	30
Martha Graham Dance Company in "Steps in the Street" from "Chronicle"	39
US choreographer Anna Sokolow instructs a class at the Dance Company of NSW, Woolloomooloo	45
Dancer Pearl Primus performing	54
Palestinian girls take part in a ballet class at Qattan Centre for the Child in Gaza City November 10, 2015	74
Daily life in Erbil	95
Hussein Smko and Amanita Jean in the duet "Antoinette," Battery Dance Festival 2019	102
Women wearing a yellow vest (*gilet jaune*) dance and hold banners in Le Mans, on January 13, 2019	114
Palestinians perform a traditional folk dance called "dabke" in Khan Yunis, Gaza on October 10, 2018	119
Martha Graham in "Spectre—1914" from "Chronicle"	152
Leslie Andrea Williams in "Spectre—1914" from "Chronicle", 2019	158
Blakeley White-McGuire dances at Socrates Park, New York City, 2019	166

PREFACE AND ACKNOWLEDGMENTS

On a clear September day in 2016, I boarded a flight to JFK in order to take up a fellowship in the New York University Center for Ballet and the Arts. I was awaiting the publication of my first book, a conceptual study of dance and politics, due two months later. My fellowship was to be spent inquiring after ballet beyond the West, looking at various documentation showing how ballet was danced around the world.

As an activist raised in the pro-Palestinian Israeli left which I joined when I was thirteen, I was breathing a sigh of relief. The vote to leave the European Union, which had shaken the UK just three months before I was pondering my new beginning, had drained energies from progressives on both sides of the debate. I was secretly relieved to be escaping its aftermath, without knowing what New York City would offer me (I had only visited it very briefly before, and was always overwhelmed).

Little did I know that the election of Donald Trump to the White House, two months after I had arrived, would shake up the way that America perceived itself and how everyone else saw its position in the world. Little did I know, also, that I would be joining a now-historic Women's March a few days after the November election, and organizing another anti-Trump march a month later.

This book was born out of an urgency galvanizing people around the world to reflect upon the position of the arts, and dance specifically, in a time of rising tensions and divisions, of the election of reactionary leaders to parliamentary institutions, but also in times of rising organization and activism. The beginning of the twenty-first century saw waves of protest— around different causes and within different contexts—bodies were marching on the street, together. And those moving bodies galvanized questions of the place of dance within this new wave of activism.

This book enquires into what it means to be radical in dance; how do our new forms of activism relate to those that occurred in the course of the twentieth century, and what is the responsibility and the mission of the twentieth century dancer-activist? The book uses diverse case studies from around the globe, centering the movement and words of dancer-activists themselves, telling their stories, which are different but also share a similar characteristic: the belief that dance can and will make the world a better place, and that it is especially urgent in dark times.

This book is an unashamedly activist text, which sees writing as a mode of praxis, of radical being in the world. The collapse of categories of "objectivity" within the political discourse pushes writers in all fields of thought to reflect upon their role as scribes. Thus, selecting case studies that are anti-racist, anti-sexist, and asking for more humanity—challenging the status quo rather than freezing old traditions or settling for a dire present—led the selective assortment in the text. The book is a text about activism that also queries the challenges of chronicling the now; how our present time reflects the century that has passed, and how we may write about the art of now—dance—as a way in to reflecting on writing about activism in the present. The book utilizes a range of methodologies: interviews, participation in events, and historiographic and archival research. The book was born out of necessity; of cases and ideas that came to me in various modes of conversation, through intimate time spent in the studio, attending public events, researching in libraries, and examining the ever-changing present. Every book is by its nature incomplete, yet this one felt at the same time urgent to write and constantly expanding in the range of information and case studies that fed into its argument. More than anything the book was written about the dancer-activists who spin its argument, and for all those who believe dance can and must work to make a better tomorrow.

The book is at once indebted to generous institutional support and intimate friendships that enabled its writing.

Part of the argument of this work is that radicalism necessitates a supportive environment to rise and be sustained. It has been a great pleasure working with Bloomsbury/Methuen, and in particular Meredith Benson, who has understood the ethos of the book and its praxis from its beginning. The biggest of thanks go to my editor, Anna Brewer, a visionary whose brave work is opening up new spaces and conversations in dance where they would otherwise not happen. She is an inspiration and an important part of the argument of this book.

I am deeply indebted to the Center for Ballet and the Arts at New York University (NYU) where I was a resident fellow in the fall of 2016. It is from that space that this work emerged. Thank you Andrea Salvatore, the praxis at the zenith of CBA, for never-ending kindness and truly inspirational work. Thank you to the visionary work of Jennifer Homans; it has been a joy and a privilege sharing an intellectual space, and a deep thank you for opening a space for all who care for the beauty of ballet in our fast-changing world. Thank you to my fellow fellows: John Heigenbotham, Jonah Bokaer, Debra Levine, Meryl Rosofksy, Melissa Klapper, and Emily Coates for transformative conversations. Thank you to my office-mate Dana Caspersen for conversations about praxis and love for ballet. A very special thank you goes to Pam Tanowitz, whose own work captures the sublime and brings me hope in dark times, for introducing me to Anna Sokolow and for visionary work that has changed the way I understand movement.

I have had the great fortune to be in conversation with the Martha Graham Dance Company since 2012. Marnie Thomas Wood, a pioneer and an important inspiration in her own right, has opened up for me the richness and depth of Graham's work. Her interpretations and passion have left a mark on my understanding of dance—and Graham—forever. Jennifer Patten, Director of the Graham School, for solidarity, generosity, and for sharing her vision as well as practice in my own time in the school in 2016—thank you.

Special gratitude goes to Oliver Tobin, director of resources at Graham, for his guidance and generosity which enabled me to continue Graham conversations across all oceans. His work is transforming the Graham archives and enabling so much new research to emerge.

A very deep thank you goes to Janet Eilber, Artistic Director of the Graham Company, whose visionary work is opening up new vistas for the Graham legacy and dance more broadly to reach many new hearts. Our conversations never failed to show me endless perspectives of Graham's work in history and performance, but Ms. Eilber's interpretation, passion, and commitment to hold the radicalism of Graham's work in practice has pushed me to do the best I can to do the same in writing.

Kim Jones's pioneering work on "Chronicle" has broken new grounds in the study of the work, and her reading is a significant interpretation that has transformed the reading of the work. I am deeply grateful for a year of truly inspiring Graham classes in London.

Thank you to Samantha Geracht, Artistic Director of the Anna Sokolow Company, Sokolow stalwart sorority symbol, for talking patiently through Anna Sokolow's work, for being an exemplar of her humanity, and for discussions of the challenges but also the never-ending grace of presenting work about humanity and for humanity.

xii   PREFACE AND ACKNOWLEDGMENTS

Jennifer Conley has generously shared her deep understanding of the transformative power of dance beyond centuries and has been a role model and exemplar of ethics in practice and theory throughout the process of writing.

Thank you to Kim Segel for talking with me about the Johannesburg Youth Ballet and sharing her own experiences generously.

Phil Chan's visionary work is transforming the understanding of ballet in the twenty-first century. Thank you for sharing your ethos in conversation and example.

Jonathan Hollander has painstakingly sustained and opened up activist spaces for dance for many years. His generosity and example enabled the work of so many to prevail in dark times. Thank you for sharing your ethos in conversation and for always opening up new spaces by facilitating conversations and connections.

Hussein Smko's generosity in friendship and in art is beyond measure, and it has been a true privilege to chronicle his work in Chapter 4 of this book. Thank you for sharing your world and your art without borders and always insisting on the power of dance and humanity. Amanita Jean has reminded me of the power of dance to connect and bring people together; thank you for sharing your art and story so generously.

Thank you to Dahlia Scheindlin and especially Amjad Iraqi, for work on an earlier version of analysis of the dabke and for allowing me to use it after it had been published in 972 Mag.

Thank you to all artists discussed in Chapter 5 for sharing their work generously; Sivan Rubinstein, (and Dr. Sarah Fine for facilitating this connection and for her example and generosity), Simon Birch and Isabel Cuecha Camacho, who has spoken openly and inspiringly on the process of creating "Impronte" and performing it over a duration of time.

A deep and special thank you goes to Marina Warner, whose ethical exemplar has often sustained some hope for me in my own moments of darkness, and it has been transformative encountering her visionary work.

It has been a humbling experience and unique experience having a vista into the Stories in Transit project, (and especially Hannah Machover), truly a unique ray of light in very dark times.

Most beloved Graham Crackers, Diane Auriol, Kristen Hedbgerg, Yuting Zhao, for never-ending conversation on thinking of dance history, dance praxis, and Martha Graham around the world. You are an example. Megan Curet—a chance meeting in London transformed my life in New York, how

I understood dance, social justice, and choreography. Thank you for your example and inspiration and never-ending generosity. Leslie Andrea Williams, for inspiration and for sharing with me so generously your art and the really special moments in dance history that you are creating. Diane Cavero for conversations about "Chronicle" and for living the praxis, and for a truly galvanizing workshop at the Royal Academy of Dance.

I met Andrea Weber too late in this project for her to suffer its full consequences but it would not have been completed without her example of integrity and care for the world through dance. I thank the dice that conjured Ms. Weber's introduction into my life. Thank you to the Wednesday and Friday Cunningham crew: Anna Chlenova, De'Ondre Goodley and Emmalee Hallinan for solidarity in dark times and for all the bounces.

My understanding of social justice has been indebted to transformative conversations in which I was lucky to partake. Thanks go to Jeanne Morefield for reminding me that it is always a good idea to revisit Edward Said and for being an exemplar of integrity in writing and action. Jodi Dean, for paving the way for radicalism to exist in theory and for generosity in conversation and example. Amelia Horgan, whose work is pioneering a new thread of radicalism in feminist philosophy, for writing solidarity when I needed it the most. Sarah-Emily Duff, who sets a high bar for integrity, for facilitating new conversations for me and always expanding how I understand justice in the world. Bridget Kibbey for sublime music, sisterhood of steel and pink bubbles, always.

A very special thank you goes to dance and political theory sister Glory Liu, who read the entire manuscript and pushed me to think further. Her own work and commitment to rigor in dance and political theory has changed my conceptions of the field.

This book is firmly rooted in activist praxis and would not have been written without conversations with my activist crew. Alon-Lee Green and Sally Abed of Standing Together, a pioneering socialist Jewish–Palestinian social justice movement, reminded me that where there is struggle there is hope. Shaqued Morag, General Secretary of Peace Now, the movement in which I grew up since the age of thirteen, is sustaining a vision of peace in hard times. My work on Eleanor Marx has taught me of those who are sustaining and furthering her ethos on the ground in the GMB, a union she founded in 1889 as the National Gas Workers and General Workers Union. Jan Wadrup, for insisting on socialism of the heart and always being kind. Start Richards for work on Eleanor's 165th birthday party and

xiv PREFACE AND ACKNOWLEDGMENTS

for your solidarity (and for all the cats). David Hamblin, who works tirelessly to preserve and further Eleanor's ethos in the GMB and outside of it. Sarah James, winner of the 2018 Eleanor Marx award for outstanding trade unionist in the GMB: you are an example of Eleanor's work. Thank you for never-ending sisterhood. Barbara Plant, president of the GMB, for furthering Eleanor's work in your own vision.

In February 2020, the Oxford Think Human festival hosted an evening I produced and curated on the theme of dancing human rights. My thanks to all that enabled this to happen: Gary Browning, and especially Thomas Andersen and Laura Baldock, who live the praxis of thinking and being better human beings in their daily work. Thank you to all the artists who shared their work: Body Politic, Eliot Smith Dance and Blakeley White-McGuire. Emmy Touslon, generously shared her spirit and ethos with me on the evening and in the process of writing. Michelle Coringdton-Rogers, an exemplar of humanity and generosity, teaches me every day.

This work came into being through many meetings with dancers, rehearsals classes, and conversations. Thank you to the American Dance Festival for opening a space for conversation about solidarity, for the generosity of all who shared their time and insight. A special thank you to Cecilia Whalen, my Graham and Baldwin friend, and to Amber Johnson, for friendship, inspiration, and for always dancing ahead with me.

In December 2019 I was able to present this book at Maison Nouvelle de Recherche Paris 3-Sorbonne Nouvelle. Thank you to the organizers of the conference, Ceclie Schnek, Mary Christine Devinau, and Rafael Molina. Special thank you to the students of act dance studio for conversations over my stay in Paris and beyond it.

It takes a lot of chuzpah to write a book that sees itself as a first. Many visionaries have paved the way for these dancing steps to follow.

Lisa Appignanesi, for generosity, uncompromising rigor and understanding of beauty and justice in the world, intertwined, for inspiration and for sustaining a vision for the role of writing in dark \times.

Shami Chakrabarti: visionary, trailblazer, exemplar of integrity, for her work that galvanizes and inspires, and that ensures that all are free and can equally share the beauty of the world.

Rachel Holmes, unwavering role model in writing and action, for deep understanding and unflinching commitment to justice in words and deeds, generosity, inspiration, and for opening the space to Go Ahead.

This book was written against a lot of challenges and would not have been written without the never-ending generosity of friends and family. Tamara Sharon-Ross—you are my example of all that is good in the world. Lee Peled has shared a barre and friendship with me for over twenty years, and inspires me every day. Yoni Bar On for always being there and enriching my life. Adi Shoham, for always understanding justice deeply and being the most generous of friends.

Nothing would be possible without my family. My aunt, Tirza Posner, understands the power of beauty in the world and supports me in never-ending generosity. Thank you for Walter Benjamin and conversations about ballet. My mother, Gabriella Mills, is my exemplar of resilience and kindness, and has been my example in standing up to what is right since I can remember myself.

This book was written for those who are doing the actual work of social justice through dance. It is a book about the dancers, for the dancers. Most specifically it would not have been written without the friendship and conversation of two women. Leah Cox, in her visionary work in the American Dance Festival, is opening up new spaces of solidarity, insists on humanity in example and theory, and is my role-model in radical dance. Blakeley White-McGuire, your work in all avenues has transformed the way I understood dance and humanism, ethics and integrity. I cannot put my thanks to both of you in words. I owe you bubbles.

This book is dedicated to the memory of my father, Harold Mills. He taught me how to love dance, how to understand people, how to always try to be a better person, and to see my responsibility toward those around me. I miss him more than I can ever put in words but every dance I'll ever dance will always be for him.

All mistakes and errors are my own.

1 IF WE CAN'T DANCE, WE DON'T WANT TO BE PART OF YOUR REVOLUTION

"*If I can't dance, I don't want to be part of your revolution*": a misquote from one of the twentieth century's most influential activists and thinkers, Emma Goldman, has become a popular slogan for placards and tea towels. "Red Emma", the anarchist who was imprisoned for her advocacy for contraceptive rights and whose lifelong resentment toward capitalist structures of power, who arrived on the shores of America, a poor refugee working in sweatshops herself, provides a more useful way of elucidating the theory of this book in the actual instance she recalled in her autobiography, *Living my Life*:

> I threw myself into the work with all the ardour of my being and I became absorbed in it to the exclusion of everything else. My task was to get the girls in the trade to join the strike. For that purpose, meetings, concerts, socials, and dances were organized ... At the dances I was one of the most untiring and gayest. One evening a cousin of Sasha, a young boy, took me aside. With a grave face, as if he were about to announce the death of a dear comrade, he whispered to me that it did not behoove an agitator to dance. Certainly not with such reckless abandon, anyway. It was undignified for one who was on the way to become a force in the anarchist movement. My frivolity would only hurt the Cause. I grew furious at the impudent interference of the boy. I told him to mind his own business, I was tired of having the Cause constantly thrown into my face. I did not believe that a Cause which stood for a beautiful ideal, for anarchism, for release and freedom

from conventions and prejudice, should demand the denial of life and joy. I insisted that our Cause could not expect me to become a nun and that the movement should not be turned into a cloister. If it meant that, I did not want it. I want freedom, the right to self-expression, everybody's right to beautiful, radiant things. Anarchism meant that to me, and I would live it in spite of the whole world—prisons, persecution, everything. Yes, even in spite of the condemnation of my own closest comrades I would live my beautiful ideal.[1]

Returning to the origins of the quotation here is crucial not only to correct false histories and misquoting of radical women, but because the actual statement by Goldman very much sits at the heart of the ethos of this book. Emma Goldman's dedication to the cause—and to dancing—is the underpinning argument of this book: the inextricability of dance from agitation, and especially seeing dance as activism and movement as a lived ideal. This has been an underlying narrative of politics, especially in the turbulent twentieth century. The book starts from asking the question: How do people live their beautiful ideal as activism through dance?

This is a book about dance and activism, or rather about dance *as* activism. The book is about women and men who believe that dance can serve the beauty of their causes. This book pursues a theoretical argument as well as a historical argument. First, it aims to place center stage the work of artists who see dance as essential work toward bringing forth a better future in different corners of the world. The book aims to show how historical interventions that burst into the world a hundred years ago resonate today, at the closing of the second decade of the twentieth century.

This is a book about the *praxis* of radicals. It is a book about failures as well as successes, it is a book about rehearsals and walking to and from rehearsals, about strikes and about sit-ins, about birthday parties and break-ups and tears and happiness; all those elements which are part of everyday life of a dancer-activist. The book focuses on dance that was able to project a vision for a better world, at times, or to trouble what seems as unavoidable justice at others. The book focuses on a century that commences in the 1920s and ends as we enter the year 2020. These are not coincidental choices, but rather two placeholders or unique moments of history in which people rose and took to the streets to claim their rights. This book does not attempt to provide a comprehensive theory of activism; its understanding is that dance, like activism, holds unique power by providing its agents with extra-verbal meaning. The book is a chronicle of the times that have passed, of the dances that have been danced, and of the processes that are galvanized and yet beginning. The book returns to the concept of action that is central to political and critical theory and is at the heart of the concept of activism.

This book is a first. There are no conceptual or theoretical studies of dance and activism for it to rely on, and in so being it proposes ideas that, it is hoped, will be taken by many others and developed in their own modes of thinking. The book and its specific analytical, theoretical, and political premises arise from a burning and timely theoretical aporia.

The field of writing on dance and politics has been fast expanding beyond its founding moment. Randy Martin's work in the field as well as Mark Franko's ongoing contributions in the world of dance studies have been significant. Alexandra Kolb's book *Dance and Politics*[2] from 2011 added much needed layers to the study of these two worlds. The *Oxford Handbook of Dance and Politics*[3] was a significant intervention in the field of the study of dance and politics; collecting and collating the work of the most profound and important scholars in dance studies into a handbook is an intervention and creation of a canonical resource. Most importantly for the ideas behind this book, *Dance, Human Rights and Social Justice*[4] was a specific look at how ethical and political burning issues are handled through dance, though in the form of a collected volume.

Important interventions challenging the white and male dominance of the field came from manifold sources (and in fact, as this book shows, have always been present both in the field of dance practice as well as writing). It is crucial to cite here Thomas DeFranz's *Dancing Many Drums*[5] as well as Thomas DeFranz and Anita Gonzales' *Black Performance Theory* (2014).[6] Brenda Dixon Gottschild's *The Black Dancing Body* (2003)[7] brought center stage voices that had shaped black dance, but most profoundly, dance, as the book highlights the significant place black dance has in American dance. Jacqueline Shea-Murphy's *The People Have Never Stopped Dancing* (2007)[8] discusses Native American dance over the past thirty years. These are all important interventions in dance writing; however, it might be significant to highlight that nearly all center on American dance from various perspectives.

In political theory the work of Erin Manning[9] and Carrie Noland brought discussions of the body to political theory, much in the context of what was then termed "the embodied turn," galvanized by the

IF WE CAN'T DANCE   3

pioneering work of Jane Bennett.[10] However, none of these studies aimed to look at activism and indeed the focus on "politics" as a field of study allowed for competing interpretations of politics as a field of study and action, and most of them weren't derived from the agents studied themselves, the dancers. Moreover, all these works occurred before the major political upheavals that galvanized the arguments of this book occurred.

This book responds more strongly to a different strand in contemporary writing coming out of political theory, radical theory, and radical democratic theory. Whereas politics continues to be discussed by scholars who do not settle upon definitions of concepts such as justice, equality, and democracy, these issues have moved to being discussed on the streets and on the march. Events unfolding around the world and especially in Anglo-America from 2016 have forced theorists and scholars to reconsider their approaches to politics, in theory and practice. These processes have been ongoing in many circles for a long time, specifically in fields of study such as African-American studies or Women's Studies, which had seen themselves as antagonistic to the method and ethos of detached reflective thinking sitting at the heart of Western philosophy and political theory. However, the election of Donald Trump to the White House, the rise of right wing governments worldwide, and Britain's ongoing debates around leaving the European Union brought a force of urgency to academic work and life in circles that had been mostly sheltered from the need to take to the streets and reflect upon action from the position of those inducing it. From the women's marches in the USA, which galvanized a mass movement and return to direct action in the UK around Brexit, and in particular ongoing strikes in the higher education sector facilitated by the University and College Union (UCU), many academics in the Anglo-American world who had been theorizing about politics and its methods were forced to consider those as *praxis*. The owl of Minerva was beating her wings fast, and the time to withdraw and reflect using analytical disembodied constructs about questions of justice was running out.[11]

However, there are strands of change and responses to these processes in writing. Most have been initiated, perhaps unsurprisingly, by women, and within feminist studies; the long tradition of feminist action as theory and theory as action has generated new responses to the burning issues of our time. And so, this book, examining dance and activism, is a response to new strands of writing tapping into long-existing traditions

4　**DANCE AND ACTIVISM**

that had become very urgent. Bhattacharya, Fraser and Arruzza's *Feminism for the 99%: A Manifesto*,[12] Lola Olufemi's *Feminism, Interrupted*,[13] and Allison Phipps's *Me, not You: The Trouble with Mainstream Feminism* were a critical response to the rise of the #MeToo movement and return of feminism to be a hotly debated issue in action and theory. The collapse of Hilary Clinton's campaign and withering of hopes of the first woman president of the United States, together with normalizing of misogyny and sexism around the world, attacks on hard-won reproductive rights—those rights for which Emma Goldman gave energy and time (sometimes in prison); attacks on gender studies programs, on LGBTI+ people all brought questions of feminist strategy into the mainstream in a quick and dramatic arc. All these studies cited are a questioning of how much mainstream feminism, focused on representation and debates around legal structures, can aid in challenging these new attacks. Furthermore, all these studies question how structural inequalities and marginalization (including racism and anti-queer sentiment and discourse) within feminism itself hinder it from attaining its radical possibilities. Intersectional justice sits at the heart of this book's argument, and the critique issued in these books and others very much inform my own theoretical approach.

Another profound theoretical inspiration for this book is the longstanding radical work of Jodi Dean. Her *Communist Horizon* was a study of the Occupy movement and brought to discussion a grassroots activist uprising as a field of study. Her most recent intervention, *Comrade: An Essay on Political Belonging*,[14] asks about the use of comrade rather than ally in the context of the bigger context of solidarity and genuine partaking in struggles as active participant, not onlooker, which is the heart of this study of dance and activism. The move is, then, from politics to activism, from theory to praxis, from that which had passed and can be dissected and analyzed to that which unfolds in the now. There are many challenges and problematics that arise from this move, thus the analytical structure and the underlying assumptions of the study will be set out here.

And yet, reflecting on the many theoretical discussions that have galvanized thinking that led to this book, its motivation comes always from dancers. Martha Graham premiered her great call for humankind's responsibility to each other in the face of rising violence and war, *Chronicle*, in 1936. The work *Chronicle*, in Graham's time and understanding, as well as in those of the many generations who danced it, gives this book its organizing structure, spine, and impulse. Graham's understanding of dance as action is vital for this book's conceptual structure. Graham said "Theater is a verb before it is a noun, an act before it is a place."[15] Drawing on this constellation the book uses the term "chronicle" as a verb before it is a noun; a way of living rather than a title, praxis before it is a dance work. A central motivating question in this book is how do we chronicle radical action, in dance and word? What is the relationship between theory and action in remembrance in writing? How can the body tell stories about events unfolding in the here and now into a future we do not yet know? This is a tension that cannot be resolved in writing and leads to methodological implications. Radical dance understood as action includes within it a component that will only be understood in hindsight. Many of the case studies, or indeed historical case studies received, are unfolding in the very recent past, or the present in which the book is written. They will unfold further in the future—after the book has been written. Thus, an extra temporal-philosophical layer joins the argument, which queries writing about action that aims to take place in a future that has not arrived yet.

However, it is not the argument that theory is necessarily conservative, able to only write on events in the past and must accept its fate as such. The understanding of the term "radical" in the context of both the theory and action of this book draws on centering dance and the words of the agents themselves. The understanding is also of action that opens up vista for justice for more human beings; rather than radical movements that aim to undo those processes of democratization. In the context of the specific analytic framework with which the book works, radicals are seen as those who aim to provide themselves and those around them with the space and language to tell their stories in their own way. This is a key premise that will be revisited and probed throughout the book.

The book works in a conceptual framework that places the notion of praxis centrally. This concept has had various enunciations and articulations, though for my own reading two main sources are significant. First, and foremost, Karl Marx, in his *Theses on Feuerbach*, in the third thesis, where he writes:

> The materialistic doctrine concerning the changing and circumstances and education forgets that circumstances are changed by man and that the educator himself must be educated ... the coincidence of the

6 DANCE AND ACTIVISM

changing of circumstances and of human activity or self-changing can only be comprehended and rationally understood as revolutionary practice.[16]

In order to understand his articulation of praxis, one of the core issues that moves people to change their own lives, the problem of alienation, will be discussed next. My argument works within a conceptual tension between two core concepts: that of solidarity and that of alienation, where the former is the focus and the latter acts as its generative impulse. Praxis is conceptualized as the space between these two concepts (as will be elaborated in this chapter).[17] Praxis, drawing on Emma Goldman, entails living one's beautiful ideal; the ability to pursue radical imaginaries in an embodied shared experience, which in turn reconfigures shared futures. This definition is drawn from the case studies and will be revisited through them. However, the chapter now proceeds to interpret these concepts in the context of the argument. In order to present the underlying logic for the book's argument, I move into the analytical structure of the book here.

Alienation

The concept of alienation has long been debated within political theory and critical theory. Many studies and discussions have attempted to connect it to various fields, ideas, and traditions. An extensive and recent study by Frankfurt School–indebted Rahel Jaeggi brings the concept into the twenty-first century.[18] Jaeggi proceeds to define alienation as a problem—a relation of relationlessness.[19] Jaeggi argues that "alienation is a failure to apprehend, and a halting of, the movement of appropriation."[20] "Alienation is the inability to establish a relation to other human beings, to things, to social institutions and thereby also—so the fundamental intuition of the theory of alienation— to oneself."[21] She proceeds to locate two different traditions that gave rise to conceptual discussions of alienation: first, Marx, most fundamentally in the 1844 manuscripts, and second, Heidegger and the existentialist tradition that follows. For Marx, alienation is a disturbance of relationships that one has or could have to the world.[22] Marx poses the concept in his Economic and Philosophical Manuscripts of 1844, four years before his theses on Feuerbach that generated the focus on praxis. In a chapter entitled 'Estranged Labour' he discusses how the worker becomes himself a commodity and writes that "the worker is related to the product of his labor as to an alien object."[23] As humankind is creative and able to solve its problems through labor, and as people are able to connect to their peers and environment, alienation from labor leads to alienation from the self and society, too.[24] For Heidegger, alienation is a failure to apprehend what is "ready to hand" as "present to hand," along with a failure to apprehend the world as the totality of what is given rather than as a practical context.[25] Following from Heidegger's discussion and his emphasis on inauthenticity arises the concept of bad faith, the inability to exhaust agency, to be the story teller of one's own story and to withdraw one's voice from one's own action. Jaeggi revisits the discussion of alienation in both Heidegger and later, Sartre, in his conceptualization of "bad faith."[26] Sartre defined alienation as "being an other to oneself."[27] Whereas this book and argument do not rely on an Heideggerian-existentialist reading, the conceptualization of alienation through this tradition is indeed productive as it shifts the focus to the individual to make her own choices and create her own narrative. The creativity accentuated within existentialism is central to this book's argument too, and helpful to understand the different traditions' engagement with the concept of alienation.[28] Moreover, another author whose work responds to alienation of her time, drawing on and giving a collective reading to Heidegger's intervention, is Hannah Arendt. Together with Marx, Arendt saw the emphasis on Vita Contemplative as central to the tradition of writing of her time. Her quest to centralize the Vita Activa was the main impulse of her 1958 work *The Human Condition*. Whereas her own analysis will not be central to this book's argument, Arendt provides a useful layer when reflecting on relationships between art and activism in the face of alienation. Her emphasis on storytelling is vital for my own argument. The epigraph to her "Action" chapter is a line taken from Isaak Diensen: "All sorrows can be born if you put them into a story or tell a story about them."[29] In her own words she writes: "that every individual life between birth and death can eventually be told as a story with a beginning and end is the prepolitical and prehistorical condition of history, the great story without beginnings and end."[30] Arendt's famous insistence on the ability to reveal oneself in word and deed, as the quintessence of political act, is tied to the idea of the life story at the same time being the pre-condition for action as well as its zenith. The emphasis on storytelling is crucial for the reading of responses to alienation that will be presented in my own argument.

There are several problems that Jaeggi raises with regards to both these avenues and traditions of discussions of alienation. Most fundamental is the essentialist conception of human nature that underpins both these traditions. In order to be alienated from authentic being one assumes that an authentic being once exists and must be re-apprehended. Both Marx and Heidegger belong to traditions from a past world, which do not include thinking of intersectionality and how various oppressions can yield variants in our world and in the visions for justice one is able to project. Essentialist thinking drawing on metaphysical assumptions was part and parcel of their theories. Jaeggi discusses much of this problematic and yet her own discussion (and many others cited) suffer from further problems that will push the argument forward. She rephrases the problem in terms of a problem of willing[31] and use of the term "appropriation" as a form of praxis; "there is an interesting tension in the idea of appropriation between what is previously given and what is formable, between taking over and creating, between the subject's sovereignty and its dependence."[32] Jaeggi's discussion, drawing on the discussion of many of those who came before her, is a first and foremost philosophical discussion. The second part of Jaeggi's study is a discussion of four hypothetical case studies of alienation. The examination of philosophical discussions through hypothetical life stories is a reference to the tradition in which she is working—from Adorno to Sartre—yet generates a discussion of alienation that is not a problem of practice.

This book, focusing on activism, examines alienation as a practical, not philosophical problem. It agrees with Jaeggi's critique of the challenge of essentialism and moving away toward unraveling possibilities as responses to alienation. Yet these new stories in becoming, the book shows, are being told by activists in our world through tangible ways. The focus is on dance, as, it will be argued in the book, the body is both subject and object; both the material and the maker, the creation and the creator.

The working definition, then, drawing on these discussions of "alienation" that I utilize in the book is: Alienation: a condition by which through economic, social, and political conditions people cannot tell their own stories in their own voice. Alienation was chosen as an organizing concept due to its explanatory force, which allows us to understand why so many governments around the world have swayed to the right, providing authoritarian answers to existential questions and displaying inability to counter everyday alienation in an increasing neo-liberalized and capitalistic way of thinking. The underlying problematic of this book can be now stated: How do people work to overcome dislocation from themselves, their societies, and their work by telling their life stories through dance? Alienation is taken to be a problem of

IF WE CAN'T DANCE   9

praxis, a tension that facilitates other forms of connection. The concept of alienation hence is read in dialectical tension with that of solidarity.

Solidarity

In order to articulate the conceptualization of solidarity the argument returns to Marx, yet not Karl, but his daughter, Eleanor, whose life and work allow for a dialectical response to the problem of alienation that haunted both their lives and works, as indeed ours.

The source for this book's thinking of Eleanor's categories of action— and indeed my own introduction to her—is Rachel Holmes's 2014 biography, *Eleanor Marx: A Life*, that not only restored her to her rightful place as a giant of the international left, but asks questions about her omission from the canon. Eleanor was "the practice to her father's theory," Holmes shows forcefully throughout her work.[33]

Jenny Julia Eleanor Marx was born in 1855 while her father was working on *Das Kapital*, the book that would change social and economic theory forever. The youngest surviving child of Jenny and Karl, she was raised in an internationalist household with both her elder sisters, Laura and Jenny, conversing in French, her parents in German, and yet she, born in Dean Street, London, among the hustle and bustle of poor Victorian London, was the only Marx to be born in England. Her immigrant father turned to Shakespeare to improve his English, and Shakespeare became the Bible of her childhood home, with the family often enacting favorite scenes in the living room. Eleanor's passion for stage was developing alongside her sharp reasoning of the economic oppression that was the landscape of her childhood hinterlands—the theory of which was written across the wall when she was playing as a child. And yet, as opposed to her father, her initial impulse was to act as well as think, and she truly brought these two categories together in her work.

Eleanor Marx provides us with a blueprint of an activist that is as timely today as it was in the period in which she intervened. A brilliant economic and political theorist in her own right, Eleanor Marx was driven to organize and work in the world in order to alleviate the suffering that patriarchal capitalism inflicts on millions. Thus, she is taken here to be a prototype of an activist, *sui generis*, who may guide the argument forward. Holmes reflects how Eleanor's favorite motto, "Go Ahead,"[34] was

10 DANCE AND ACTIVISM

the underpinning narrative of her life's work; she sought to live the struggle that she reflected upon her entire life. Looking at Eleanor Marx's interventions in theory and practice the chapter moves to extract a concept of solidarity drawn from her work.

Eleanor Marx Aveling and Edward Aveling, her common-law husband, published *The Woman Question (from a Socialist Point of View)* in 1886 after writing it in 1885.[35] For Eleanor Marx, writing was a way to overcome the injustices of her present, never just for herself, but for women and men like her, in her time as well as in a future she did not yet know. Her writing was not disengaged from her work as an organizer but rather stemmed from and responded to it.

"The position of women rests, as everything in our complex modern society rests, on an economic basis."[36] This is the zenith of the argument, presented clearly at the first point of theoretical intervention. "The woman question is one of economics, and one of organization of society as a whole."[37] Treating the position of woman without seeking the cause of it in economics is treating the symptom rather than the disease, she explains to her reader. This is the radical spirit of Eleanor Marx in all its force, which allows us a vista into her understanding of the concept of radicalism and its implications toward understanding temporality. Marx does not want to see little tweaks and amendments to current society under arguments that will be known as lesser evil; she works to overhaul the current world toward a society in which all human beings are free and equal. Her action is grounded in the present and yet works toward a future she does not yet know.

"There is no more a *natural calling* of woman than there is a natural law of capitalistic production, or a *natural* limit to the amount of the laborer's product that goes to him for means of subsistence."[38] Here, Marx moves into her clear, powerful exposition of structural oppression.

And first, a general idea that has to do with all women. The life of woman does not coincide with that of man. Their lives do not intersect. In many cases do not even touch. Hence the life of the race is stunted. According to Kant, "a man and a woman constitute, when united, the whole and entire being; one sex completes the other". But when each sex is incomplete, and the one incomplete to the most lamentable extent, and when, as a rule, neither of them comes into real, thorough, habitual free contact, mind to mind, with the other, the being is neither whole nor entire.[39]

Thinking of this statement in the context of Jaeggi's definition of "alienation" as inability to establish relationships to others and to oneself, we see a conceptual connection here between alienation and structural oppression (which sat at the heart of both Karl's and Eleanor's work). However, for an activist, this statement was not the end but the beginning of thinking of alienation and oppression and, moreover, of responses to it. At the heart of any radical change, only through addressing structural oppressions in an overarching action will free and equal human beings be able to have intercourse devoid of violence in the home and outside of it. To answer the woman question one must overhaul society radically and consider the multiplicity of spheres of life influenced by sexual oppression. All parts of life should be examined in order to overhaul our current oppressions and work toward a better tomorrow.

Beyond the specific context of the text and its underpinning core problematic, this is a forceful articulation of structural oppression. Lives that do not intersect, phenomenological experiences that do not meet in the everyday, are the deepest evil those fighting for progressive politics must counter. This is also the hardest challenge as there is a lack of lived knowledge of another's oppression and conditions that bring about alienation in the twenty-first century. But this means that in a society sustaining oppression and allowing lives to lack intersection, in Eleanor Marx's time as in our times, "the life of the race is stunted." The work of progressive politics is to transcend those divisions and show how human beings are implicated in each other's fate.

Marx continues to present her position and vision for socialist-feminism: "women, once more like the laborers, have been expropriated as to their rights as human beings, just as the laborers were expropriated as to their rights as producers. The method in each case is the only one that makes expropriation at any time and under any circumstances possible—and that method is force."[40] In order to understand this statement better, it can be read together with this argument later in the text: "we disguise neither from ourselves nor from our antagonists that the first step to this is the expropriation of all private property in land and in all other means of production. With this would happen the abolition of the State *as it is now*."[41] Marx knew that radical struggles must take into account the lives of those who mobilize within them in the here and now. She was one of the founders of the National Union of Gas Workers and General Labourers in 1889, still fighting strongly today for equality and justice as the GMB union. Eleanor Marx defends a radical vision of social democracy but steers away from authoritative tendencies within the left as well as anarchism. And yet, her focus is always on collective action, on working together to overhaul oppressive structures toward a radical future unraveling in her actions here and now.

It is worthwhile pausing on the construction of the argument and Marx's careful crafting of quotations throughout the text. After referencing Engels she quotes from Shakespeare,[42] Mill on marriage (while criticizing his lack of understanding of economics),[43] Shelley,[44] Mary Wollstonecraft on the need for equal access to education,[45] Henrik Ibsen,[46] her friend Olive Schreiner's heroine of the novel *Story of an African Farm*, Lyndall Gordon,[47] Tennyson,[48] and Isabella Beecher Hooker.[49] Here we see the brilliance of Marx's mind as well as her intellectual voyage at its clearest. Only a polyphony of voices allows her to show all sources from which she draws and thinks. Marx understood the radical power of culture. In her own work she mobilized that radical power and here she crafts it effortlessly into her theory. Literature and theater are never disengaged from writing and organizing; they are a way to understand other periods and other places, as well as to mobilize lessons learnt from them for a better world for all. Mill and Engels are crucial for her understanding of feminism, and yet she shows solidarity-in-writing to Mary Wollstonecraft, the foremother of feminism, and her friends and contemporaries Olive Schreiner and Isabella Beecher Hooker (whom she met while sojourning in America). By tracing Eleanor's influences from Engels through Wollstonecraft to Schreiner we have an intellectual map of Eleanor Marx the thinker as well as a guide to understanding her legacy as a whole; theorist as well as translator, cultural pioneer, and critic. Understanding Eleanor's praxis necessitates that we, as readers, look at context beyond text, and yet here the context, Eleanor Marx's work, is woven into her method and provides a view of what being a radical in action and thought entails for her.

It is necessary to read Eleanor Marx's method as exemplified in this text together with her work outside of writing; this text is crucial in understanding oppression and alienation, but the responses she offered were in her lived praxis. Eleanor Marx was a cultural pioneer, who saw possibilities for societal transformations in and through culture. Holmes contextualizes this text, *The Woman Question (from a Socialist Point of View)*, in the context of another ongoing work Eleanor had engaged with: the first ever translation of *Madame Bovary* into English, on which she worked in the same year, 1886. At the same time, another major project upon which Eleanor was working as she wrote this text was producing and presenting the pioneering work of Henrik Ibsen on the London stage. The first ever reading of *A Doll's House* was in her front room, with George Bernard Shaw acting opposite her.[50] She loved both Shelleys—Mary and Percy—and intertwined quotations from their work into her own, showing continuation in radicalism across ages through culture. Culture and politics were deeply interlinked and culture was a forceful way to present both constraints of our present times as well as visions for a better tomorrow. Moreover, fighting for bread and roses, for the beauty of life (which had galvanized the work of Emma Goldman whose radical dance started this discussion), at the same time as caring for the necessity of its most basic demands were part of Eleanor's lifelong work. A lifelong dedication to Shakespeare, the family bible,[51] as Holmes shows, while writing and lecturing on culture were part and parcel of Eleanor's work. Everyone has the right to enjoy art—a central pillar of her own life, according to Eleanor Marx—and art and culture are vital in projecting a progressive idea of a just society in becoming.[52] Thus, we may learn about the praxis of Eleanor Marx as exemplary and aiding in the argument of the book: transcending divides between theory and practice, culture and politics. A pioneering activist who unraveled better futures than that which she could have imagined for herself, she established solidarities from which we still benefit today, whether formally, through foundation of organizational structures, or ideationally, through elucidating specific commitments to justice that still inspire women and men to action today.

Returning to the text in the context of this book and deepening its reading poses us with a wider question: what does it mean to be a radical activist? How does a subject living in conditions of extreme inequality agitate toward a world they do not yet know? Marx asks, "What is it that we as socialists desire? What is it that we expect? What is that of whose coming we feel as assured of the rising of tomorrow's sun? What are the evolution changes in the condition of woman that we anticipate as consequence of these? Let us disclaimer all ignition of the prophetic."[53] The text started from Eleanor Marx noting that society is in a position of unrest; here she is asking what is the direction of the unrest. Earlier in the text she notes that "certainly, socialism is at present in this country little more than a literary movement. It has but a fringe of working men on its border. But we can answer to this criticism that in Germany this is not the case, and even here now socialism is beginning to extend among the workers."[54] Marx is aware of the fact that she is speaking from the radical

14   DANCE AND ACTIVISM

outskirts of society. She is not claiming herself a hegemony. And at the same time, this position of agitating through writing brings her to a substantive point that once again shows the radical thinking she brings forth in this piece. In the latter part of the text Marx addressed certain issues, controversial and at times still volatile in our day, from divorce to polygamy to prostitution. More than a century later the feminist movement will still be torn over those issues with all sides claiming access to the absolute right. Marx, when discussing divorce, writes that "our answer is this—the union between men and women, to be explained in the sequel, will be seen to be of such a nature as wholly to obviate the necessity of divorce."[55] The emphasis here is on the term *the sequel*. Eleanor Marx understands that many issues burning in the heart of her society as well as in the hearts of women and men of her time are structured in the oppressed psyches they inhabit. It is only when leaving the society as it is known at her time, when, in her own words, a psyche that exceeds "the limits of society of today,"[56] "can these issues be resolved."[57] Our visions, our hopes, and our frustrations are the product of a world marred by alienation. The detailed map of our societal lives can only be established when we leave this delimited frame of mind.

The *Woman Question (from a Socialist Point of View)* gives a clear and forceful articulation of structural injustice, "lives that do not intersect," but at the same time allows one to construct a forceful conceptualization of solidarity. A text that emerges from her lived experience as an organizer as much as from her theoretical work, drawing upon and always returning to lived experience, the text shows the gravest iteration of structural injustice, those lives that do not intersect, while creating a framework in countering it. That framework necessarily transcends divisions between thought and action and allows action occurring in the present to unravel into a future the radical does not yet know. Alienation was an impulse that galvanized Eleanor Marx's life and yet her response to it was never in theory only, nor in essentializing what human life was like before alienation had occurred. As a radical she knew only that the future would unravel the answers, in which more lives would intersect, and woman and man could look into each other's eyes and hearts. Solidarity was at the heart of Eleanor Marx's radical praxis, and this solidarity transcends boundaries between thought and action, present and future, and physical and metaphysical. Most profoundly, the answer to structural injustice is always in collective action, in creating new solidarities to counter deep alienation.

This book is inspired by Eleanor Marx's quest to "go ahead!"—her focus on lived experience and her understanding of the longer view of history, which centralizes the concept of praxis, woman, and man and all collective responses to evils and oppressions that structure their lives. The book accentuates social and economic structures that influence both possibilities and constraints for activism. At the same time, the book also argues that by narrating a life-story that is unique and individual the individual who tells the story as well as the collectives that listen to the story change. Those lives that previously did not intersect have a moment of coincidence that enables solidarity to emerge.

Moving on, the argument can proceed to the conceptual framework underpinning the book. The book works in a dialectical tension between alienation and solidarity, which become reconfigured through the concept of praxis. At the same time, as part of a four-part dialectic always unraveling toward another unknown future, the book also utilizes the verb *chronicle*, which sees the telling or retelling of a life story as an intervention with a possibility to alter imaginaries and open up new horizons for action. The argument now moves to define these concepts as an underpinning for the argument.

Alienation, our inability to create a connection to oneself and another, is reconceptualized in this work as women and men's inability to tell their story in their own way of expression. This reiteration allows us to examine artistic life as the center of analysis. The lack of ability to tell one's own story in one's own way, whether to oneself or to another, and moreover with a hopeful horizon that includes a future in which that would be possible, emerges from these lives that "do not intersect," from lack of the ability to raise one's voice equally in society. The response to alienation is always in collective reconfiguration of our lived, shared, societal structures, which allows for a future in which more sharing in lives that do intersect is possible.

Solidarity is collective action, together unraveling toward a better tomorrow, drawing on the past but aimed toward the future; "going ahead" together, in the words of Eleanor Marx. Solidarity may arise from a conscious effort but may be unconscious; the act of solidarity may arise from impulse or reaction that in turn creates an action. However, solidarity always aims toward an interest greater than that of one person, aimed to reconfigure a shared future. Solidarity emerges when more than one life story is considered, when more than one life is taken into account; when a future that includes many voices, and in particular those voices

16   DANCE AND ACTIVISM

who are not heard the loudest, takes over our streets. Solidarity is a generative process; in its practice it includes toing and froing, making mistakes and learning from them. Solidarity can emerge intentionally or unintentionally; it depends on the circumstances of lives of people who are able to act together against the forces of their present, but this action is not always forward planned and contemplated. The ability to foresee in action "the sequel," a radical future that is not yet here, is reconfigured through working together to allow more lives to intersect and more stories to be told and resonate. Solidarities allow for more than one story, one point of view, to be held; they diverge and at times dissent against frameworks of our times that may be seen as necessary (hence the connection to the theme of this book, the radical component of dance), and, following Eleanor Marx, they aim toward a different time in the future, one that we do not have access to in our present.

Praxis, in the context of this conceptual framework, is the space of action entrapped between alienation and solidarity. It is the space that unfolds from the action *itself,* which is encapsulated in the deed (though may be accompanied by word). Drawing on Rachel Holmes's conception of Eleanor Marx as "action responding to [her father's] theory," the shift to praxis, looking at work done in the real world rather than debated and narrated theory, allows for dancers as activists to take center stage. Changing people's lives collectively as well as changing individual lives occurs through radical reconfiguration of our shared societal frameworks. Praxis is the rejuvenation and change in which human beings change their shared life. Praxis is one's lived experience toward a radical future, unraveling from conditions of alienation toward new solidarities in becoming. In order to focus on praxis, though, consideration of what the role of this book, or any other work of writing is required. For this reason, and as the fourth part of the dialectic (mirroring Eleanor Marx's "the sequel," contributing an open-ended addition to the classical configuration of thesis, antithesis, and synthesis), the conceptual framework utilizes the concept of the chronicle. This concept draws in its entirety on the work of Martha Graham and will be examined in the next chapter. However, in the context of this conceptual framework, chronicle is the act, whether in verbal or non-verbal ways of communication, of bringing radical praxis that has happened or is happening into shared consciousness, allowing for new solidarities to emerge. Chronicle, as the next chapter will elaborate, is a verb; it is a progressive action that emerges from the effort to retain and learn from radical action. Thus, the act of writing or dancing a story of radical praxis is significant in and of itself. Alienation can create solidarity, through processes of constantly reconfigured praxis; in order to know these processes, we may chronicle them, allowing more stories to be told and more lives to intersect. Each one of these concepts will be examined in depth in writing on dance—as praxis—itself, but the chapter now moves to the methodological and analytical structures that underpin the book's narrative.

First, following the Marx family legacy, this is a book written in a historical materialistic method. The moving body is the most primordial material humankind possesses and is interpreted in the context of its social relationality. This book looks to the material conditions from which movements of dissent arise rather than focusing on individual "dissenting voices," feeding into "Great Man" narrative (which may be mildly tweaked into "Great Woman"). People are part and parcel of their environment, and in order to understand the origins of radicalism, we must turn to the economic-political context of its rupture.

Second, this book attempts to think of the narrative of the whole life story. Human beings—including dancers—live a full life that encompasses much more than their moments on stage or even in the studio. This book tries to seek a holistic retelling of life stories, asking about the full life a person lived, not just a moment on stage crucial for the works analyzed.

Third, this book asks about the dialectic between alienation and solidarity sitting at the crux of humankind. Those moments in which people were posited as antagonistic to each other yet found ways to overcome divisions and argue for a better humanity—for all receive the limelight in this discussion. The analysis is always of a dialectic: not seeking to reconcile it but to enfold the placement of these pulling forces within dancing human beings' lives.

Fourth, and last, the book asks about the process toward that period Marx termed "the sequel," in which all structural oppressions will be done away with and we can live as free and equal individuals. This is an unashamedly radical book—it does not focus on those who nurture a status quo underpinned in a racist, sexist, and economically exploitative world, but on those who are able to dream a better world is possible. Thus, this book follows in Eleanor Marx's footsteps and aims, too, to go ahead; to listen to those claiming a new tomorrow they do not yet know. The discussion moving from alienation to solidarity along the four methodic pillars discussed leads to an emphasis on creative and communal responses to constraints that disallow human lives to flourish to their full.

This book aims to transcend divisions between theory and action. As such it will not operate as many political theory books—including those focusing on embodied practices—do, which is to turn toward a case study, then elucidate it in theory. This method of writing merely reconfirms the division between theory and action: "here, reader, you had the action; now here, for you to make sense of it, the theory." All the people whose stories this book tells made sense of their actions in the process of performing them. Thus, the book asks the reader to listen to their voices better and do away with previous conceptions of theorizing. Several methodical reflections will now be countered before delving into the dance.

Method

The book asks two central questions that act in dialectical tension with each other throughout the argument. The first question is what does radical praxis, examined through the unique prism of dance as activism, entail? The second question is what does it mean to chronicle a present unfolding into the future, either in words or dance? In order to pursue those questions some primary methodological assumptions will be presented first.

Why focus on a century of radical dance? This question is crucial for understanding of the method used in this book. The underlying assumption and argument are that there is continuity as well as change in various strands of radical dance as activism. At the same time, sensitivity to the context of creation and performance means that no performance can be the exact same performance twice, as the bodies performing it and the situations in which it is undertaken are different. In terms of method, the shift is thus for the voice of the dancers-activists, rather than the historiographers/critics/researchers, to take center stage. The book operates in a dialectic between the argument arc and the polyphony of voices to which it responds. It is argued that it would be impossible to cohere and create a linear narrative of all radical dancers in the book, from New York to Syria to Delhi to Gaza; all radicals are radicals in their own way. The argument, then, does not attempt to meld all these voices into one voice that it narrates, but rather narrates those voices and then presents the organizing argument opposite them. The book also attempts to respond to, rather than theorize and abstract from, the dancers' voices. Using a wide array of methods from close reading of dances, historiography, and interviews, the book shows different ways in which radical dancers "live their beautiful ideal." The argument acts as a chronicle, not explaining but curating, not imposing an authoritative voice but bringing together on the page conversations that otherwise would not have occurred. Thus, as a contemplation on writing as a radical act, it also asks to centralize the dancing body, not the writing hand.

Moreover, where possible, words as well as movement of the artists discussed are presented. This is not to reduce politics within dance to the spoken word, but more to allow people to tell the stories of their lives, give the context from which their work rises in their own words. Awareness of the limitation of identity of one theorist who is always watching from her own place, allowing more voices to enter the argument verbatim means different points of view, sometimes contradictory, are allowed to inhabit the same space.

In a world that revolves around a white, middle class, Western heterosexual being as the default and the norm, this book seeks to look for voices that challenge this norm. The book seeks to illuminate those who strove to make the world inclusive of more voices not at the mainstream of discourse. Hence nationalistic, anti-internationalist, exclusive activism is not covered here. This a moral and political decision to focus on progressive politics. The book is a dissent against a world that normalizes attacks on the vulnerable under the facade of "neutrality" or even "discussion," allowing for oppression to continue and sustain. This book is in itself an activist text—trying to change the discourse of dance and politics, both. Drawing on the sources presented above the aim is to undercover structural inequities and silencing by way of expanding analysis to those voices that challenge power structures and current political configurations. The focus is also on adding more voices to our political discourse as well as diversifying that discourse. The line between a status quo that is unashamedly white and the entrance of white supremacy to locations of power is a fragile one, thus the book aims to include variety of different voices that usually do not sit at the center of analysis in dance studies. From Emma Goldman's insistence to include the beauty of the world—including dance—in revolutionary praxis the book presents a selection of case studies unraveling from 1920 until the sequel in which we are living. The book takes on board learnings from critical race theory, from current discussions, to the influence of pioneers such as W. E. B. Du Bois and in particular James Baldwin, who ask how "white" came to be considered the default, and especially how racism within the canon implicates all in society. Baldwin especially showed the hefty cost all bear from a predominantly white America, and the easy slip from white hegemony to white supremacy.[58] At the same time the book starts from a firm belief in people's ability to transform their lives and act against oppressions that delimit them. Racism, like all oppressions, is a creation of man and can be overhauled. The book looks at pioneer dancer activists from anti-racist movements such as the civil rights movement and the anti-apartheid movement in South Africa to contemporary anti-racist struggles in Palestine, Syria, and the USA. The book focuses on the dancer activists and attempts to open a space in which they tell their own stories in their voices, in deed and word.

The term "activists"—those who can be part of these generative solidarities that allow one to imagine a different future—can expand beyond intentional actors. Not only choreographers or dancers can be seen as activists in this broad conception of solidarity; students of a ballet class, or audiences whose perceptions are transfigured watching a dance performance, are necessary for this conception of activism. The shift to collective action and away from a singular individual allows for a reading of the context and different agents who allow radical action to occur.

The works discussed were viewed and researched in a variety of ways, from video access to live performance to extensive rehearsal viewing. Where possible, the text includes some footage of the work discussed in the form of YouTube clips. This is not to take away from the force of live performance, but to open vistas to readers who may not be able to access those in the process of reading the book. It does not also tell the reader what the process of writing and research entailed, but rather reflects on how technology may open new doors to dance and invite new audiences into theaters.

This is a feminist work drawing on a feminist argument. The book asks about people of all genders changing their lives when their voices are suppressed elsewhere, a key ethos of feminist activism and theory. Writing on all genders the book asks how women and men remake their lives, utilizing their bodies, their most primordial material possession.

The conceptual framework does not attempt to employ a universal and overarching conceptualization of its core concepts. Instead, each case study allows a different interpretation of solidarity, alienation, and praxis as well as a different lens on the praxis of chronicling radical dance. The underlying method of the book is curation; and so the conceptual map allows one to curate different perspectives of these conceptualizations rather than a coherent and overarching singular articulation. Each dancer-activist adds a layer of signification to the meaning of these concepts in their unique context.

This book does not claim that all dance is inherently activist; in some of the case studies, the creators and choreographers discussed have created a wide body of work that may vary in its degree of offering a radical future through dance. The book focuses on some case studies to allow a conceptual framework to be developed and examined, rather than to present a necessary and overarching connection between the two terms: dance and activism.

The last question to be asked is about the argument arc—why a century? Why start in the 1920s? In fact, like most historiographical research, the book starts from the background to revolutionary dance in the 1920s and ends in a non-conclusion that transcends the moment of the end of writing in 2020. However, part of the argument in the book emerged from new conditions for thinking about activism as well as dance. Much of the historiography of the earlier days of modern dance in America, in particular, was influenced by the "red scare," McCarthyism, fear of various progressive causes still labeled "other." Many histories retold, especially in the second chapter, are retold in the context of changes in American democracy; in particular, the resistance on the streets seen in the Women's Marches, discussed in the fifth chapter, the understanding of bodies in movement, and what is perceived as radical are reconfigured. The Workman's Circle, an organization to which the mother of one of the protagonists of the second chapter, Anna Sokolow, took her as a child, was now becoming a central anti-Trump organizing force. Madison Square Garden, in which another central voice in this chapter, Pearl Primus, danced against racism was often passed in the women's marches, and of course Union Square, the geographical and conceptual locus of the next chapter, which acts as a question about beginnings—of the argument, of radical dance—was the hub to countless protests. This led to a proposition that transcended this specific contingency: bodies remember and carry narratives. They remember repression, but they also remember possibility for collective emancipation in movement and for empowerment in solidarity. The focus in the book throughout is on moments in which histories converge and bodies find possibilities to create solidarity in motion in the face of stark alienation.

22 DANCE AND ACTIVISM

Martha Graham in "Spectre–1914" from "Chronicle." Photographer unknown. Courtesy of Martha Graham Resources.

The second chapter looks at a unique moment in time in which dance and activism in the USA held a close relationship at the burst of modern dance onto the aesthetic scene. The beginning of American dance is explored in the work of three women: Martha Graham, Anna Sokolow, and Pearl Primus. The focus of this chapter is on beginnings of action and transmission within a uniquely radical time. The chapter also asks about the continuation of these legacies and how they are lived experience today, in the words of Graham herself, as proponents of action embodied in dance. The dialectic between beginnings and action sits at the heart of this chapter.

IF WE CAN'T DANCE   23

The third chapter, "Ballet beyond Borders," centralizes questions of form and intentions. Focusing on a form of dance that is often accused of anachronism as well as sustaining cultural and political wrongs, ballet, the chapter shows specific and direct use of the form for emancipatory potential. The chapter looks at case studies in which alienation is entranced in highly volatile lived conditions, from apartheid South Africa, to Syria to Palestine, and shows how the force of solidarity through ballet is mobilized; and moreover, how the force of solidarity transcends the boundaries of the form from its intended beginnings.

The fourth chapter, "Erbil/NYC: Break/Dance" focuses on one artist who was educated through the internet in breakdance and then brought his artistry to its hub in New York City, Hussein Smko proves that dance and technology, both, force us to reconsider how people connect and transmit movement in our times. The chapter works in dialectic between technology and transmission, focusing on the latter. The chapter challenges singular narratives of transmission that in fact see dance as merely a commodity in which the dancer has no agency, thus returning to the essential problematic of the concept of alienation. In turn, this hugely hopeful story shows how solidarity may be found in dance through unexpected modes of communication and new technologies.

The fifth chapter, "Steps on the Street: Revolution DJ," focuses on the use of dance in demonstrations and protests at the tail end of our decade. From Chile to Lebanon, from New York to Delhi, more and more people join dancing lines that expand within marches. What function does dance hold in such contexts? What is the unique solidarity that dance brings within the march? This chapter revisits the work of Eleanor Marx as it especially probes questions of gender and activism at the center of its discussion.

The sixth chapter, "Dance as a Home," focuses on the use of dance to connect life stories of refugees to those living in times of increasing anti-migrant discourses. From community project to artistic performances more and more conscious efforts are used to create bridges where they do not exist and relieve some of the most atrocious humanitarian crises of our times through dance. The chapter draws on Edward Said's work on exiles and examines dance focusing on refugees as a form of thinking, the ability to reflect upon the world from the point of view of an exile. The chapter acts in dialectical tension to the rest of the book as it focuses on the responsibility of those who have a home toward those who have experienced being an exile or a refugee.

The seventh and last chapter, "Spectre, Haunting," is a non-conclusive conclusion. The chapter aims to asks: Where does activist dance go forth in our just-beginning decade and a new century, while revisiting some protagonists of the book (and some others who correspond to the action in it closely)? Both Martha Graham and Karl Marx used the concept of *spectre*; the chapter asks how we can proceed productively from the non-resolution of the tension between alienation and solidarity. What does this dancing discussion offer to our own interpretation of Eleanor Marx's concept of the sequel?

Yet, it is Martha Graham whose steps pulse the first beats of the discussion. In 1936 Graham premiered what was to become one of the central works in her canon, "Chronicle." The book draws on the title (as well as sub-titles of the work: "Prelude to Action," "Steps in the Street," and "Spectre—1914"), as an embodied metaphor of the work as a whole is crucial for the argument of the book. It thus takes a central place within the next chapter. Graham chronicled her times, and this book chronicles her work as well as that of many women and men who came after her.

People have always been working together to improve their shared world. Change in the world occurs in leaps as well as small steps, strides, and gallops. Change is not one-directional; the world is not becoming unequivocally more generous toward its inhabitants. That change unfolds and starts from one singular woman walking down the streets of the Lower East Side in the 1920s, whence her danced revolution will explode and transform many lives around the world. These radical tensions, bubbling under New York's hot pavements, facilitate the danced rupture of the argument of the book.

IF WE CAN'T DANCE **25**

2 PRELUDE TO ACTION

Emma Goldman, whose demand to include dance in her activist praxis spiraled the first chapter's argument into action, was key in the social and political landscapes that are the background for this chapter and beginning of the argument of the book. A photograph from 1916 shows her agitating passionately for women's rights over their bodies at Union Square, a center for radical organizing and action in the first part of the twentieth century. Bare-headed Red Emma agitating to a sea of hats creates a moment in time, a photograph that will change radical histories, and will remain inscribed in the history of Union Square. But she is not the only dancing revolutionary who will leave her mark and explode the argument into motion. All three luminaries whose danced revolution starts this argument were choreographed, inspired, and galvanized by the problem and danger of alienation and provided a robust response through danced solidarity.

Dissent was bubbling underneath the tiles of New York City's Lower East Side's streets like lava, quickening many women and men's steps. From Goldman's mass orations (which often resulted in her imprisonment), to other forms of organization, the city was a home to some of the most prominent radical voices of the early twentieth century. The Communist Party USA's Headquarters were a short walk from Union Square, on 235 West 23rd Street. Following the 1929 Stock Exchange crash and the Great Depression, strikes and workers' meetings often took place in Union Square, making it a hub for socialist, communist, and trade unionist organizing.

But the streets around the Union Square area were hubs for radicalism of various kinds and in manifold forms; and one woman whose studio was a short walk from Union Square was about to forever transform modern dance and modern art beyond it. Her danced revolution started just a brief walk from Union Square, on 66 West 12th Street.

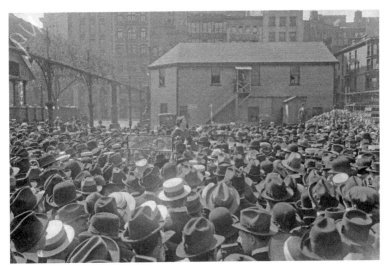

Emma Goldman addressing a rally in support of birth control in Union Square, 1916.

Martha Graham: Embodied Chronicle

Martha Graham (1894–1991) was a pioneering force and the mother of American modern dance. Born to a middle-class family of Irish-Scottish descent, and training with Ruth St. Denis and Ted Shawn in her earlier years, she moved to New York in the 1920s where all forms of radicalism were about to change the century ahead. At an early stage of her dancing life she sought ways to change the way dance—and the world around it—were perceived.

The crash of the New York Stock Exchange in 1929 created a watershed moment in American social-economic history and at the same time galvanized mass grassroots organization. The New York landscape became scattered with breadlines; hunger and desperation developed into anger and mobilization. Radicalism was a fact of life and a very visceral response to terrible suffering and poverty. This was a time of reconsideration of what were considered given truths, and reconsideration of what human action may create instead of the capitalism that had brought so much devastation to the lives of Americans across the land, and to the hub of capitalism, New York City.

Martha Graham and Dancers first appeared on the stages of New York on April 18, 1926, yet 1929 was a profound watershed moment for Graham's career. In 1929, famed dance critic John Martin noted that Graham's "strides in the past year, both as a solo dancer and choreographer, place her in the first line of modern dances, whether native or foreign."[1] "Heretic" premiered on April 14, 1929 and on January 8, 1930 Graham presented her solo "Lamentation," a reflection on grief and emotion/motion, which "revolutionized the way people thought of dance."[2] The 1930s were a decade of premieres of very significant works for Graham—all responding to and echoing themes she saw around her: "Heretic" from 1929 was a work contemplating the price of being a heretic, very reflexive of Graham's positioning of herself as an individual counter to the group, "continu[ing] to resist the movement even as the curtain falls."[3] "Panorama" from 1935 is a rallying cry for social activism,[4] "Imperial Gesture" (1935) looked at greed and imperialism, and "Deep Song" (1937) was a response to the Spanish Civil War and normalization of man's inhumanity to man. In 1936, Graham premièred "Chronicle," her response to the rise of fascism broadly and the increasingly loud winds of war and devastation echoing throughout Europe and the world.[5]

The temporal and physical contingencies that created radicalism in Graham's work as well as in American political history have been thoroughly examined and discussed thanks to the centrality of her career within American dance. Mark Franko's *The Work of Dance* argues that dance in the 1930s in New York was able to produce ideology, not as a commodity but as a continuing sensuous experience, which made it effective.[6] Franko's analysis focuses on two works, "Primitive Mysteries" and "Frontier," which are significant for the background of the argument yet do not sit at its crux.[7] Significantly, Graham's 1936 work "Chronicle," which underpins the spine of the book as well as this argument, is mentioned in passing comment by Jane Dudley as "having some very good movement material."[8] At the same time, a review from Owen Burke in the *New Masses* hailed "Chronicle" as "brilliantly and stirringly anti-war, anti-fascist";[9] this work firmly consolidated Graham's place in anti-fascist, left-wing circles.

Stacey Prickett provides a rigorous overview to the origins of "Workers Dance" and in particular to tensions and reconciliation with Graham in her essay *From Workers' Dance to New Dance*. The provides a condensed and precise overview of organizational dynamics in the 1920–1930s dance world as well as relationships to other organizations and

GUILD THEATRE

FIRE NOTICE: The exit, indicated by a red light and sign, nearest to the seat you occupy, is the shortest route to the street.
In the event of fire or other emergency please do not run—WALK TO THAT EXIT.

JOHN J. McELLIGOTT, Fire Chief and Commissioner

SUNDAY EVENING, DECEMBER 20, 1936, AT 8:45 P. M.

MARTHA GRAHAM
and DANCE GROUP

LOUIS HORST, Musical Director

Celebration .... *Louis Horst*
Dance Group

Frontier .... *Louis Horst*
Martha Graham

Primitive Canticles .... *Villa-Lobos*
a. Ave
b. Salve
Martha Graham

Primitive Mysteries .... *Louis Horst*
a. Hymn to the Virgin
b. Crucifixus
c. Hosannah!
Martha Graham and Dance Group

INTERMISSION

Chronicle .... *Wallingford Riegger*
Dances Before Catastrophe
a. Spectre—1914
b. Masque
Dances After Catastrophe
a. Steps in the Street
b. Tragic Holiday—In Memoriam.
Prelude to Action
Martha Graham and Dance Group

Dance Group: Anita Alvarez, Thelma Babbitz, Bonnie Bird, Dorothy Bird, Ethel Butler, Aza Ceskin, Jane Dudley, Frieda Flier, Marie Marchowsky, Sophie Maslow, Marjorie Mazia, May O'Donnell, Kathleen Slagle, Gertrude Shurr, Anna Sokolow, Mildred Wile.

Concert program for the Martha Graham Dance Company at the Guild Theatre, December 20, 1936. Courtesy of Martha Graham Resources.

artists. Prickett, too, sees 1926, the year of Graham's first concert, as the year when a revolution in dance and dissent through dance both emerged.[10]

The most extensive study of the social-political history of the emergence of modern dance, as well as of Martha Graham's career, was written by eminent dance historian (and former Graham dancer) Ellen Graff. *Stepping Left: Dance and Politics in New York City 1928–1942* provides a deep interpretation of the societal configurations in which Graham and others worked.

Graham came from a different background to many of her dancers, and her politics were often more complex. Certain left-wing circles critiqued her "for dealing with a subject matter that was too personal, too mystical and too divorced from contemporary social issues as well too abstract to understand."[11] However, it is widely agreed that "Chronicle" was both created and received in a different vein, seen as explicitly anti-war,[12] and indeed marking her emergence as a political choreographer.[13] Much has been written, also, on Graham's privileges in the context of her social-economic environment[14] as well as within the choreography itself. At the same time, little attention has been given to the moving bodies carrying Graham's legacy, in her time and after it, as well as her positioning of herself in the context of her social-economic environment.

Celebrated Graham dancer and scholar Kim Jones studied the work "Chronicle" in the context of its choreographic era and provides a deep introduction to its long and fraught performance history that leads to a vital and cohesive discussion on the work. "In a 1936 Program (for Martha Graham and Dance Group, all female dance group founded in 1926) Chronicle consisted of five dances presented in three sections: Dances before catastrophe (including 'Spectre—1914' and 'Masque'), dances after catastrophe (including 'Steps in the Street' and 'Tragic Holiday—in Memoriam') and 'Prelude to Action'".[15] The work was grounded in its social-political moment and was received with great accolades, resonating with its forceful message. At the Guild Theater, at the hub of New York City, Graham premiered "Chronicle" on December 20, 1936. This was a complex dance responding to a complex moment in history, and, crucially, premiered in a complex place in radical history too. "Chronicle" feeds into a moment in Graham's work that reflects her consideration of her voice as well as her responsibility as an artist. Jones's theoretical approach, which sees transmission as process, and moves the focus to the dancing bodies transmitting the dance, is crucial in the context of this argument.

Graham's refusal to participate in the Berlin Olympics, a crucial turning point for Jones as well as for this book's argument, read together with "Chronicle," was not only derived from her own position but was grounded in the social-political context in which she was working. Many of her dancers were Jewish and the polyphony of voices that allowed radical art to emerge on the Lower East Side, she grasped intuitively, was one of the key enemies of the Nazi state. On February 14, 1937, Graham testified before the American Committee for Anti-Nazi Literature, reporting on the changing mood in Europe and pleading with artists to be watchful of the world and sincere in their art. Graham argued for united resistance and for artists to know their place in the movement against a rising tide of fascism and the suppression of individual voices. This was a clear action Graham took while listening to those working with and around her. It was an action of solidarity.

"Chronicle" is a work of its time, as this short social history of its emergence shows, and yet its life transcended the historical activist moment from which it had emerged. The program notes for the original premiere of "Chronicle" made clear that the work is not about an "incident" or real life, but rather about the emotional states that result from living fully as a human being.[16] This brings the discussion back to the analytical focus of this book. In the reading put forth, "Chronicle" is an iteration of danced solidarity in response to alienation. "Chronicle" was premiered comprising five sections: Dances before catastrophe ("Spectre—1914"; "Masque"), dances after catastrophe ("Steps in the Street"; "Tragic Holiday—in Memoriam"), and finally "Prelude to Action."

Janet Eilber, artistic director of the Martha Graham Dance Company since 2005 and much revered Graham dancer, discusses the return of the work to Graham's repertoire:

> I first saw *Chronicle* as an audience member in the late 1990s. When I was a dancer in the Company, *Chronicle* didn't exist. Martha created it in 1936 and it was performed for another year or so. I believe the last performance was in late 1937 or early 1938.[17] In 1938, MG added the first man to her company—Erick Hawkins, others soon followed including Merce Cunningham and Martha started to experiment with narrative—such as *Punch and the Judy* and *Every Soul is a Circus*. *Chronicle* and most of her abstract group dances from the 1930s (casts

32   DANCE AND ACTIVISM

of all women) were shelved and forgotten. Almost none of her works from the 1930s had been filmed. Fortunately, in 1964, original cast members helped to reconstruct *Primitive Mysteries* (1931) and filmed it. Otherwise it would be lost. In the 1980s, the Graham Center took on several other reconstructions such as *Celebration* (again with original cast members returning to the studio) and *Panorama* (Yuriko reimagined a section of this work using a smattering of film clips of the original cast). In the late 1980s, Barry Fischer, a doctoral student at NYU, discovered a film of "Steps in the Street" and reconstructed it at NYU. Somehow, the Graham Center received a copy of the film and Yuriko reconstructed it for the student company that she had created, the Ensemble (now called Graham 2). Yuriko could not find the original music, so she chose another work by the same composer, Wallingford Riegger. Riegger had originally composed that score for Doris Humphrey with the title *New Dance*. After Martha's death, film clips of "Spectre—1914" and "Prelude to Action" were uncovered and reconstructed by a group of Graham alums led by Terese Capucilli and Sophie Maslow. The original *Chronicle* had five sections; the Company now performs three.[18]

"Chronicle" as it is performed today is a triptych comprised of three surviving dances. The curtain opens on "Spectre—1914."[19] A lone woman sits on stage, a large skirt encircling her. Her movements are sharp and furious. The skirt is an extension of her body, providing an image larger than herself shifting in space. The horrors of the past war are haunting her; she is calling out against them reoccurring in the future. This is not a metaphorical cry of action; but a sharp visceral presentation of the pain of carrying the trauma and actuality of war. Presenting a lone woman onstage allows for the depiction of the individual as at once entrenched in their society as well as always able to act, to cry out against injustice. The women of "Chronicle" are the face of the cry against war, those who carry its weight and call out against it. A review from 1936 in the *New York Sun* by I. K. describes this section as "taut, inhuman gestures of response to the offstage trumpet and drums might be interpreted as the unwilling but uncontrollable participation of humanity in war . . ."[20] And yet the dance itself as well as its setting within the complete work is an act of powerful resistance. Human beings' lives are entrenched in violence and cruelty, but the same bodies that are able to develop war machinery and gun powder are able to provide the means to resist it. Coupling that

PRELUDE TO ACTION   **33**

message with the versatility of technique exhibited on stage, the work exemplifies to the audience just how much power a moving body carries in the world. At the same time "Spectre—1914" is a reminder of the power of the moving body to act against the powers that are aiming to destroy humanity.

It is necessary to pause here and reflect on the temporality embedded within this section of the work "Chronicle." Graham's return to 1914 in warning against the winds of war shows an intricate and complex understanding of temporality. The work chronicles, in its very performance, how human beings perceive time. At the time of performance 1914 was in most audience members' memory yet the devastation and radical changes of the two decades since, especially from the end of the 1920s, meant it was vital that the moment be inscribed anew upon audiences' psyches and bodies. Graham's return to the moment a world war broke out is not a metaphor but a performance of actuality of suffering and trauma that most Americans were carrying in their bodies. This is a lived past calling individuals to use their power to make a better future.

The second surviving section, "Steps in the Street," returns the audience to their—and Graham's—present. "Steps in the Street" is one of Graham's most famous ensemble works.[21] A group of individuals—alienated from each other as well as from their surroundings—move with a dejected array of movements, occasionally breaking that mold into a movement of rebellion and resistance. There is a leader who creates a dialectic between group and individual but it is clear all are living in their surroundings and very much in their present. The work again presents very actual lives of dancers as well as audiences, with one section entitled "the breadline." Breadlines were part of the architecture of the Lower East Side, where Graham made her own steps in the street and most likely what the audience members would have encountered when they left the Guild Theater, where the work had been performed. Yet the power of the work is in its ability to abstract from the literal social and political architecture while presenting a wider brushstroke of the present. Graham here is chronicling her own time, writing the present of her body and her dancers' bodies. The breadline is painfully of its time, part of the dancers' and audience members' psyches; yet also transcends the time of performance and allows numerous breadlines and others who have suffered alienation and hunger to have their stories told onstage. The work in its choreographic construction allows for multiple points of view

34 DANCE AND ACTIVISM

which converge in unraveling a new and better future, creating a space for dissent against the social and economic conditions in which Graham was creating.

"Steps in the Street" is divided into three sections: devastation, homelessness, and exile, as three iterations of the consequences of war. This is perhaps one of the strongest statements about alienation in the modern dance canon. The feeling of fear and anxiety is transferred from the dancers' bodies, self-enclosed as they mobilize Graham's signature move, the contraction, evoking emotional intensity within themselves and audience members both. The movement is sharp and angular— exemplifying Graham's movement vocabulary at that point, but also highly effective in portraying what living in postwar society, where individuals are without community, feels like when it is entrenched in the human body. I. K. comments on this work: "'Steps in the Street', conveys to the mind a world of the unwanted—the unemployed shuffling along the avenues, now and then bursting forth in rebellious movements, succumbing once more to a futile resignation."[22] And yet, the work is also a powerful contemplation on solidarity acting to oppose alienation. An all-female ensemble work powerfully together—often moving without music, thus having to be completely and utterly attentive to another person's moving body in order to move within and without their own. For the dancers, performing "Steps in the Street" is an act of tremendous empowerment through solidarity, showing the possibilities of the human body in the starkest of times to work together and counter alienation in collective motion. Graham opened up possibilities of examining what ensemble work can mean to counter conditions of stark alienation. For her dancers, then and in the times that followed, creating an all-female work that allowed them to choreographically investigate inter-group relations gave the dancers the possibility of empowerment on stage that slipped outside of their lives as performers. This is not just a metaphorical statement about resistance; "Steps in the Street" is an étude that shows the moving bodies within it, as well as those in the theater, the force of togetherness in the face of harsh alienation.

"Steps in the Street"[23] is a work about Graham's present as well as a contemplation about the present more broadly. The last part of the surviving triptych, "Prelude to Action," is a danced meditation that unfolds into the future. This section that closes the work is a rallying cry to act against injustice. Bringing together the soloist who had danced "Spectre—1914" with the ensemble from "Steps in the Street," the dialectic

PRELUDE TO ACTION   35

between group and individual takes center stage. But this is not a repetition of Graham's work's heresy (and the price individuals pay for being heretic), but rather a performance of the force of an individual to lead a collective, the power of one to influence the bodies of many; the possibilities each and every human being has to act against injustice. The movement in this piece is different in its registers than the first two works; the desperation and seeming possessiveness of "Spectre—1914" and alienated motion of "Steps in the Street" is replaced by purposeful and motivated action. For the dancers the entire work from its commencement is a powerful articulation of the human body in action. To execute the movements the body has to be in complete and utter command of every one of its cells. Thus the technique and performance of all parts of "Chronicle" are in fact for the dancers a means to inhabit their body powerfully, to gain absolute command of it, in the face of harsh and degrading living conditions.

"Prelude to Action" is unique in its temporal understanding. Ending the work (as it did in the original) with a call for action suggests that the action never ends, spills over from the stage to the world outside the theater, to each and every audience member's responsibility to act against the impending war. The work ends on an open-ended future. The call for action is not pre-set and determined; it is a calling for any individual who is part of a group to galvanize such action and to make tomorrow better for all.

The work—and this section especially—were powerfully received in its time, as leading left-wing critic Owen Burke observed. "'Prelude to Action' is restrained, taut dance of gathering energies, gathering forces. There is no goal marked but following the catastrophe the direction is plain. Right now there is an amassing of strength; there must be no repetition of [death, despair, mourning]. 'Steps in the Street'! for sheer artistry of movement, for brilliance of choreography, for the rush and force of energy there is little on the concert stage to equal . . . 'Steps in the Street' . . . or 'Prelude to Action'. . . . Chronicle uncourtly is the most important work of the current season."[24] Another review sees this as most powerful part of the piece: "'Prelude to Action' was the title of the last number of Martha Graham's opening sequence in her latest dance creation 'Chronicle' (Wallingford Riegger). Appropriately enough, this was the keynote of the evening."[25] There is a temporal urgency in the work that is central to its understanding. "Chronicle" is a work about remembering as well as projecting a different future, about action and

36 DANCE AND ACTIVISM

beginnings. The work is radical at the same time that it is about emerging radicalism as well as how to record it. "Chronicle" is an urgent intervention in its time, but it is also a contemplation about the relationship between this intervention and other time spheres to which it relates; the warnings issued by the past as well as hopes derived from the future.[26] "Chronicle" is a work of solidarity, about solidarity and for solidarity, that in its creation and performance counters the alienation of the time it was premiered and that which followed.

Graham's written articulation of temporality in 1937, in the period in which "Chronicle" was performed, is helpful to move the argument onward. "Throughout time dance has not changed in one essential function. The function of the dance is communication. The responsibility that dance fulfill its function belongs to us who are dancing today."[27] Graham places the statement in her specific social and political context: "we are making a transition from 18th to 20th century thinking. A new vitality is possessing us. Certain depths of the intellect are being explored. Great art never ignores human values. Therein lies its roots. This is why forms change;"[28] "The modern dance, as we know it today, came after the World War. This period following the war, demanded forms vital enough for the reborn man to inhabit."[29]

Beyond the political context for the emergence of modern dance, what is striking here, and illuminating for this reading of "Chronicle," is Graham's understanding of time and commitment within dance as a moment of crystalized action: "Dance was no longer performing its function of communication. By communication is not meant to tell a story or to project an idea, but to communicate experience by means of action and perceived by action."[30] This is an activist reading of dance, unfolding from its urgent present time rooted in its social and political landscapes. However, dance as a form of political action is not merely an iteration of other messages; "all this has nothing to do with propaganda as known and practice. It only demands the dance be moment of passionate, completely disciplined action, that it communicate participation of the nerves, the skin, the structure of the spectator."[31] The moment of embodied commitment transcends all other modes of protests yet is always engrossed in processes in which audience and dancers alike participate within.

"Chronicle," in the context of Graham's work in that era, is a zenith of crossroad between beginnings and action, a step that goes into an unknown future, and yet faith in the human body that is able to work

PRELUDE TO ACTION   37

within itself to also act in the world and make it better, not repeat mistakes and carry past burdens. Graham's work is an active intervention as it allows the dancer to become an activist within one's own skin, to galvanize the body from its inside out, to be in its total command. Steps in the street cannot be executed without purpose, thus the steps in the street can always make the march better for all.

There was little metaphor when Graham choreographed around the rising alienation of her time. At the same time resistance through solidarity was anything but metaphorical to her, too. On March 13, 1936, the same year she premiered "Chronicle," she turned down an invitation to perform at the Berlin Olympics. It is worthwhile revisiting her explicit statement here:

> I would find it impossible to dance in Germany at the present time. So many artists whom I respect and admire have been persecuted, have been deprived of the right to work for ridiculous and unsatisfactory reasons, that I should consider it impossible to identify myself, by accepting your invitation, with the regime that has made such things possible. In addition, some of my concert group would not be welcomed in Germany.[32]

This is a statement of solidarity both in its own right, as an artist bearing responsibility for the actions she takes in the world with great integrity, as well as an overarching statement of solidarity to her dancers and the environment in which Graham worked. The leader galvanizing action was a dilemma structuring artists' works outside the theater. Graham herself became that leader calling for action and galvanizing the power of resistance and boycott, in the name of responsibility toward others. Already a celebrated artist with a substantial following, this action made headlines and provided an exemplar for radical action. Moreover, this is a sage reading of Graham's environment and her dancers' worlds. Undoubtedly, she came from a different background to many of her dancers who, she predicted correctly, would be in existential danger in Nazi Germany, thus she used her privileges to act in solidarity with them. Graham's refusal as a public personality was a verbal counterpart to her choreographic call to arms. Graham was a member and speaker for the Committee for Anti-Nazi Literature symposium, and spoke of "the manner in which art and education in Nazi Germany have been turned to imperialistic uses, not through changing the structure of the education system, or changing, say, the movement in dancing, but by changing the

38   DANCE AND ACTIVISM

Martha Graham Dance Company in "Steps in the Street" from "Chronicle." Photographer unknown. Courtesy of Martha Graham Resources.

entire basic philosophy of which these things are taught and applied."[33] Moreover:

> Miss Graham's plea that dancers be watchful of their world and sincere in their art, carried over the emphasis that the very real and terrible development taking place in the world leave no one unaffected. Spain is at present the scene of tragedy and horror; all Western Europe is looking on, vulture like; America has its own enemies within. Such hysteria can be curbed only by unified resistance against it, and dancers and other artists must know and play their part with others in that resistance.[34]

This statement is crucial and illuminating. Fascism seeps into the human body, allowing its philosophy to inhabit the viscera and make it a tool for violence and war. But human beings can resist and work within the body, just as her own system of movement allows for a novel philosophy to take hold of human flesh. Every individual holds responsibility to act in the face of rising forces of evil, and yet the force of the group always transcends the individual. The work's afterlife aids its conceptual structuring of this book.

A Graham luminary who had worked closely with Martha Graham since the 1950s and has been central in the transmission of her legacy, Marnie Thomas Wood, talks about her own relationship to "Chronicle" and its potency in 2020, when she tells the story of her encounter with "Chronicle":

> I first encountered sections of Chronicle when I returned to NY to run the Graham School in 2003 and was asked to set Steps in the Street on a group of young college dancers. During the years I was in the Company [1958–68], Chronicle was not part of the repertory and revivals of early works were limited to specific works featuring Martha's dramatic roles in El Penitente, Frontier, Primitive Mysteries. What was truly apparent in learning and setting Steps was how powerfully it spoke of the gathered energy of the twelve women moving with the intense command of their collective focus. The original themes of homelessness, hunger, and anxiety drawn from the political framework current at the time of the dance's conception were vibrant and carried contemporary strength of the message with no sense of being outdated. Steps in the Street is about issues facing everyone in a collective outcry that speaks from a common urge. It was rewarding to set this work as it is essentially a dance that moves with a young and vibrant freshness. even now.[35]

Thomas Wood has been central in the company's work on Graham's repertoire, and her reflections on staging the work are vital in understanding the twenty-first-century bodies that dance it:

> Following this first encounter with Chronicle I then had the opportunity to observe the Company working through the full dance, and then participate in setting all three sections of Chronicle (again on college dancers) and appreciate how deeply this work inspires outstanding dancing at the solo level as well as in group collectiveness. Working with young dancers in Martha's solo brought out challenging dynamics in that exacting portrayal. The group work in Prelude to Action is a fitting conclusion to the ever-increasing build of the entire work.[36]

Wood has a unique perspective as an authority on reconstruction and staging, encountering "Chronicle" in various contexts within different periods of time:

40 DANCE AND ACTIVISM

I find Chronicle a work in which young dancers can excel. It has physical and expressive demands that are definitely part of the message of the dance and it taps contemporary strengths of technical and dramatic depth that bring out the best in those performing it. This is not a dance that is "dated". I believe this work appeals on the very basic level of how effectively the movement tells its story.[37]

"Chronicle" gives this book its galvanizing drive toward its argument, and will be revisited, in the context of its performance in the twentieth and twenty-first centuries, in its last chapter. The impulse to say what is right, to stand up to in justice, and to dance in solidarity with one's fellow woman was underscored in its premiere and yet continues to live. "Chronicle" is a work about time and about telling a story; it is a chronicle of the act of chronicling and, more than anything, about that fact that dance is simultaneously of its time and outside of its moment of emergence. And so from the immigrant cast on the Lower East Side to those steps in the street that continue to our current world, "Chronicle" remains a powerful iteration of the force of the collective to resist evil done to the individual and transcend its moment of emergence as a timeless message to stand up for what is right.

Graham's work "Heretic," from a similar time, represents a red thread through her life's work. The weight and price of resistance, of being an individual voice, was a narrative that found many different iterations in Graham's canon, although in "Chronicle," the work ends with the individual and the collective draw forces together, in a statement of solidarity, a call for action. Martha Graham was herself a heretic and opened the door to many heretics after her. One such heretic is apparent in an early photograph of Graham from 1931; Graham, clad in white is juxtaposed with her company. In that company a young dancer called Anna Sokolow can be seen; her own steps in the street made a vital and radical intervention in American dance history.

"Go Ahead and be a Bastard": Anna Sokolow

Anna Sokolow's parents arrived on Ellis Island in September 1907, from Russia, with five dollars in their pockets. Anna was born in 1910. She recalled later in life:

In the European Jewish tradition, the man was really the scholar, and the woman he married and her family took care of him and their children. When they came here, a lot of them had to change and they did. They learned to cope with the system and realized that they had to earn a living. Well, my father was totally bewildered by it, and he could do nothing. Eventually my mother, with her great energy, stepped in and took over. I think this happened to quite a few of the families who came here.[38]

Anna Sokolow's introduction to activism was by the context of her upbringing; feminist, socialist, and Jewish.

"My mother was a real working-class woman," Anna proudly stated in her later years. "She was a member of the ILGWU and a staunch socialist. Her idea of a great man was Eugene Debbs. People like my mother really fought for the proper conditions for workers in these days."[39] The Sokolow household kept kosher, high holidays were observed, and Shabbat candles were lit.[40]

Anna, a rebellious spirit from childhood, encountered dance by chance through the Emmanuel Sisterhood. "They had something going on every day after school ... Elsa Pohl was the dance instructor. She was tall and very impressive and everybody loved her. We never missed a class—we listened to her as if she was a goddess. She could infuse us with a delirium about dance."[41] She narrates her own encounter with dance: "One day, I remember just looking in the room and seeing them dance around, and I liked it. So I asked: 'could I join?' They said yes, of course, and that was it. I joined the class and fell madly in love with dancing."[42]

It was the community organizing around culture that enabled Anna Sokolow's further education. The Lewisohn sisters, who were important organizers and patrons to Martha Graham and founders of the Neighborhood Playhouse, aimed to provide the immigrant children of the Lower East Side with possibilities to expand their horizons. The stated object was "to train East Side youngsters to sing, dance, speak and mime, in order to transcend their environment by exercising their imagination."[43] Founder of the Playhouse Irene Lewisohn wrote: "Emotion, like a dream, must find an outlet; and through the temperament of an artist that emotion will find its natural form."[44]

An early testament to the societal and artistic power of the Playhouse came from British revolutionary suffragette Sylvia Pankhurst, who had visited the Playhouse in its original location, in the Henry St. Settlement,

42 DANCE AND ACTIVISM

in 1911. She had seen a children's performance and met the Lewisohn sisters, and was profoundly affected and changed by her visit. Her recollections of the experience (recently published and contextualized by Katherine Connelly) provide a snippet of the goals and achievements of the Playhouse as an artistic-activist institution: "So life appeared to me, till the cold, hard world outside dimmed the brightness and warmth glowing in my heart, and seemed to bolster up anew new barriers I had thought to surmount."[45]

The Neighborhood Playhouse moved to a new location in Grand Street in 1915. The Playhouse presented folk dance and festivals around Jewish rites and ceremonials, with an emphasis on ritualistic posturing, mass movements, and processionals (with a clear influence of Dalcroze).[46] In 1920, a professional dance company was installed in the Playhouse. Anna joined this company probably in 1925. Anna's main dance teacher at the Playhouse was Blanche Talmud, although through the Lewisohns she met Bird Larson.[47] After 1928, Martha Graham joined the faculty,[48] and Anna Sokolow participated in her first performance with Graham on January 8, 1930.[49]

Sokolow's biography can teach us a lot about the lives of her peer dancers, the founding casts of Martha Graham, and members of her circles, as well as give us an important context for her own unique contribution. Young modern dancers of the 1930s came primarily from working class families and thought of themselves as workers. Dancers were attracted by the potential social content of choreography and the notion that dance was a potential agent of change.[50] Sokolow's first performances from 1929 were held against the dramatic backdrop of the stock market crash.[51] Her audiences were people who, like her family and her, sought to engage arts to nourish their souls, but also to provide a way out of current present into a better world. Anna Sokolow testified:

> The unions were really my first audience. They would present programs where poets or writers would read their work and singers and dancers would perform in their halls. I remember going on a tour sponsored by the Jewish Fraternal Order with a singer, an actor, and a musician. We toured up to Montreal, over to Chicago, and down to Washington. It was about a two-month tour and we got fifty dollars a week, a lot of money in those days. We traveled on slow trains and buses and no body complained about things like that. As I remember, it was a wonderful audience. They understood us.[52]

PRELUDE TO ACTION 43

Anna Sokolow's first works were entrenched in their context, much like the streets from which Graham drew her steps, the hub of radicalism in which she lived. The titles for her first dances are very telling: "City Rhythms" and "Immigrant and the City" presented in the student program at the Neighborhood Playhouse on May 20, 1931; the anti-war trilogy comprising of "Depression," "Diplomacy," and "War," in 1933; "Homage to Lenin" in October 1933; "Forces in Opposition" in 1934; and "Strange American Funeral" in 1935, showing the misery and alienation at the heart of American culture, through mourning the wrongful deaths of hundreds of miners and steel workers. The year 1937 saw "Case History no.---," looking into the alienated individual in society, a motif at the heart of her great work, and "Rooms" (1955), which will be discussed later in the chapter. A review of this piece read it as "a burning indictment against society and the first great revolutionary dance characterization." "Anna Sokolow depicts the lifetime of thousands of youths who roam the country as vagrants and petty criminals, who live in the slums of New York, Chicago, or Detroit. She dances, with boyish bravado, their willfulness, frustration, desperation, the hunted suspect, the third degree, the cringing crying boy killers, the last mile."[53] Also in 1937 was the premiere of "Slaughter of the Innocents," Sokolow's response to the Spanish Civil War (to which Graham's response was "Deep Song" [premiere: December 19, 1937] and "Immediate Tragedy" [premiere: July 30, 1937]). In 1939, Sokolow presented "Exile." It is worthwhile moving to the next decade and pausing on "Kaddish" from August 20, 1945. Exemplifying both Sokolow's understanding of identity and her ability to transcend it, this is a contemplation of the heavy price the Second World War bore on the Jewish people, in which Sokolow dons Tefillin, the traditional prayer accessory worn by men only, and moves, lyrically and dramatically, in an extraordinarily intense and contained motion to the sound of the "Kaddish" prayer said for the dead in Jewish tradition. Sokolow, like most Jews in the diaspora coming to terms with the news from Europe about the scale and magnitude of the slaughter of Jews, is here both very rooted in her immigrant, Jewish, and feminine identity and at the same time able to transcend it (while taking on an ungendered stage persona). Like much of her work, this choreography is grounded in her own experience, and at the same time asks questions about the responsibility of humanity as a whole. "Kaddish" is also crucial in understanding another great work she created in 1972, "Dreams," responding to stories then emerging from the concentration camps.

Anna Sokolow instructs a class at the Dance Company of NSW, Woolloomooloo.

The beginning of Sokolow's career is a unique moment from which to examine the intersection between art and activism. A highly organized labor movement welcomed and encouraged artists to explore their voice and catalyze social change. Most famously and remarkably, the New Dance Group, which claimed as its motto "dance is a weapon of the class struggle"[54] (referring to the motto slogan of Soviet drama "theater is a weapon"),[55] created collective pathways for exchanges of expression between workers and artists. Dances were choreographed based on a word to which the workers could relate: unemployment, hunger, and unionism.[56] Early plays protested the way black people were treated.[57] In 1936, the same year Graham premiered "Chronicle," Anna premiered her first evening of dances on April 5.

An important component of this book's argument is the shift away from theoretical readings that reduce people to the conditions from which they arose. Whereas Anna Sokolow grew up in the immigrant, labor-organized movements of the 1930s, her focus and audience was

PRELUDE TO ACTION   45

humanity as a whole. A commentary from 1935 marks her work as different to her peers: "Anna always managed to be more the artist than the agitator. The urgency of her message never displaced her from the realm of dance."[58] It is visible, here, that the commentator sees these two terms as exclusionary; in the argument of this book they are read as dialectic.

Anna's statements elucidate this message and push it further, in dialectic tension. In a text from 1966 entitled *The Rebel and the Bourgeoisie* she starts by stating:

> I hate academics. I hate fixed ideas of what a thing should be, of how it should be done. I don't like imposing rules, because the person, the artist, must do what he feels is right, what he—as an individual—feels he must do. If we establish an academy, there can be no future for the modern dance. An art should be constantly changing; it cannot have fixed rules.[59]

The focus is first and foremost on action, on the individual creating and unraveling work for others. There is a calling to be courageous in the self, to explore one's inner stories despite societal policing: "To young dancers, I want to say: 'do what you feel you are, not what you think you ought to be. Go ahead and be a bastard. Then you can be an artist.'"[60] There is a high price for bravery, but going ahead is the only option for activism, whether in dance or elsewhere.

Much like Graham's focus on the now, Sokolow understands modern dance as art of the present unfolding toward the future. "The important thing is that the art being created now be related to now, to our time. The artist must be influenced by his time, conditioned by the life around him. If he is not, if his viewpoint is limited by the past, and turns back instead of going forward. If he draws on the ever-changing life around him, his work will always be fresh and new. Art should be a reflection and a comment on contemporary life."[61] Artists are not disengaged from society and their present is always unraveling toward a time yet to come.

Art is part of society but reflects its creator's voice: "I don't believe in ivory towers. The artist should belong to his society, yet without feeling that he has to conform to it. He must feel that there is a place for him in society, a place for what he is. He must see life fully, and then say what he feels about it. Then, although he belongs to his society, he can change it, presenting it with fresh feelings, fresh ideas."[62] This is a succinct definition of a view of activism through dance—entrenched in society yet able to provide it with a vision of a better tomorrow, by appealing to shared feeling and humanity, thus presenting an alternative to what is known and accepted. This is Sokolow's elucidation of praxis. Art is conceptualized explicitly as a way to bring about social change.

Sokolow provides direct statements about her reading of alienation: "[This generation] don't want freedom."[63] Further, "Yet some people are afraid to use life, feeling that art should be something apart, sorting isolated from reality."[64] "The new generation haven't really faced themselves; they don't know what it is that they want to say."[65] This is a forceful articulation of alienation; of the fear of life itself, of being a full human being relating to other human beings.

As a concise, precise statement on alienation, it leads towards her danced statement, "Rooms," her choreographic reading of alienation. In the same essay she wrote:

> Rooms was choreographed without music. I wanted to do something about people in a big city. The theme of loneliness and noncommunication evolved as I worked. I like to look into windows, to catch glimpses of unfinished lives. Then I ask; "what is there, and why?" Then I thought of using chairs as if they were rooms, each dancer on his own chair, in his own room. Isolated from all the others though physically so close to them.[66]

"Rooms" will be analyzed in detail next as an exemplar of a danced contemplation about alienation.

"Rooms" was premiered in 1955, long after Sokolow had left the tenements of her childhood landscape and the social-economic themes that had emerged from it. Betty Walberg, pianist for "Rooms," narrates the story of its becoming: "When we were working on it, we knew instinctively that something very special was happening. It was the same feeling I had when I worked with Jerry a few years later on West Side Story; you know something is happening that is going to change the face of things."[67] Sokolow describes the work as follows: "Rooms dealt with the devastating aloneness that can grip people who cannot make contact with others except on the most superficial level. There are no heroes, no central characters. The work portrays not so much how these people act in their isolated world, but how they feel being there. The central character could be any one

PRELUDE TO ACTION   47

of us. By touching on the universality of human isolation in so direct and visceral a way, Anna created one of the enduring masterpieces of twentieth-century art."[68] "Rooms" is an ensemble work in nine parts (Alone-Dream-Escape-Going-Desire-Panic-Daydream-The End?-Alone),[69] and narrates the existential feeling of being alone. This was groundbreaking work in its use of chairs on stage; each chair was to signify a room.[70]

Beginning with the section "Alone," which starts and closes the work, the theme of alienation is brought to the forefront of the stage. Sokolow ends where she begins so that the work remains open ended, much like the argument of this book—she pushes the spectator to find the answer to the conceptual question she poses them. "Rooms," she says, is New York, is the streets, is the tenements, "is where I grew up." "Rooms" is an exemplary work on alienation and solidarity; it starts from the condition of loneliness, poverty, and harsh living conditions that provide the backdrop to an exceptionally lyrical enunciation of the human spirit that transcends them. Dancers on stage, using chairs as their rooms, boundaries of movement, also show the lack of boundaries of their spirit. Sokolow's work exposes raw, unadulterated humanity. There is no escape from the essence of who we are when watching her work; no myths or abstractions or simplifications. Yet Sokolow's work also, in the range of emotion and movement, shows the spectator the range of their possibilities—what it means, truly, to be human.

Two sections of "Rooms" especially illuminate the underlying dialectic of this book: first, the section called "Alone." In this section dancers are on stage in chairs that are connected but also alien; their movement resonates but is also disengaged. They are, clearly to the spectator, related somehow to each other, their movement echoes and shifts here and there—never didactically a unison, nor a solo showing an unequivocal triumph or resolution, but subtle interactions—here a foot mirroring another foot shifting in a similar way on other side of the stage, there a body falling in an angle illuminating another body rising on the other side. Never too symmetrical, never too organized, the movement is always deeply lyrical. A strong message here for what a danced work in concert may entail; alienation is a profound condition in which similar utterances are made in close spaces and solidarity—Sokolow's choreography and, moreover, the audience response to it—is a step forward to subvert it. Anna commented on this section: "Each person in a chair is alone in a room, and they are looking out of the window. The room is very small and they don't know who lives next door. They don't know who they pass on the

48   DANCE AND ACTIVISM

stairs going up and down. In the first section you see all eight of them projected. It is called 'Alone' so it's like saying alone, alone, eight times."[71] The dancers are alone, but together, in front of an audience; and so they are not really alone.

Another hugely poignant element of this work is a solo termed "Escape."[72] A woman, alone on her chair, performs both everyday gestures and elaborate, emotive, lyrical movement. Who or what is she trying to escape? Her surroundings? Her own being? The depth of emotive movement here is explosive. Confined movement shows the expansiveness of the soul, transcending a very bounded space in which it unfolds; the piece reveals the depth of humanity in the most constrained of spaces. Sokolow commented on this section: "The next room is called 'Escape'. You see a girl with an evening dress on and she has the greatest romantic image of herself. She thinks she is Greta Garbo waiting for a lover to come in."[72] The generosity of swaying limbs and the expression pulsing from within act in tension to the set showing highly constrained, separate lives. Escape from alienating lives on one's own is always impossible, in the dance and outside of the stage.

Yet Anna Sokolow's work, in "Rooms" and beyond it, was to elucidate action that came from the spectre of alienation, from the dangers of extreme and oppressive segregation, of people unable to tell their own stories. The impulse for action is crystalized in her work as well as in her words: "You do not ease up on action. You take action," she began. "There is far too much contemplation, dreaming, and much too little movement. Go forward. Reach. Demand to be seen or heard or experienced."[74] Sokolow was a woman of action, striving to elucidate the beauty and horror in humanity so that people could see the depths of despair but also the utter beauty human life entails. The stripped-down movement, far distant from Graham's dramatic gestures, exposes the raw underpinnings of human life for better and for worse, and when watching her work one is forced to confront one's options.

"Rooms," like Graham's "Chronicle," arose from a specific time and context and yet transcended it, exemplifying Sokolow's work that started from specific social conditions and yet was able to discuss humanity beyond it, as a whole. "Rooms" saw early and immediate success and became part of many companies' repertory, beyond Sokolow. A review from 1956 comments: "Rooms is a powerful, deeply penetrating exploration of man's aloneness ... Miss Sokolow has given her subject stunning theatrical treatment through movements which are striking as

PRELUDE TO ACTION   49

pure dance action but also revelatory of the individual dreams of each of the participants."[75]

Sokolow's career expanded and included many accomplishments and collaborations in her own company and beyond it, becoming a foundational figure of modern dance in Israel as well as Mexico. The Sokolow Dance Company is presenting "Rooms" as part of their 2020 season. Samantha Geracht Myers, a celebrated modern dancer who studied with a variety of luminaries from Sokolow's generation (as well as Anna herself), comments on programming "Rooms" in 2020: "When Anna made 'Rooms' in 1955 she was looking at how isolated people were feeling even living on top of one another in a tenement building. In 2020 we are all feeling just as isolated even if we have access to 24-hour social media. While the world is very different in many ways, the basics of how we feel as people have not changed at all."[76] Alienation changes in its articulations but remains a challenge haunting our humanity.

Jennifer Conley, a former member of the Martha Graham Dance Company and admired specialist in modern dance, who had performed Sokolow's works, narrates the visceral experience of dancing Anna Sokolow's work in the twenty-first century, from sitting on a panel with Samantha Geracht Myers to performing in Lyric Suite:

> I remember saying something about experiencing life and culture of another period through embodying these "historic" works and passed the mic down the line when Samantha leaned over and said, "you should really learn one of Anna's works." And that was it. I said yes, and asked her what piece. She said she would need to talk with Jim (May)[77] about that. A few months later, I was in a studio with Samantha and starting the process of learning the "Andante Amoroso" solo from Lyric Suite. Samantha said that was Jim's suggestion, and he was posing a challenge to Samantha because she had never danced that work. The experience presented a new horizon of possibility for both us. The process was a long one."[78]

No two processes of learning dance works are exactly the same, and yet it is telling to listen to practitioners whose bodies contain different histories as they reflect how a new history enters the viscera. The process of entering the world of Sokolow in the twenty-first century is through solidarity in transmission, and that solidarity remains in the process of learning and performance:

50 DANCE AND ACTIVISM

After I learned the complete piece, we parted for about two months. I recall her [S. Geracht Myers] saying I shouldn't rehearse it like crazy, but instead let it "simmer." Foreign of a concept as that was for me, I followed her instruction. The next time we rehearsed it was amazing to feel the material flow out of me. I was surprised with how much information was retained in my body memory with so much time between rehearsals. That was when I started to believe in the power of less being more.[79]

Conley relates her process with the work of Anna Sokolow to her previous training, like Anna's own beginnings, in Martha Graham's technique:

On this note, going into Sokolow material from Graham is a process of stripping away all the "beyond human" intensity/energy/imagery ... There is a sense of reality in Sokolow's work that was new to me. It is a movement away from theatrical spectacle toward what postmodernists would call pedestrian—but it is neither of those things. For example, the chairs one stage in "Rooms" are just that, real chairs. Nothing decorative, abstracted, or metaphorical. The chair, is the chair, is the chair. And for every dancer that performs that work, they know what it means to sit down in a chair and to get out of that chair. That makes it incredibly accessible.[80]

Yet, accessible does not mean easy on the heart. Sokolow's drama was the drama of the life around her but was able to transcend its immediate context and inhabit many bodies that followed her. Conley comments:

It's not opera. There is not a tragic divine vibrato in the body like I feel in Martha Graham's work, but it is an experience that is engaged deeply. There is a feeling that I must go deep, go deep within but there is no character or image to armor myself with ... it is just me out there moving, perceiving, experiencing and that makes me feel totally naked and transparent! It is not grand, but it is human. Every moment leads to a choice, a different choice from night to night based on my awareness of that moment. It is a fascinating thing. When I speak with people who do improvisation, we are referencing the same experience except I'm actually working within a determined structure. The boundaries of that structure do not feel confining in the least! So I feel naked and free.[81]

PRELUDE TO ACTION   51

And then there is the transmission of a history into the present through performing a work that brings something new to every new body it inhabits. On the process of working on Sokolow in the twenty-first century, Conley says:

> The moments of looking at something and then looking away or turning within in deep grief and despair really recalled my own experience witnessing the atrocities of that day. It was not cathartic. It was depressing, because you really have to go there, fully and when you do there is no release. Taking a bow after that work felt odd. I recall Anna in an interview in the early 80s (I think) saying that after a performance of "Dreams" in Holland the audience was silent. They did not applaud, and she felt that was the perfect response to that piece. "How do you applaud for something like that?" This is the realism that I experience in Anna's work, it is a theatre of the real. I was deeply moved and felt immediate political importance of that work today.[82]

The response to a work on alienation can be by providing quiet solidarity; by being there, witnessing, and being a living, breathing body receiving these messages and acknowledging them.

Gerarcht Myers provides an urgent and necessary vista through a profoundly intimate knowledge of Sokolow's work in our current times:

> Sokolow's works are deeply human and personal, venturing into the human condition in places of horror and places of love, treading into the depth of the psyche stripped so bare that both the performer and audiences are drawn through her choreography to deep feeling. Simultaneously, Sokolow's style is just abstract enough to be timeless. Well known for her searing social commentary, the non-literal style of Sokolow's dances of eternal truth speaks to the events of today and reminds us of her unwavering belief in the triumph of the human spirit.[83]

This may act as a non-conclusion for a work that had emerged from a specific social-economic context and yet has been transformed by many tubulations and changes in its context of performance. Every layer of meaning that emerges from a moment of performance changes the meaning of the work. Perhaps it would be more accurate to refer to this phenomenon of works as transmitted from their time to another; not as "timeless," as all dance is always performed in certain bodies who live in social-economic conditions. The process of transmission into new eras allows us to pour new meaning into these works that survive beyond their moment of premier, becoming a piece and a memento *of a new time.*

In 1955, the year "Rooms" premiered and provided the world with a musing on people's responses to confined spaces, one young dance luminary and activist resisted her confined space and changed history forever. On December 1, 1955, Rosa Parks refused to sit in her segregated space on the bus, shortly after young Emmett Till was viciously murdered and lynched in a year that would be crucial to the civil rights movement, changing the course of American—and world—history forever. The third exemplar of activist dance in the first half of the twentieth century begins from that epoch.

"Through Dance I Have Experienced the Wordless Joy of Freedom": Pearl Primus

Pearl Primus was born in Trinidad in 1919 and came to New York in 1921, where she burst onto the world stage in 1943 in her debut as a choreographer.[84] Her artistic influences show the breadth of her praxis; she studied with Martha Graham, whose work began this discussion, as well as with Paul Robeson, whose solidarity work and activism truly transcended borders from the USA to Wales.[85] In terms of her specific placement within African-American dance and culture she was inspired by Katherine Dunham as well as Dafora dance theater.[86] Pearl Primus inhabited movement praxis beyond borders of discipline, education, and performance.

Pearl Primus's life and career elucidates the struggles and challenges of black communities whose cultures are collapsed by mainstream writing and cultural curation into "non-white," having to deal with the urgency of racism in their midst, while the effort to be attentive to various influences and languages that form the self sustains (while white Americans and Europeans are granted an ever-expanding space). Her biographers comment that in NYC, West Indians were segregated by race

PRELUDE TO ACTION   53

but integrated by ethnicity and class:[87] "West Indians were considered 'black' immigrants in a city of immigrants, but race structured their life chances."[88] Migrants were often the subjects of Primus's art as well as a significant part of her audience.[89] White supremacy structured her life, as it did, and still does, so many artists, yet Primus's voice and commitment to integrity shone bright in her times and transcended it.

Pearl Primus performing. Photo by Gjon Mili/The LIFE Picture Collection via Getty Images.

Primus's education in the very white New Dance Group (she was encouraged by Anna Sokolow) presented her with lived lessons on structural racism, yet its politics enabled her to subvert and carve a space for herself and others. Martin wrote on her debut in the 92nd Street YMCA that she walked away with the "lion share of the honors."[90] She was featured in a major anti-racist rally, crucial to the history of the civil rights movement, at Madison Square Garden in 1943,[91] upon which John Martin commented:

> The young lady who leapt so high in the middle of Madison Square Garden a couple of weeks ago at the Negro Freedom Rally is named Miss Pearl Primus. She is in the very middle of the Garden on a star-shaped stage, and twenty thousand people were sitting around her. Every time she leapt, folks felt like shouting. Some did. Some hollered out loud. Pearl Primus is a dancer. She was dancing a dance called Jim Crow Train, and another dance called Hard Times Blues[92] by Josh White and Waring Caney. She is a dark brown young lady. She got low down on the ground, walked, turned, twisted, then jumped way up into the air. The way she jumped was the same as a shout in church. She did not like the Jim Crow Train, so she leaped way up into the air. And it was like a work weary sister suddenly shouting out loud on a Sunday morning when the minister started singing, Jesus knows just how much I can bear.[93]

"When Pearl danced 'Jim Crow Train' she was dancing for herself, for her family, and for all those Jim-Crowed. The political was deeply personal."[94] Martin continued to enact the societal experience of pre-civil-rights black Americans. Martin raised race even when he declared Primus the premier dancer of the season. In spite of the sheer brilliance of her dancing, the critics needed to define her as a *black* dancer, using racist discourse and understanding, associating the immense energy and precision of her movement language with racial categories. Structural racism means that some dancers are only allowed be radical in categories bestowed over them by the group that oppresses them. However, Primus was a fierce fighter against racism. Speaking of her preparation for this rally she said:

> I know we must all do our part to beat Fascism and I consider the battle against Jim Crow in America part of that fight, which is taking place on

PRELUDE TO ACTION **55**

the battlefronts of the world ... even one of us can wield a weapon against Jim Crow and Fascism and my special one is dancing. I shall continue to protest Jim Crow through my dancing till victory is won.[95]

Her art both supported the war effort against fascism and protested against racism.[96]

Whereas Emma Goldman and Martha Graham were measuring steps in their streets, Griffin notes that Primus was walking the same streets as James Baldwin. "Not everything that is faced can be changed, but nothing can be changed until it is faced,"[97] Baldwin penned, and it was Primus's life's work to show those things that people work hard to avoid so that they are changed and more lives intersect. Primus was an intellectual as well as an artist, for whom dance became a way of bearing witness to what her studies revealed, and her discipline as well as her activism stemmed from this conviction. A desire to eliminate white supremacy, racism, and discrimination was the impulse that brought an incredibly diverse body of work together in a cohesive narrative.[98]

Pearl Primus spent her life enquiring around links between identity and culture as a base for action. In a book that chronicles the work of progressive women artists during the Second World War, *Harlem Nocturne*, Farah Jasmine Griffin notes that Primus's calling was "to use the language of dance to represent the dignity and strength of black people and express their longing for freedom."[99] Primus saw dance as a means of contributing to the ongoing struggle for social justice.[100] This was significant as she introduced a new context for the marriage of black aesthetics and politics.[101] She lived a new praxis, which would open the doors for many who came after her.

The positioning of Primus as a "black dancer" pushed her to action. In July and August 1944, she went to the American South, in a trip that transformed her art,[102] and found that racism was raw and present. Out of this backdrop she created "Hard Times Blues." Primus said:

In the South of the United States many people still live in extreme poverty. They are forever indebted to the landowners who live far away. This dance is a protest against the system which robs the people of the ruins of their labour.[103]

In 1954 she went to study in her native land of Trinidad,[104] and later travelled to Africa where she was given the name "a child returned home"—Omowale.[105] At the same time, her associations with radical circles marked her out in the eyes of the American authorities. Primus placed African dance and aesthetics in parallel to modern dance, creating a dialogue between both forms and showing both were a longing for freedom and dignity, an approach later referred to as Afrocentrism.[106] She gained a PhD in anthropology from NYU in 1978. This understanding of the relationship between theory and action stands out in the context of this chapter; Primus sought to chronicle her own journey, and that of many others, as part of her praxis. By so doing she unraveled solidarities that have changed the lives of many others who came after her.

Unlike both Sokolow and Graham, Primus was also a member of the Communist Party.[107] For her, the racial problem in America was a problem of democracy.[108] Primus's early dances ranged a wide variety of issues, from her debut in "Authentic Dances" and "First Shine" in the New Dance Group Festival Program in 1941, through to 1943's "A Man has just Been Lynched" at her professional debut at the 92Y, a dance that she would later develop into "Strange Fruit," and "Hard Time Blues," "Jim Crow Train," "The Negro Speaks of Rivers," and "African Ceremonial" in 1944. "Hard Time Blues" as well as "Strange Fruit" came out of Primus's visceral response to the stark racism in the South, danced to a song that references sharecroppers, a comment on their everyday hard work, performed by the folk singer Josh White. This was a dance about a man resisting his degrading situation, the exploitation of his labor, and the racism that structured his life. The lyrics as well as the depiction of the harsh conditions of work in which the dancer moves is poised in dialectic to the physicality of the dance, which shows resistance and empowerment in motion. "Hard Time Blues," read in its context, is a brave iteration showing how various forms of oppression (racial, economic, and societal) are interlinked and hinder all Americans from living a fully liberated life.

Concerts were cancelled because of Primus's political dances, especially "Strange Fruit"[109]—a work to which this part of the chapter is dedicated—and pickets assembled outside her shows in the Midwest. Maya Angelou, who was greatly inspired by Primus's work said: "Don't be naive! This is the would-be United States of America."[110] Dance as activism is dangerous to those structures it wishes to challenge. Just as Rosa Parks's refusal to sit in an assigned place was as galvanizing as it was inspiring, Pearl Primus never accepted simply being termed a "black dancer," nor the space assigned to her in the circles she worked within, including those which saw themselves as radical. Her own thinking and words ruffled feathers

PRELUDE TO ACTION **57**

among all groups—those she was rebelling against and those she empathized with. An interview from the *New York Times* claims that when she began performing African dances in the 1940s, Primus encountered resistance from black audiences who, she said, "had been taught," to be ashamed of their heritage as "primitive."[111] This has now been changed, much thanks to her work as well as other pioneers working to claim their own stories in their own voices. Later, when she danced in Africa, she encountered resistance there, too, which pushed her to claim, in 1988, that "the African-American has a technique of movement that is special to the United States," and not found elsewhere among black people. "I am not talking about professional dancers who have studied other techniques," she explained. "But if you take six dancers from Chicago, Florida and New York and put them in the same studio, you will see a technique of movement that is the same in timing and emphasis."[112] The punishing regime of structural racism represents a double marginalization of people who are seen as "others" in the USA (or other countries whose discourses are underpinned by white supremacy) yet when they return to the homelands from which their ancestors were expelled, they are strangers there, too. This was a struggle that spun Pearl Primus's career and yielded creative results that changed the course of history.

> It goes back to the movement people were forced to do on the slave ships. They were made to dance. There was little space aboard, but they had to exercise or they were whipped or thrown overboard. So, you got a kind of movement that was different for a sociological reason. It was not the movement that came out of Africa. And you do not find it in the Caribbean. Because once they reached shore, what happened? In South America and the Caribbean, the slave quarters were away from the master's quarters, and the slaves could indulge in dances—which also had French and Spanish influences. But in the United States, dancing by slaves was forbidden. If you go into certain churches today, they don't say, "I dance." They say, "The spirit dances."[113]

In her activist dance, Pearl Primus opened spaces for telling a unique story, which opened up doors for many others who would come after her, yet arose from pain and exclusion.

Primus states her message as a clear, concise definition of praxis:

58 DANCE AND ACTIVISM

Dance has been my vehicle. Dance has been my language, my strength. In the dance I have confided my most secret thoughts and shared the inner music of all mankind. I have danced across mountains and deserts, ancient rivers and oceans and slipped through the boundaries of time and space. Dance has been my freedom and my world. It has enabled me to go around, scale, bore through, batter down or ignore visible and invisible social and economic walls.[114]

Primus's dance starts from the inner depths of the soul, though in so doing dismantles the constraints from within which it is performed. The walls disable some people from telling their own stories in their own voice. Dance has a social weight; all the more for someone who faced obstacles that many of her peers did not face. At the same time, dance aims to change society as a whole, as Primus writes in a program note: "I dance not to entertain but to help people better understand each other. Because through dance I have experienced the wordless joy of freedom. I seek it more fully now for my people and for *all* people everywhere."[115]

Pearl Primus experienced structural—and physical—racism, and her dance challenged those attitudes and behaviors head on. At the same time, her dance aimed to emancipate womankind and mankind as a whole, realizing that alienating one part of the population leads necessarily to the loss of humanity in all its parts. Primus states as her mission statement:

Throughout the ages man has danced. He danced because he had something to say, and he danced for the joy which comes with rhythmic movement. As he pounded the grain, as he prepared for the hunt, even as he worshiped, he danced. He translated into this language of gesture his longings, his ecstasy, his tears, his laughter, his prayer. Man danced!

Tonight we dance with a twofold purpose. We wish not only to entertain you but to bring you a part of ourselves, that we may grow closer in the bond of brotherhood and so move one step closer to world peace.[116]

For Primus dance has a heightened mission of activism in her time, though dance in its essence always changes the societal configuration in which it is performed. Much like Anna Sokolow, she sees alienation as a key issue in contemporary society, when she discusses the metaphor of the mask:

[H]ere in the United States, the psychological mask must also be removed. Unless the manipulator is allowed to be, all growth can be aborted. The mask cannot grow. It is a shell which can be outgrown. The manipulator can become a prisoner inside. Worse yet, the wearer can grow into the structure of the mask, distorting it and at the same time being distorted by it. Soon it becomes too late to struggle. In hiding the self, the self has been destroyed.[117]

This discussion of alienation resonates with the price paid by alienating, as well as alienated forces. It is a clear and urgent calling to center the issue of alienation in discourse as well as in dance. The consequence of alienation and violence for the oppressed as well as for the oppressor became the subject for one of her most celebrated works, and an enduring call to end racism.

Over a fine New York City lunch in 1940, Pearl Primus and Billie Holiday spoke with lyricist Lewis Allan, a.k.a. Abel Meeropol, a high school dance teacher at de Witt Clinton High School in the Bronx, about his poem "Strange Fruit." The poem evokes the pain of African Americans in an era in which many white people considered lynching a legitimate method of dealing with a person of color who dared to challenge their oppression. Primus went on to choreograph "Strange Fruit" (originally named "A Man Has Just Been Lynched"), which became one of her most famous works. Premiered in her first recital in 1943, "Strange Fruit" was to become a landmark work in modern dance, in anti-racist artistic activism, and in Primus's career.[118]

"Strange Fruit" was the most harrowing of the solos that Primus created. The dance was initially performed to the accompaniment of the poem, and readers at various times included the actors Gordon Heath and Vinette Caroll. But when Primus performed "Strange Fruit" in silence the dance developed its greatest impact. The audience could hear the gasping intake of breath, Primus's fists beating on the floor, and her footfall as she runs and throws herself to the ground. The dance ends with a run that Pearl describes "as gathering the consciousness of mankind to this act of cruelty and injustice." Finally, under the "unbearable weight of the act, the dancer succumbs and falls to the ground. With a final thrust of her fist, as if she is stating that such despicable acts must never occur again."[119] The physical iterations are not a metaphor for resistance but are resistance in themselves. "As you come up, it's not just flinging the arms up as the run begins, it's almost as if you're gathering the consciousness of mankind. You're gathering up everything in order to make that last final pull down gesture that this injustice must never be repeated."[120]

Primus discussed the dance in a 1988 interview: "'Strange Fruit,'" for instance, is concerned with "a deep psychological thing, and I came out of that period of dance." She continues to place the dance within her archive: "The dance begins as the last person begins to leave the lynching ground," Primus said, "and the horror of what she has seen grips her, and she has to do a smooth, fast roll away from that burning flesh. The hurt and anger that hurled me to the ground in that solo were translated into an anger that took me into the air in 'Hard Times Blues.'"[121]

Based on the famous poem by Lewis Allen, a white author, the solo does not contain his image of "black bodies" hanging from the trees. Instead, Primus took the daring step of identifying herself with a white woman in a lynch mob.[122] This is an act of resistance by a woman who was pigeonholed by the racist world in which she lived. It is a dance that is drawn from her deepest experience and yet in its very being unravels beyond her and the racist structures underpinning her life. The dance raises crucial questions sitting at the heart of activism that creates solidarities, about integrity and responsibility. Primus dances about the connection between wrongdoers and those who are silent in the face of a wrong, showing that the boundary between those two categories is more precarious than it may seem. The fact that the dancer represents an onlooker makes a crucial point about the culpability of the audience—whether metaphorical or literal—about wrongs and rights and, on a positive reading, the possibility of an audience member resisting and enabling a solidarity of radical dance to emerge.

Her biographers note on "Strange Fruit":

Pearl made it clear that "strange fruit" was so personal that she would rather withhold rights to the dance than see it performed badly. She was not talking about technique ... she was referring to the artist's capability to transmit the infinite and critical nuances of intention and meaning so the solo could rightly illuminate its fundamental question and response: How has mankind allowed such injustice? All such acts of cruelty must never occur again! The breadth and scope of Pearl's artistic, cultural, political and anthropological beliefs merged within the accusations lodged in this dance.[123]

PRELUDE TO ACTION 61

The dance is constructed choreographically within a tension between running and reaching, opening up and collapsing to the floor. Is there an inevitability of injustice? Are those witnessing acts of horrific violence constrained to their space? Primus's movement language is expressive yet driven, potent and focused; this isn't an emotive cry but a call for action. The reaching out of arms, especially, is in tension with running and falling; a very physical fall, surrendering to forces of harm, of violence. The feeling of danger as well as the quest to escape it is very present in the performance.

Reading this dance in its context adds further layers to its potency. This is a dance performed by a black woman about a white woman witnessing a racist lynching, shying away from injustice and not acting in the context of horrific wrongs. The music was sung by another heroine of the civil rights movement, Billie Holiday. This dance, today, needs little explaining, showing its power as a piece of danced activism. This was all the more so in the time of its premiere, before the change galvanized by the civil rights movement broke into American history, when the danger to black bodies was present everywhere. Primus's bravery is still urgently inspiring in our times, as she dared to challenge the responsibility of her spectators, including those who see themselves as radical and progressive.[124]

The lasting potency of this dance can be revealed in its reception. Yemenite-Israeli dancer Ahuva Anbary commented on "Strange Fruit":

> I remember a solo, a wonderful solo. She did circle falls. She would fall and rise in circle five or six times. It was like Graham but different. Graham falls don't lead with the hops . . . instead of sliding into a split and then to a fall, she did it from standing up. She did a hitch forward, falling into the arm, going sideways a little bit with the body, going into one arm only. Then when she reached the floor, she would shift to her left leg and turn the right leg backwards, turning herself around. She would rise from the knees, into the body and then into the arms, using the arms to rise without putting weight on the knees. She pushed into the hips, into the knees, into the arms and always got applauds on that.[125]

Dancer Michelle Simonns, who performed the dance later, comments:

> So when I went to perform it downstage left and made the run, at this point it was a lynching, but Bosnia and Herzegovina was there, the

Holocaust was there, every horrible thing that human beings have done to each other on this planet ... it bothered me terribly that Muslim women were being raped ... Buchenwald, the death camps, all of that. Lynching, too ... that's what made it become so deeply, deeply, deeply real to me.[126]

The wrongs against which Pearl Primus bravely stood up enabled many other women who came after her to challenge racism in their midst.

Luminary writer, activist, and dancer Maya Angelou started dancing in 1945. On seeing Pearl Primus:

I'd never seen anything like it. I'd never seen such strength and grace at the same time. I'd seen beauty but never almost a raw strength with the grace of a sigh. I couldn't contain my tears at the beauty, and ecstasy is what I remember of Ms. Primus dancing. She seemed to stand without a plie and lift herself and had those very thick thighs, and she was like a gazelle. And so she saw me and saw me weeping and she came over to me and I told her I was a dancer ... she gave me a time the next day and I came without music and a leotard and I just danced. And she said, "you are a dancer. You are a dancer". I told her the little I had of training and said if I would come to New York she would give me a scholarship to study with her. And that's all I could think of for months.[127]

Pearl Primus was an exemplar of solidarity both on and off stage, and enabled many women who followed in her footsteps to raise their voice against injustice.

Primus sums up the impact of this truly unique dance in her own words, which allow us to bring this discussion to its next step. "I didn't create 'strange fruit' for a dancer," she explains. "I created it to make a statement within our society, within our world. And therefore, it was made with my body. When I danced it, I wasn't a male or female. I wasn't the wind. I wasn't a tree. I was a concept."[128] Dance as activism, as elucidating responsibility and the power of dissent in response to horrific, constraining frameworks, is anything but a metaphysical move. Dance as activism is the sole dancer gathering her audience's consciousness to resist the evils of her time but also those that follow. The ability to not be silent at the face of ostensible violence shows the power of solidarity. Primus's biographers Peggy and Murray Schwartz comment: "Pearl did

PRELUDE TO ACTION   **63**

resist the racism, lack of money, political opposition, and the social conditions of dance. She would always turn her negative feelings into positive action, and find the energy to say, 'I'll dance'!"[129]

And her dance changed her life, as well as those of so many who came after her.

Dance as Intervention, Dance as Action

Did Martha Graham ever run into Emma Goldman and discuss revolutionary dancing? We will never know. But what is clear is Goldman, Graham, Sokolow, and Primus, in different ways, all made dance and revolution interchangeable and created revolutionary, danced praxis that inhabited many bodies after they had died. The beginning of the century chronicled in this book is also the beginning of unfolding dialectics. Action has a start, and this chapter explored three paralleled beginnings. All ubiquitous in their own way, considering them together paints a picture of radical steps burning through the streets of New York City. Three dancer-activists who responded to conditions of alienation by offering solidarities of different kinds, and more than anything "lived their beautiful ideal," as Goldman stated, and presented three groundbreaking interpretations of praxis in dance as activism. They all, in different ways, opened up new solidarities that continue to this day. The social-economic background from which modern dance arose gave it an activist impulse, crystalized in works now canonical, and living in many other dancer-activists' bodies. However, other forms of dance, less bound up in stories of resistance outside the studio, gave the world different forms of dance as activism. The next chapter explores one such form, ballet.

3 BALLET BEYOND BORDERS

Pearl Primus was a strong voice in the modern dance tradition, which in its radical beginnings was susceptible to interruptions and forms of activism deep inside the studio and theater. She was also a strong voice in the civil rights movement that transformed the history of America (and yet showed how much work has to be done, still). At the same time, the argument pursued in the book is that the entire world of dance is open to radical action, not just modern dance or dance created in the early twentieth century, a temporal moment which was, as argued in the previous chapter, uniquely revolutionary politically as well as aesthetically. This chapter seeks to examine radical dance within another form of dance, which preceded modern dance and was the form against which it rebelled: ballet.

Every day millions of dancing feet within rooms, studios and outdoor spaces assemble in a particular ritual. The barre, that physical support that enables the commencement of the ballet class, as well as ballet class as a concept in and of itself, carries within it an ethical and epistemological weight that is independent of the performative history of ballet as a concert art form (which is usually the focus of research on ballet). The ballet class can take many forms and shapes, and yet some elements of it always recur; from the *plié*, the soft melting of knees enabling the dancer to execute any movement in their vocabulary, to the *tendu*, swishing the foot against the floor, which is the first encounter the feet have with the earth, the surface from which all dancing springs. These concepts are indeed rituals that unify an enormously diverse community of dancers worldwide.

Some rituals find new arcs in their unfolding. Ballet represents a repetition of set movements and set customs and events, whose unfolding can be foreseen and yet gains new meaning out of different contexts and the different bodies who move within it. This chapter operates on a twofold plane. First, it asks: What does it mean for the discipline of ballet to read it away from the Western canon from which it emerged, complete with its power relations and effects on a variety of politics? Second, the chapter asks: Can—in what way can—ballet be a radical art form? Can ballet be used to revolutionize other forms of life and to question conservative configurations of authority?

Focusing now on ballet as well as activism allows us perhaps to understand this form of dance and its radical implications. You cannot freeze a pirouette. You cannot stop a jump mid-air. In its movement vocabulary ballet capitalizes on the absolute living-in-the-present. The fact that no move can be replicated means that ballet needs to stabilize itself in other ways so it can be passed on. Ballet epitomizes the tension between presentness and stability; between the absolute now and enabling the replication of that absolute now. This is a dialectical necessary relationship that lies at the heart of ballet as an art form. Ballet is a reflection on the present through the human body. Ballet entails succumbing to the absolute now, which may entail vulnerability or fragility in other fields of human experience; now being able to draw on stable resources or indeed plan for a stable future. At the same time, in its movement vocabulary that draws on the past as well as the need to pass it on, ballet creates systems of inscription and thus becomes a fragile language written in the now. A ballet dancer is never without a space, as they require their bodies in order to enunciate their vocabulary. Dance is a spatial art form—drawing on the body and utilizing it as vehicle for expression. Ballet gives living-in-the-now a spatial stability in its method of expression. Whereas ballet can be perceived as an ephemeral art form, it is grounded in the first physical contact to the world—the human body. The human body requires physical support networks in order to survive. Humans are first and foremost material beings. As such we need to be able to plan for some kind of spatial stability that transcends the now. Relying on the human body only, with no spatial stability beyond that, reveals the most essential fragility of the human existence and the limitation of humanity's physicality.

Dance, broadly, is the art of the present, and ballet, specifically, has been understood as an art of the extreme living in the moment. At the same time, ballet projects into the future. Every jump starts in anticipation of landing; every turn in anticipation of ending. Ballet requires a strong ability to imagine the future in order to perform its vocabulary. Sustaining a movement vocabulary that draws on the past but requires ability to

66 DANCE AND ACTIVISM

imagine the future and yet always lives in the absolute present exemplifies the complex temporality of human life. Ballet also reveals the complex temporality of human interactions. Hence, ballet gains significant importance when performed in moments of political transition; when living in the now can unravel new futures.

Pausing on the beginnings of ballet is helpful to focus the argument. There are few forms of dance that have received as rich and elaborate an interpretation as ballet has in one book, Jennifer Homans's *Apollo's Angels*, which changed the field of discourse around ballet. A rigorous narrative of ballet and its many incarnations up to the late twentieth century, Homans's book provides a rich cultural history of the well-known moment when Louis XIV's devotion to dance would change the course of ballet and dance history forever.[1] Homans discusses the relationship between the "full blown absolutism" of Louis' reign and the development of ballet in his court,[2] as well as an engagement with "good marriages," purification, and noting "true" from "false" nobles.[3] Louis founded the Academy of Dance in 1661, noting that "The art of dancing ... is most advantageous and useful to our nobility and to the other people who have the honor of approaching us, not only in the time of war, in our enemies, but also in time of peace in our ballets."[4] Unlike modern dance, which was created against the backdrop of the radical movements of the early twentieth century, ballet was championed and consolidated as an art form by a king with an absolutist vision of politics. The cultural backdrop for ballet's founding moment sought to conserve and centralize power, not to disperse it and allow more voices to intervene in the governing of people's lives.

However, in the context of the argument of this book, it is useful to go beyond those beginnings and ask about the radical potential of dance not in terms of its creators and their intentions, but rather in the dancing bodies that mobilize the form itself. This chapter shows that ballet can be radical for those who choose to engage within it while challenging the intentions of its so-called "creators" and inspirations. Thus, this is an attempt to create a history of ballet through its dancer-activists, away from "great man" narratives that necessarily replicate the power structures within which they are embedded. The underlying question is: Can ballet as a form in itself enable radical action, when read either away or directly against its conservative historiographies?

It should be noted here, also, that this chapter does not engage in efforts to expand outreach or change dynamics within companies or schools that belong to the hegemony from which ballet arose and that still retain disproportionate power in discussions of power within dance discourse. Ballet companies in the US and Europe that attempt to tackle issues of representation and reach within their existing institutional frameworks will not be discussed here. This is for a twofold reason. First, the chapter attempts to look at the underpinning structures of ballet as a form growing away from a specific history (and, in many of the case studies that will be discussed, independently from it); discussions of equality within institutional structures that still adhere, to a large extent, to the politics from which ballet arose, would not serve an argument that looks at a counter-history of ballet. Second, outreach programs in ballet companies are to a large extent additions to the contemporary institutions, structures, and underpinning ideas of ballet—they by no means try to radically alter them (as do, whether intentionally or not, the case studies chosen for this chapter). The only two examples, discussed toward the end of the chapter, that hail from the regions from which ballet originated and consolidated itself as a canonical art form are Final Bow for Yellowface (USA) and Ballet Black (UK). However, both these case studies operate independently and, indeed, scrutinize companies that seek to keep ballet as a form in a known and accepted manner, rather than to reconsider and augment its very foundations.

Pearl Primus was a brave and groundbreaking anti-racist activist in the United States during a critical time in the twentieth century. At the same time, on the other side of the globe, many other human beings were trying to undo the yoke of racism that hindered their development. The history of the struggle against apartheid in South Africa is key to the history of activism in the twentieth century. The chapter now turns to the role ballet played for those who lived those years of struggle.

"No One is Born Hating Another Person Because of the Color of his Skin"[5]

It would be impossible to write a book about the history of the twentieth century without referring to one of the most disciplined, brave, and resilient anti-racist movements the world has known: the anti-apartheid movement in South Africa. Attempting to break down boundaries in conditions of harsh race segregation and struggles between settler-colonialists and native populations, whose land and labor was exploited to consolidate an imperialist model, a long history of anti-apartheid activists struggled until their efforts' culmination in a significant moment for progressive causes, still celebrated worldwide: Nelson Mandela's election as the first president of non-racialized South Africa in 1994. All elements of culture were vital to the campaign, which in its later stages relied upon, and was successful due to, a cultural and academic boycott. Dance was also important to Mandela himself, as shown in celebrations in 1999, when an 81-year-old Mandela joined singer Johnny Clegg in an impromptu public performance of anti-apartheid song "Asimbonanga," and said, "it is music and dance that make me at peace with the world."[6]

Ballet was an area in which racial tensions were enacted and played out, but it was also a field in which lives that would otherwise not intersect met in extraordinary circumstances. David Poole was studying to be a schoolteacher at Zonnebloem College at the Cape Town Colored Institution in District Six, when his paths crossed with a Muslim boy called Johaar Mosaval, who, a year or two previously, had started showing an enthusiastic interest in ballet.[7] Both developed successful international careers, studying in England and touring internationally. His biographer, Richard Glassone, recounts an incident in which Poole, who belonged to the "Cape Town coloured" population, was performing and the art master questioned whether it was indeed Poole dancing, exclaiming, "but sir, he's dancing with white girls!"[8] Poole was able to pass as "white" but Mosaval was not allowed to perform with Sadler's Wells ballet in 1954 when it toured South Africa, as the theaters were operating a strict color bar.[9] Mosaval remained with the Royal Ballet until 1976, when Poole was able to invite Mosaval to perform with the CAPAB (the Cape Performing Arts Board) ballet he now ran, which until then was operating under strict apartheid laws, to dance the title role in "Petrushka."[10] Poole also took part in anti-apartheid marches and tried to exemplify what a man of color could achieve, even under apartheid.[11] He died in 1991, never living to see the overturning of apartheid.

Poole, in his time with CAPAB, produced ballets that tackled explicitly issues of race inequality and apartheid, most notably three ballets: "Le Cirque" (1972), "The Rain Queen" (1973), and "Kami" (1976). Both "Le Cirque" and ""Kami" dealt with apartheid policies; "Le Cirque" was an attack on government repression and "Kami" was a grim tale of interracial marriage and its violent implications in its contemporary contexts. The work he and others had done to open up ballet to different voices transformed the perception of ballet as well as race relations. Presence on stage is a fact that cannot be removed, and yet opens up futures and imaginaries previously not considered possible.

Like many dancer-activists in this book, Poole put much energy and resources into education, seeing it as an essential part of creating action in the world. Another fascinating story from the struggles against apartheid shows the efficacy of ballet in creating change in the world. The story of the Johannesburg Youth Ballet touches upon some of the struggles and triumphs of Poole's career, and articulates his passion for education. He created a charity, Dance for All, bringing dance to underprivileged areas of non-white South Africa, as well as the David Poole Trust Fund, which still works toward supporting young artists in Cape Town. Perhaps one of the most remarkable things about the Johannesburg Youth Ballet, founded in 1976, is that it did not explicitly engage with the politics of its time, though they certainly structured its history. Its founder Audrey King was quoted in an *Evening Express* article from 1977 saying, "I am not politically minded, and so I wasn't surprised because I couldn't see why there should be any opposition."[12] Accepting an invitation to perform in the Aberdeen festival, King formed the racially integrated Johannesburg Youth Ballet (JYB). This time in South African history was especially volatile; the Soweto Uprisings (June 16, 1976) heightened political unrest, and yet the founding of JYB met with no opposition, a fact that may seem still surprising to the reader today. In the same interview she is quoted as saying: "Many of the Africans travel to rehearsals through trouble spots at some personal risk.[13] The members get on extremely well with each other, thanks to an opportunity they have hitherto been denied." Accounts by JYB veterans recount the experience of rehearsals and especially touring as a rare opportunity for interracial socializing that transformed the lives and understanding for all members of the company. One of the pieces performed in Aberdeen was called "What are We?" King states:

> In it I try to convey my belief in life and in humanity, I am trying to say that you, me, we have the power within us to make the world a happier place than it is at this minute. The young are the people who are going to have to live in this world, and if I can engender in a few people in my class this idea, I have done something. You can't change the whole

world—you can only throw a pebble in the water and watch the ripples go out.

It makes me very happy to know that what started out as an almost impossible dream of mine during the years of apartheid, has survived so long, and that the Company is still giving young dancers and choreographers an opportunity to present their talents to the public.[14]

This is a critical intervention in understanding praxis through dance, in response to alienation. And King's work unraveled new solidarities that changed the lives of those who partook in them. Yet the focus in the JYB was always on the artistry, integrity, and reverence to the art form. Any understanding of dance as activism that sees aesthetic excellence as antagonistic to a socially progressive understanding of art may turn to this example—exemplar—as grounds for a counter argument. King is remembered with reverence and admiration though she was, like many others within the ballet form, uncompromising and perfectionist. Her motto was "If something is worth doing, it's worth doing well!"

For those who danced in the Johannesburg Youth Ballet, the company was a possibility to engage in excellent training that would otherwise be barred to them. However, engaging in an art form that was made available to many is only part of the radicalism of the JYB. Allowing non-segregated interactions in a time in which this was illegal allowed the young dancers, both in training and on tour, a glimpse of a future yet to come, with a profound, incessant, and sometimes uncompromising focus on excellence in the present. Changing lives in the present allowed for a glimpse of a future yet to come as a lived experience. This is an instance of creating solidarity through dance, which in turn enabled its activists— both students and King as founder of the company—to experience a future that wouldn't arrive till decades later, that of life without racial segregation.

The extreme rigor demanded in training for ballet and the short-lived careers of ballet dancers mean that the focus is always on the now. This may seem like a contradiction to reading art as a visionary praxis, going toward the future, but as the underlying argument of this book has stated, the temporal frame in which this book works is a present expanding into a future. Hence the focus on the now can facilitate creating social change in lives of people for many years to come. This feature is crucial for some struggles that are very much still ongoing, as the next case study may teach.

BALLET BEYOND BORDERS   **71**

"Going around the House Like a Butterfly"

Revolutionary activist and the first president of post-apartheid South Africa, Nelson Mandela, said after the end of apartheid: "we know too well our freedom is incomplete without the freedom of the Palestinians."[15] The lessons from the anti-apartheid struggle in South Africa resonated twenty years after the end of apartheid as another battle against racism is still being fought on another side of the world, where the beginning of the twenty-first century is greeted with rising tensions and acute responses in dance.

Amid rubble and intermittent war sounds, bombing and shooting, Gaza is the largest open-air prison in the world.[16] The predictability of the escalation of violence—Gaza was twice the target of large Israeli military operations in 2014 and 2018—together with the unpredictability enacted on the human psyche by war are the backdrop against which 1.8 million Palestinians live their daily lives in a routine that is anything but routine. The daily life full of war and violence creates a setting in which predictability is that of the unpredictable. Against that backdrop, in 2015, after Israel's 2014 offensive, fifty pupils were registered in the Al Qattan ballet school, all of them girls.[17] The initiative started among contradictions. The strife of finding an instructor in a society organized as a prison was resolved by finding a Ukrainian married to a Palestinian.[18] By the time of the founding of the Al Qattan ballet school some of the children enrolled, aged five to eight, had lived through four wars. War creates an abnormal routine and brings a perverse rhythm to human life. In her book *The Unwomanly Face of War*, Svetlana Alexievich writes: "we didn't know a world without war; the world of war was the only one familiar to us, and the people of war were the only people we knew."[19]

For children (almost half of Gaza's population is under eighteen), this perverse rhythm generates life and changes it forever. Maria was six years old when the center was founded. She had been suffering since the 2012 war and 2014 threw her into escalating distress. Her mother said: "After the first ballet class, she came home as happy as a bird. She did the moves she had learnt, and she was going around the house like a butterfly." Another student, Bana, said: "I used to imitate ballet dancing that I saw on television or on YouTube. Now I am learning it for real and I just love it."[20] This isn't merely a use of metaphor or imagery, but rather a testimony to the ability of ballet to expand our horizons and imageries as human beings. Learning ballet in the physical world is crucial for the students of Al Qattan. The dance becomes part of the dancer's body, never to be removed from it, in conditions in which bodies are facing constant dangers. UNICEF, the United Nations Children's Fund, estimates that 400,000 of Gaza's almost 900,000 people under eighteen need some form of psychological care.[21] Thus, dance serves a unique feature here of unraveling imaginaries for deeply traumatized children. For the children of Gaza, ballet serves a life affirming, arguably essential role. The ability to unravel the possibility of thriving as human beings depends on their imagined possibilities. Action can transcend its beginnings and, in its unfolding, it expands its imitator's horizons. Activism, here, may be extended to those whose lives are structured by alienation and extreme violence; learning to expand one's imaginary allows for a counter-future to a harsh and violent present. Al Qattan offers the young students a place to cultivate and explore their praxis.

The case study of a ballet school in Gaza brings into question the position of the ballet class in and of itself as a resource for solidarity. In a community where life's pace has been unhinged and unsettled by war, the daily practice of a ballet class serves a crucial role in creating the pace and routine of a normal every day. Although learning ballet from a phone or TV (which will be a running theme in this book) provides a vista into the art form, being part of a physical ballet class provides a different intervention, especially in conditions in which physical vulnerability is part and parcel of lived experience. "For real," here, in Bana's statement, does not only mean with real teachers and in embodied presence but with a full community that is present physically despite many obstacles. This solidarity unraveling in the ballet class acts in tension to alienation.

What purpose can the ballet class, in and of itself, serve as an act of activism? The determination of these young girls and their families can aid us in understanding deeper thinking regarding the ballet class as an institution, especially in times of heightened violence. As ballet is rooted in action it is never a metaphysical source of solace. In the ballet class muscles are trained in order that in performance they are not exposed to the spectator. Ballet technique, more than any other dance techniques, centers around the hiding of the effort needed to execute graceful movement. The embodied balletic being works extensively on flesh in order to appear weightless. Practicing to be a butterfly in a house that has no walls can provide a powerful performative iteration of the example,

BALLET BEYOND BORDERS   73

Palestinian girls take part in a ballet class at Qattan Centre for the Child in Gaza City, November 10, 2015. Photo by Majdi Fathi/NurPhoto via Getty Images.

showing the complex place ballet can have in human beings' lives, as it can open up other imaginaries otherwise seemingly impossible.

The sequence of moves executed in ballet classes around the world—from the first *plié*, through *tendu*, through center work and finally *port de bras*, creates a symbolic structure that is resilient yet executed only in moving bodies. The disembodied *plié* has no meaning in the world. Thus, the ballet class is a symbolic structure that transcends the bodies executing it, yet depends heavily on the bodies executing it to survive. When the girls of the Al Qattan center can't arrive at their ballet class, no *pliés* take place there. There is no ballet class without moving bodies; its existence relies on the physical ontology of its agents. If there is a metaphysics of ballet, and that is in no way certain, there is certainly no metaphysics of a ballet class. And so, in response to a community facing alienation from humanity, enclosure in an open-air prison, the affirmation of physicality of moving bodies is a forceful way of resistance, focusing on the ballet class in and of itself, regardless of ballet's performative element. The ballet class as an institution, a space of activism in and of itself, can be a source of solidarity: working toward a common goal, developing a sense of integrity toward the technique, and providing community and togetherness in extremely harsh conditions.

Moreover, in its need to transcend the absolute present in which it exists, ballet creates a movement language that can be passed on and that enables the recreation of sequences of motion. This movement language has its own rules and acts independently of verbal language. Practicing to be a butterfly is anything but a metaphor. It is a possibility to repeat and practice a future not yet here through a present in becoming, a present that is offering a better life for children whose home is rubble and whose future may seem otherwise bleak. This is not only imaginary play projecting a different future, but practicing, consolidating, and creating a movement language that in turn, practiced in a class, creating solidarity, brings a better future perhaps an inch closer.

While chronicling a century of violence as well as resistance, it would be impossible and wrong to ignore the harsh conditions that structure the lives of young pupils in Gaza, as it would the hard lives of those, not too far away, in Syria, where people have been living through one of the harshest and longest civil wars in the region. It is from that social-economic context that the next case study is derived. The solidarity emerging here is between the teacher, the young dancers, and their spectators and parents; all are able to experience a sense of shared space allowing a different future to unravel.

Ballet, Home, Syria

Born in a Palestinian refugee camp in 1990 in Damascus, Syria, Ahmad Joudeh is the uncontested face of Syrian dance. The ongoing conflict in Syria, which escapes definition and has brought incessant news of violence and wrongdoing, has not only cost a deadly price in attacks on human lives; it has also assaulted the culture and histories central to the ethos of many Syrians.

Living through a civil war bears a heavy price on any and all. Joudeh is no different. He has lost five of his relatives over the duration of the conflict, and the ongoing trauma of the conflict continues to arc the narrative of his life. But, uniquely, another arc accompanies his life story: that of dance. He saw his first ever ballet performance when he was eight, and aged sixteen he joined the largest ballet company in Syria, the Enana Dance Theater. This was five years before the Syrian Civil War broke out; thus Joudeh obtained a powerful tool with which to tell his story as well as—very practically—to get away from his now burning homeland.

Joudeh is currently based in Amsterdam, where he dances for the Dutch National Ballet, one of the most esteemed dance companies in the world.[22] It is vital to realize, here, that much like in the case of those young dancers in apartheid South Africa, as well as the subject of the next chapter, Hussein Smko, dance changed Joudeh's life very practically as a way to cross borders. The transformation of his life was pragmatic, not just symbolic; he received a way out in an international language. "Dance is my passport," he says. The price of his choice to dance was very personal and very heavy; Joudeh became estranged from his father, who did not accept his choice to dance. More broadly he says: "I have no connection to a home."[23] The condition of homelessness as a sister concept to alienation runs as a thread through this book and will be discussed in full in its last chapter; this is a case in which dance can offer a conceptual home in lieu of a physical one. Praxis transforms the relationship the dancer-activist has to their surroundings and how they see their relationship to the world.

Yet the relationship is more complex, as indeed are the conditions in which it unravels. The Syrian conflict, unfolding from an authoritarian regime galvanized by neoliberal policies inflicting suffering on many and unclear boundaries between sides in the fight has also brought about the physical ruin of a country, as well as the symbolic ruin of its culture. The site of Palmyra, in the region of Homs, which included neolithic archeological artifacts, was ruined by Daesh and destroyed the facade of the carved theater. This attack was met by many around the world with deep shock and grief (many articulated, though, their conflict in perceiving this attack as particularly heinous in the context of a hugely bloody civil war). Have we become so completely immune to attacks on people that attacks on culture—as part of the physical infrastructure of human construct—can elicit more empathy? And what does this teach us about our alienation from the Syrian people?

Ahmad Joudeh challenged this conceptual tension when he decided to return and dance on the ruins of Palmyra. He said: "Dancing in the Palmyra theatre was my way to fight Isis. It was my way to tell them: you can kill people, but you can't keep me from dancing. It was a dangerous thing to do, we couldn't stay there longer than one hour, and it was 50C [122F] in the sun. But I did it because I knew I would never have the chance again. And I was right. Isis have destroyed the theatre now. I cried for two days when I heard the news."[24] Thus, the rare intersection of human movement and a cultural devastation that is always very

76   DANCE AND ACTIVISM

physical—the attacks on these artifacts are exemplary of the physical control Daesh achieved in the war. In the context of the book's argument it is necessary to pause on this extraordinary moment. This is where the material and the symbolic blend; where an attack on a physical site is an attack on a history of human work that had given it symbolic weight; and where "ruins" gains a dual interpretation: not only the remains of the site after the devastating act of violence, but also as a verb, the act of ruining in itself.

And yet opposite the act of ruin, transgressing the boundary between the physical and the material, stands the act of dancing: in its blurring these boundaries further, but showing resilience and resistance. Joudeh's decision to return and dance in Palmyra is an act of solidarity with all whose labor gave this site its symbolic meaning. His dancing tows the line between the physical and symbolic, too; and it is his own body that transcends the line. In the face of violence and oppression he is offering redemption through dance. His praxis shows respect, perhaps even mourning, for those whose work was demolished by the actions of Daesh. Thus, we see a profound case of tension between alienation and solidarity. Daesh's attacks on Palmyra are an act of devastation and alienation of people from their ancestors' work. At the same time, it exposed the alienation of much of the world outside of Syria toward its people. However, Joudeh's act is not of mourning but of creating new symbolic meaning through his intervention in the site. It is his own working body that is creating new meaning. And in that act he exposes the invisible yet resilient solidarity people have with one another across generations and across different historical periods. Daesh may kill people and attempt to destroy property, but they can't kill the dancing human spirit, which is the same that created the deep and rich meaning of the site of Palmyra.

This case study pushes us to think about the ontological significance of ballet, especially in moments of great political crisis. Ballet is grounded in the physicality of the human body. At the same time it draws on a constitutive tension: between being present and leaving a lasting effect as well as between discipline and freedom. Ballet is located in the tension between motion and stability and cannot ever be reduced to one side of the axes. When human life is more in becoming and lacks affirmation; when structures that organize and give meaning to human life, and give them political ontological (or ontic) weight are in crisis, ballet can supply a counter impulse; it can give some stability to lives experiencing political instability.

What is the significance of dancing among the ruins of Palmyra? Joudeh's honest articulation of himself and his place as a non-resident of the world, always in exile, pushes this interpretation into subtle readings of this action. The dancing body against the ruins is a move toward thinking about ballet's ability to give further ontological weight to the creative spirit. Ballet is read here as physicality in motion. It is a way to create further presence in the world. As argued above, this process starts with being based in the now, the present, and working on the body in systems of discipline.[25]

However, this is always ontology in motion. An equilibrium is always momentary; there is always only now. Dance is a physical art form, ballet aspiring to ephemerality; demanding a robust physical training to appear effortless. Ballet allows the body to add what will be termed here as an "ontological layer"; the language, the disciplining that becomes part and parcel of the body itself.

At the same time, as material beings living in a fast-shifting material world, this ontological complexity allows the body to confront and subvert other complexities and challenges. The ruins in Palmyra are not only dust and rubble showing man- and woman-made artifacts disappearing because of violence and war. The ruins of Palmyra signify an attack on human culture, on the ideas, norms and ethics that shaped Palmyra and sustained it for as long as it did.

When Ahmed Joudeh dances in Palmyra he brings into a clash the ontology of his body—enriched by years of training and disciplining in ballet—and the ontology of the ruins in which he performs; culture attacked by war. The dialectic of materiality and dance are evident here in the most extreme way. The human body is able to invent a complex system of signification—ballet—but also to create wars that bring down cultural memento moris and wash away complex material histories. The human body can create but also ruin, and that is true of itself as a material. The dialectic played out of alienation (here through destruction) and solidarity (here from a moving body to a history that has been physically attacked) creates a powerful act of resistance and subversion. Joudeh doesn't only dance with the rubble, but with the women and men who created the complex structures and ideas that have been dismantled by violence. This is an act of solidarity with material, with history, and with those made absent by war. Alienation, in the reading underpinning this book, relies on a reading of the materialistic conditions of life. In this case, an act of radical action reconfiguring the relationship between the

78   DANCE AND ACTIVISM

body and its physical surroundings allows for new, radical solidarities to emerge. This is a crucial intervention in the reading of praxis offered in this book; this reading always also relates to the material world from which it emerges, and, as Joudeh powerfully performed, to which it may return.

Thus far the argument has started from looking at ballet as a powerful mechanism of the now, able to transform people's futures without intentionally focusing on social change as a goal; then the argument moved to look at the development of systems of signification in the ballet class as an alternative place of dwelling, a structure for solidarity that becomes significant especially in situations of extreme warfare and violence; and ended with looking at the ontological complexity of the ballet-dancing body and how that complexity may enable acts of solidarity in unique situations. Ballet as a world has resources to allow its practitioners to subvert systems of power in places where they seem always irredeemable; a far cry from the origins of the form in the court of Louis XIV in Paris. However, questions must be raised about the performance of ballet and its place in the still-developing arc of history; indeed a crucial question throughout this book. Unlike many of the forms of dance discussed in this book, ballet has a canon that in part dates back to almost immediately after its origination in the world, and quite often encapsulates politics that are far from radical (even for their time, let alone for our times). How, then, can this alternative reading of ballet as a radical art form be squared with ballets performing racialized, gendered politics that are oppressive to those who perform in them? How can one truly democratize and radicalize this form of dance when the canon is drenched in racism, sexism, and mocking of the poor and with its slaves? How can ballet serve an emancipatory form of movement when it presents daily scenes that pastiche people of color, demean women, obliterate non-heterosexual relationships from the stage, and force its participants to perform daily iterations of highly conservative narratives that are jarring and harmful to those who participate within them? Surely having a more diverse range of voices would change nothing if the narratives themselves are marginalizing those voices and, moreover, may be harmful and oppressive to those forced to perform degrading stereotypes of their identity? Activism in revision of the canon occurs at the same time as initiating activism within the people who make it a living, breathing canon. The approach to the canon and the attempt to radicalize it will be the focus of the next and final part of this chapter.

BALLET BEYOND BORDERS 79

The Canon Must be Fired! Ballet and the Long Arc of History

The question of the politics of the canon is in itself complex and encapsulates many areas of life, much beyond ballet. Feminist interventions as well as post-colonial interventions have consistently pointed out that while areas of knowledge try to diversify and open up to new voices, those texts read as "great texts" are still predominately from a very specific and homogenous part of our world with oppressive histories that are airbrushed and whitewashed out of its teaching. Any attempts to read any field of knowledge beyond its hegemony necessitates handling how works of thought and art precisely from that hegemony are handled.

The histories of ballet and race, especially in the United States, are entangled and have many inspiring examples of how people chose to work within this art form, created by a white king with a leaning toward purity of race ideas, and make it their sphere for radical action. From Arthur Mitchell and the Dance Theater of Harlem, through to Virginia Johnson and, recently, Misty Copeland, many have raised questions about who is allowed to tell their stories in ballet, how we see "classics" and especially who is excluded by this process of canonization in ballet.

In the United Kingdom, other changes in popular discourse around ballet were made in other ways. Stormzy, a popular artist famous not only for his music but for his explicit politics—from speaking out against the Grenfell Tower fire that took the lives of seventy people and injured more than seventy more, to explicitly supporting Jeremy Corbyn in the 2019 election and speaking out against Boris Johnson and his politics—took the central pyramid stage in Glastonbury music festival, making history as the first solo black artist to do so. The performance was viewed by millions as the performance broadcasted live through the BBC. Jeremy Corbyn hailed the performance as historic,[26] while David Lammy, a Member of Parliament noted for his longstanding anti-racist work, saw Stormzy as highlighting justice for black men.[27]

This performance made history in ballet history too, as in one of the songs two ballet dancers appeared, to a crowd of cheering thousands and millions at home. Ballet Black, consistently highlighting structural racism in the British ballet world, got exposure when two of their dancers performed behind Stormzy. Not only that, but during the performance

80   DANCE AND ACTIVISM

visual slides explained the fact that only as of that summer, in 2019, and thanks to the work of Ballet Black senior artist Cira Robinson, were British ballet dancers who are not white able to find ballet shoes and tights to match the color of their skin. "Ballet shoes have not traditionally been made to match black skin tones. Until now. . . . Previously ballet dancers 'pancaked' their shoes with makeup. Now there are ballet shoes to match all skin tones. A huge leap forward for inclusion in the ballet world."[28] At the same time, the rise of stars from diverse backgrounds to center stage and the spilling over of discussions of race and equity in ballet beyond its own world questions other practices rife in ballet performance, such as blackface and yellowface, as well as, more broadly, clinging to outdated cultural stereotypes in the name of preserving tradition.[29]

In parallel to this contradiction arose Final Bow for Yellowface, a unique phenomenon in the world of ballet in that it questions politics of race within ballet itself and is a dance-focused activist movement. The founders of Final Bow for Yellowface, Phil Chan and Georgina Pazcoguin, set out clearly the political and intellectual background to the project in the context of our times: "Whether we're people of color or not, once we become sensitized to how offensive racial caricatures and stereotypes can be, we're torn away from the magical experience of watching great dance, jarred by something sour in the midst of what's supposed to be the land of the sweets."[30] Going deeper into the context of the problematic at hand, the authors argue: "ballets are not presented in a vacuum, and as much as creators need to be knowledgeable about the dance history and tradition their works will be embedded within, we must also realize that everything presented happens within the context of a place and time."[31]

Pazcoguin describes their position:

In the same way that Blackface is limiting and degrading to African Americans, continuing to present an 19th century view of Asians does not allow for character nuance for Asian American dancers today. If all audiences see is the bobbing and shuffling coolie from a bygone era as the only representation of Asians on stage, what message does that send to our Asian students who dream of dancing the Swan Queen? What does that say to the Asian audience members who want to see themselves on stage, only to find themselves as the butt of the joke? What does that say to the Board member, who writes checks and involves their friends, only to see a one-dimensional representation of their heritage?

In the spirit of making the ballet more inclusive, we invite you to join us by signing our pledge and committing to speak up against Yellowface on our stages, and working to create more positive and nuanced representations of Asians in ballet.[32]

In a book Chan gives further details about the work of the organization in the context of quickly changing times:

Final Bow for Yellowface came about after a conversation with then-NYCB Artistic Director Peter Martins[33] who reached out asking for help modifying the Chinese dance in the Nutcracker. When it became clear he was going to update Balanchine's most iconic and widely performed ballet, we realized that there was the potential to make even larger change.[34]

The politics of dance, though, is never disengaged from politics outside of the studio and the theater: "Some of this feeling to do something came out of the 2016 election. We felt powerless to change the larger issues plaguing the country, but this was a small thing we could do in our little corner of the world to make it better—so we did it."[35] The attempt to transform individual lives enables the transformation of solidarity as a lived concept, opening up a vista for many new conversations to unfold. This was never in a vacuum:

We were inspired by many other parallel conversations about race and representation of Asians, most notably the Theater Communications Group's seminar "Beyond Orientalism" in theater, the various conversations around "The Mikado" and "Ms. Saigon," as well as the great work of CAPE (Coalition of Asian and Pacific Islanders in Entertainment) which does this work in film and television. We wanted to be a similar resource and voice in our community—ballet. We also stand on the shoulders of the leaders in the Black community who have been pushing this conversation, leaders like Arthur Mitchell who founded Dance Theatre of Harlem in response to Dr. King's assassination. We've benefitted a lot from the progress of African Americans in dance. This larger diversity conversation happening in ballet right now gave us fertile ground to make our arguments. I recently discovered the advocacy of Mr. Ying Hope in Toronto that was having this same discussion with the National Ballet of Canada as early as 1981! So we definitely were not the first![36]

Further, he expands about leadership through accentuating an individual voice, thus changing the face of the community, and solidarity built from individual acts of questioning resonating with others:

> What we found was that we weren't always starting the conversations locally, but often consolidating conversations happening around the country and giving cover for companies to make change while citing us an outside resource and impetus. We also realized that we didn't need to reach every person in America, or to collect thousands of signatures to make an impact. We actually just needed to change the minds of the major gatekeepers—the artistic directors of the leading ballet companies in America. Just four or five directors signing on was enough to garner us press to get the real momentum going for the larger conversation. My co-founder Georgina Pazcoguin and I both have busy day jobs—she is a Soloist with the New York City Ballet—so we needed to figure out a means of advocacy that was minimal effort with maximum impact.[37]

When challenged to think about the insistence on ballet, where other forms of dance have been—with their own challenges and structural tensions—less problematic in terms of stereotyping and approach to the canon, Chan replies:

> That's like asking why people of color choose to express themselves in English, the historic language of their oppressor. Ballet is a language too. It's a physical discipline that speaks to me as an artist. It's my home. And within ballet, I see potential for the art form and existing repertory work to be bigger and touch people. Ballet has the potential to be a universal dance language, but it has to be big enough to fit in other people and ideas. If you look at how ballet has changed from an expression of monarchy, to its power as a Communist propaganda vehicle, to its ability to express democracy and love and other complex ideas that cannot be put into words. Because of that, there is value to this plastic art form.

The process of opening up the conversation about racism in the canon also expands the possibilities of diversity and visibility on stage, enabling more voices to enter the world of ballet:

> The flip side of our work is making sure there are more opportunities for Asians to excel in the field. This means improving support for families and creating pipelines to careers through our schools. It means improving arts administration wages and access to education so that immigrant families see the arts as a viable career path. It means seeing more Asians on stage. It means commissioning works by Asian choreographers, both about the Asian experience specifically, but also just like any other artist trying to express ideas through dance. It means working harder to get Asian board members and donors. It means inviting reviewers from Asian publications to review the production, and targeting ads to Asian people. Imagine a Western ballet company putting an ad for Swan Lake or Nutcracker in Chinese at a Chinatown subway station! Or better yet, advertising works by Asian choreographers! You don't think that would do wonders to diversify the audience, school, and donor base within a few short years? As ballet as an art form invests in communities traditionally not included, we will organically see the diversification of our art form.[38]

The question of relationship between diversity on stage and in the auditorium is articulated forcefully in the book: "Some participants can simply enjoy fantasy portrayals of "other" cultures and revel in the feeling of ballet history being reenacted in front of their eyes. But the usual caricatured portrayals suggest to minority audience members that ballet isn't for them, though it sometimes pretends to be about them."[39] The project is in its essence radical—and forward looking:

> As we enter the 21st century in earnest, there are many new social issues that have permeated the dance world we've called our personal and professional home for most of our lives that were not issues for previous generations. As a new generation takes the reins at performing arts institutions around the world, we need to ask ourselves what are we repeating on stage and why?

The answer is elucidated powerfully later:

A single dominant cultural lens through which everything in the world is seen and evaluated is characteristic of Old World cultures, held together by shared racial, religious, or geographic heritage. In some places this Old World glue continues to hold cultures together, and art is created, performed, experienced, and evaluated within those cultural milieus ... But ballet is alive as an art form, and one of its homes is in New World places such as America, which, while majority White, is majority immigrant, from all over the world.[40]

This approach to dance and activism, much like the ethos at the heart of Ballet Black, who danced behind Stormzy in Glastonbury, is in the hope that it one day will not be needed in the world of ballet and beyond. Thus, the temporal outlook is uniquely radical in that the future it aims to bring about is one in which its actions will not be necessary. "My biggest hope is that Final Bow for Yellowface becomes redundant. I'd love for nothing more than for the conversation to be such a no-brainer for our artistic leaders that future generations will not even believe that this conversation had to happen in the first place for change to happen." One question that will be handled in the next two chapters is activism in the twenty-first century and its unique possibilities and challenges: "I would add that activism in the internet age also looks quite different than it has in previous times. The internet has been a great tool for us to change minds through education (putting out information to reach a wider audience) and also subjected us to a lot of online pushback, which in turn has been a constructive influence in helping us sharpen our arguments."[41]

Final Bow for Yellowface is a crucial intervention in allowing more dancer-activists to feel at home in ballet, to tell their own stories in their chosen method of expression. It is an intervention opening possibilities of solidarity in a world that is marred by structural alienation masqued as "classicism." Final Bow for Yellowface is radical as it is offering a new interpretation of praxis through ballet, which is neither oppressive nor exclusive.

Ballet came a long way from the court of Louis XIV in Paris before the contemporary activists offered it new possibilities and significations. Radical action unfolds in manifold ways and demands manifold avenues of actions; from asking who is allowed to dance, to where and how one can train, to where one can perform and which canonical interventions one can bring about. All these are possible and indeed have occurred in the world of ballet.

BALLET BEYOND BORDERS **85**

There is Only Now: Radical Ballet Going Forward

The underpinning question of this book is how radical action can find its form in dance. To answer this question the issue of form within dance must be addressed. This chapter has shown that there is potential for radical action in what is perceived to be a conservative form, that of ballet. The ability to expand its horizons both from its geographical origins and within its own history—questioning its conventions and unsettling its "traditions," allows us to reconsider the balance between configurations and norms and deviating from them in transmission. In short, the ability to transgress boundaries—both of the art form's sphere of influence as it is usually perceived, and within its own practices and mores, is an essential part of the art-form. When radical action as praxis unfolds it reconfigures its sphere of influence as well as its own organizing principles. Radical actions need a moment of departure that is able to transgress form through reconfiguration of content in its unraveling.

The origins of ballet as a dance form designed to preserve power and allow for absolutist rule determines nothing about how people use its vocabulary. This vocabulary can inform and indeed catalyze liberationist action, open up spheres for human voices in situations of explicit conflict and war. New solidarities may emerge if we listen to new voices and turn away from what are presented as "classical" but also exclusive and unitary interpretations of ballet. All the voices chronicled in this chapter choose to tell their stories in ballet. Activism in dance may emerge in new and unexplored spaces and can start in a moment of recognition that the future may be radically different. And this can happen in a ballet class.

From South Africa to Syria, from Palestine and back to New York City, the boundaries of who may practice ballet—and how—are being reconsidered and reconfigured. Ballet is action that is now transcending its own borders. This is a vital argument against essentialism in dance and dance history, both. No dance form must reiterate its founding principles in a thoughtless repetition; as carried through living bodies it changes when they shift their own history. Thus, the term "radical" which underpins this book's argument does not entail exclusion of certain forms, but rather attentiveness to their ability to accommodate the changing tides of history. Contemporary dance can be anachronistic as much as ballet can be radical. *Pliés, tendus*, turns, jumps: the ballet class

86   DANCE AND ACTIVISM

and performance can unravel a radical sphere of action and liberation. This chapter provided discussion of exemplary cases of solidarity: from an English woman in South Africa creating a multi-racial company against the law, through to ballet schools operating under shelling and bombing, allowing for little girls to feel like butterflies, to a grime artist not only making history for himself but opening a vista for understanding structural racism beyond the ballet world. The barre can be a home. Those who work to make it a home for more, to allow some certainty, an opportunity to counter and develop the body's ontological complexity, to reflect upon the body's materiality, sometimes in the face of physical ruins, with the dangers of war structuring the everyday, make it even more so, a home. The now has within it possibilities for a better tomorrow, in which more people can feel like butterflies and more bodies are valued as equal in our world. The next chapter looks at another dancer-activist whose life was transformed by dance and in turn keeps transforming the ubiquitous traditions of contemporary dance and hip-hop: Hussein Smko.

4 ERBIL/NEW YORK CITY: BREAK/DANCE

One arm can change a course of a life. One man can bring with him a new vision of dance and of connectivity. Dance as solidarity can start in a singular body, which in turn may transform multiple bodies through praxis. This chapter examines a case study that is extraordinary and at the same time teaches us a lot about core problems examined in this book: dance and activism, alienation and solidarity. This chapter looks at the role of technologies in the transmission of dance as activism and at how dance may be a way to create a new home through a variety of ways in which movement is transmitted. Dance and activism as a relationship is transformed by changes in the world, including technological changes.

The Body in Battle

Iraq is home to a thriving scene of hip-hop, breakdance, and its related dance languages (locking, popping, house, to name but a few). In tracing its origins we encounter a theorist of radical action's chicken-and-egg problem; most of the information available to the Western reader arises after the second war of 2003; and as we see from the case study and exemplar, the response of the West to the wars and conflicts in Iraq is intertwined in its effort to understand the local breakdance and hip-hop scene. The relationship between the presence of predominately American and European forces in Iraq and the development of the breakdance scene there is neither straightforward, nor one-directional. Let us begin by seeing how Western journalism understands this scene before listening to one dancer tell its story in his own words.

Paul Rockwer in *The Huffington Post* is nothing short of exuberant when describing the work done in the breakdance scene in Iraq. "It felt like nothing short of a public diplomacy *miracle* to hold together a quadrilingual program—Arabic, two dialects of Kurdish (Badini and Soranî) and English—for two weeks."[1] The journalist is enjoying this dream of multi-lingual collaboration; and yet the main language used in the program discussed, and not mentioned here, is, of course, dance. Rockwer continues:

> Perhaps the most exciting portion of the program was found in the hip hop & breakdance class. The highly athletic and energetic ADS Crew—Baghdad's only breakdance crew—worked with breakdancers from Kurdistan to hone their breakdance talents. YES Academy dance faculty instructor Michael Parks Masterson pushed these nimble artists to learn new levels of choreography and staging so that their raw talent could be transformed into new levels of breakdance *savoir faire*.[2]

Kurdish and Iraqi dancers, collaborating under the auspices of an artist who hails from the "promised land" of Broadway: this seems like an unflawed vision of togetherness. Dance is perceived as a method of building bridges; bringing people together, creating solidarity where sometimes it is hindered through war and conflict that makes human beings vulnerable, yet this can be countered in danced solidarity.

Moreover, the undercurrent narrative of this reading is that hip-hop training in Iraq is a centralized effort supported by various international institutions. Another report on the hip-hop scene in Baghdad, this time Yasmeen Sami Alamiri in *Al Arabiya*, takes the same route:

> "First Step Iraq" is the product of collaboration between the U.S. Embassy in Baghdad (which sponsored and paid for their trip) and the YES Academy, which aims to train teachers and promote youth leadership in the arts in Iraq and a host of other countries. The six young men that make up "First Step Iraq" hail from the most distant points of the country and trained together in the country's relative safe haven of Kurdistan.[3]

Dance is understood as a method to cultivate leadership; to create alternative models of being together where they are absent, fostered by large and overtly political organizations. Dance is a way to reconfigure shared experience together. Dance generates new forms of solidarity in moments of acute alienation. At the same time transmission of a form of dance to an entirely different location from its origins is never an unequivocal, linear process.

Transmission always has context; there is a direct reasoning for "bringing hip-hop to Iraq." And that process was not easy, as we can see from further reporting from *Sami Alamiri*:

> Just a few years ago, the country was awash with reports of Iraqi teenagers being killed for being "emo," a word initially coined to describe young people that listen to certain types of rock music and wear alternative clothing. In Iraq, the term started being used to describe men that have long hair or any type of feminine appearance. The insinuation is that men who look, or dress a certain way, or engage in certain types of activities (like dancing) are gay, Satanists, or a slew of other presumptions.[4]

The young men representing Iraq through their dance spoke of the same fears and discrimination back home, saying that because they wanted to dance, the community saw them as different and unacceptable. Further, according to Sami Alamiri: "'It's human nature that anytime something new happens, people see it as a threat,' said Haider, who asked to only be identified by his first name due to threats against his family in Iraq because of his dancing."[5] Since 1929, when Graham premiered "Heretic," dancers have been punished for speaking their truth. And yet dance is mobilized to counter prejudice directly; to protect those who are targets for violence; those whose stories are never put center-stage.

Sami Alamiri, in her piece on the breakdance scene of Erbil, introduces Hussein Smko's remarkable journey into the world of dance: "One of the men from Erbil, Iraq said it was actually an American soldier in 2003 that taught him hip hop dancing. He said he and some of his friends were running after an American convoy when an American soldier pulled him aside and showed him how to do the arm wave—a hip hop dance move." This small moment of solidarity between one soldier and one young boy transformed a life. This chapter tells a story of transmission and learning and chance meetings that can create dance. But it is also a story of war and violence—profound alienation—that constitutes the lives of human beings. It is an intervention attempting to chronicle the praxis of exceptional life-story. It can be narrated by many people: journalists who

ERBIL/NEW YORK CITY: BREAK/DANCE **91**

come from different corners of the globe to find a unique "story," which immediately undergoes its own processes of transmission and sharing on; but also by those whose body spans the story itself. This is where the chapter moves next.

Those Who Leave and Those Who Stay

One day I'm going to leave Iraq and go to a place where people love dancing.

ADEL EURO

In 2016 a deadly terrorist attack in Baghdad took away the lives of 292 people and injured many more. One life whose motion was made still in this attack is that of Adil Faraj, known by his stage name Adel Euro (1993–2016). He was planning to go to New York City after his graduation from law school (several days before the bombing), and join the acclaimed company Battery Dance, with which he had been training online. From watching a video of Michael Jackson on YouTube, he made dance his world, and went on to perform and teach despite often unsupportive and scornful responses in Baghdad. He was a master breakdancer and hip-hop dancer and had a law degree. He was twenty-three years old when he died.[6] The untimely and tragic death of Adil Faraj/Adel Euro brought to further Western media attention the hip-hop/breakdance scene in Iraq, and illuminated stories of other dancers who mobilize the language of hip-hop within the scene of one of the most volatile conflict areas in the world that has made many other lives fragile. The death of Adel Euro shed light on the lives of many others who engage and mobilize hip-hop to bring it to multiple and diverse audiences.

Jonathan Hollander is the artistic director of the internationally acclaimed New York–based Battery Dance Company, which champions the use of dance for good since its foundation in 1976— from international exchanges under the title "dancing to connect," to extensive work in schools and local communities. Battery Dance's and Hollander's visionary work have opened many spaces for dancer activists around the world. Hollander has contributed to this new interest in the Iraqi hip-hop scene. He says: "Over the past four decades, we have expanded beyond our home base in lower Manhattan to carry our mantra of artistic excellence and social relevance, collaboration and access to the arts around the globe. We aspire to make dances that stir the emotions and spark thoughtful consideration of issues that may be difficult to put into words."[7] Further, his inspiring artistic mission is aimed at creating solidarity where it is lacking:

> Through the abstraction of art, hearts and minds can be touched in a way that cuts through partisan divide. Our world is being swept by hate speech and heinous attacks against individuals and communities; cultural heritage is being destroyed. I feel a new level of urgency to reach out beyond our own enclaves and to listen, observe, learn and create together. That is why my recent productions have involved collaborations with artists from India, Iraq, Romania, Syria and Tunisia—and why Battery Dance's teaching artists are going into the heartland of America in addition to addressing refugee integration in Germany, and arts empowerment in South America, Africa and Asia.[8]

Hollander was supposed to give an artistic home to Adil Fraaj/Adel Euro. He was never able to take that opportunity. Hussein Smko came to New York and worked with Battery Dance on a scholarship named after Adel Euro.[9]

Hussein Smko was born on 4 October 1993, two years after the first Gulf War/Operation Desert Storm had ceased. He narrates his introduction to dance in the context of the local politics: In 1995, he saw war for the first time, when Iraqi army ambushed Erbil—the Iraqi capital of Kurdistan. One rocket flew through the kitchen window and never exploded. He did not see it, his mom told him about this, but since then he has thought of war as an alien ship of metal that may explode any minute. What he does remember is the incessant cacophony of soldiers yelling, women screaming, machine gun shots, tanks rambling, and the high pitch of sirens. He was nearly three at that time but still he remembers that clearly, to this day. In 2003, when the USA attacked Iraq and set up a military base in his hometown, his family climbed on the roof and watched F16 planes unleashing the inferno of fire and smoke over the city of Kirkuk. At that time, he was nine. When he was nine years old, a US RV stopped, and a soldier summoned him over and said "Watch!" He showed him a hip-hop dance move that impressed Hussein deeply. Hussein went online and investigated further the arm wave. This incited two years spent watching dance videos online and ultimately his becoming a dancer.

ERBIL/NEW YORK CITY: BREAK/DANCE **93**

When he realized that this was his destiny, Hussein quit school and became a street dancer. In 2007 he applied and got accepted to perform in the competition on "Kurdish Got Talent" (*Min Ciyawazim*), a program on national TV. He and his crew won third place. They formed a group called "Street Wolves" in Kurdish (*Gurgakani Sar Shaqam*) that introduced hip-hop to the Kurdish community together with all its inherent attributes: a sense of resistance to authority, individual freedom, and brotherhood. It hit the Kurdish regional headlines and became wildly successful. In 2014, while acting in a feature film directed by a Syrian Kurd, Lauand Omar, he saw his sound boom operator stopping the production because he heard gunshots. That was ISIS forces barging into the streets. The cast from the US flew back to the States, his family fled to another city along with hundreds of residents, while he and his brother stayed behind and watched over the family business, and his father was called back to service as one of the generals of the Kurdish Army.[10]

Born to a family of seven, Smko testified that he was always interested in dance but, "an American soldier started the spark in me 2003."[11] He says: "I cannot explain dancing by words . . . you will just have to see me dance. It will show how much I love this form of art, as for many artists are the same, I'm sure!"[12] He started to dance hip-hop but now sees contemporary as his favorite style. He says: "hip-hop is different from contemporary . . . hip-hop it's more for me of [sic] expressing anger; contemporary is a life story—telling and explaining different points of view in each dancer." Hussein moved to New York City in the autumn of 2016 at the invitation of Jonathan Hollander, artistic director of Battery Dance. Hussein and Adil had crossed paths in Baghdad and Kurdistan: "he was a talented young man [who] just so happened to be found dead by the dirt of the world's new leaders that are so based on greed."[13]

Discussing dance in Erbil, Hussein says:

Dancing in Iraq, Erbil is different . . . no studios and no mirrors or teachers your motivation is the person dancing next to you. It's pure love for the art. War didn't effect dancers stop dancing . . . but the government and the capacity of their acceptance for the art did!! But it was for sure an amazing start.[14]

Further, "I feel home of course back home Erbil . . . but NYC has been my second home I can say that for sure! I miss the food from home and the smells; and family and childhood friends and streets it's in us to miss that

94 DANCE AND ACTIVISM

Daily life in Erbil: A general view over the city of Erbil and the ancient Citadel on June 15, 2014 in Erbil, Iraq. The Citadel is thought to be the oldest continuously inhabited settlement in the world. In Iraq's capital city of Baghdad and other towns and cities affected by the recent conflict, people who can afford to do so have begun to stockpile essential items of food, which has increased prices dramatically. The US dollar, which is normally a relatively stable currency in Iraq, rose about 5 percent in one day making many household items more expensive. The price of potatoes increased approximately six-fold, to about $4.50 a pound. People continue to leave Iraq's second city of Mosul after it was overrun by ISIS (Islamic State of Iraq and Syria) militants. Many have been temporarily housed at various IDP (internally displaced persons) camps around the region including the area close to Erbil, as they hope to enter the safety of the nearby Kurdish region. Photo by Dan Kitwood/Getty Images.

it's important to miss it!!"[15] Hussein's impulse to move countries was facilitated by journeying within his home within dance. Dance can be transmitted in a variety of physical and ideational contexts, and yet the possibility of its telling a life story never disappears. In a world of over-connectedness, which can create alienation (as forcefully articulated by Samantha Geracht Myers when discussing performances of Anna Sokolow's "Rooms" online in 2020), technology can also allow for life stories to unravel in new ways. For radicals, turning back in time is not an option, and new technologies have to be considered in terms of dangers, but also possibilities. Chronicling the praxis of dancer-activists can take many shapes and forms, and these changes also alter our perception of relationships to other material parts of our world.

The connection created in this story between three men, in collective action, goes from one man, Adel Euro, to another, Hussein Smko, mediated by Jonathan Hollander. Solidarity transcends boundaries and can be extended from the dead to the living. Adel Euro's work—and his internationalism—created the grounds for the development of Hussein Smko's work as well as the international infrastructures upon which he drew. All the protagonists in this chapter work towards an Other; and their work chimes much further, affecting those who they do not yet know. Solidarity through dance is not necessarily more than one person on stage at the same time and can take many forms of transmission.

Hussein Smko arrived in the USA just before the election of Donald Trump as president. He was present at the discussions of the Muslim ban and resistance to it; Iraq being one of the first countries to be declared as part of the ban on citizens from Muslim majority countries entering the USA. The next part of the chapter examines the interplay between one and many, togetherness and solitude, fragility and power, as an undercurrent of Hussein's life, and consequently his understanding of dance. His spirit of openness to the world and stern commitment to dance and to ethics pushes us to ask him about listening to his life story in the language that is his praxis and in which he chooses to express himself: dance.

Not Just for You, But for the Rest of the Earth

Hussein Smko is alone on stage in downtown NYC as part of the world-renowned Battery Dance Festival, founded in 1982 and recurring annually since, telling us his story through movement. It is a multifarious story, shifting from moments of joy to moments of sorrow; it has moments of raw anger but Hussein's story is always an inspiring, galvanizing one. The movement in the work "Echoes of Erbil" shifts between looking inwards, exploring the body's vulnerability within, as a space, and expanding outward to the audience. There is raw emotion in Smko's gestures. Nothing is contained and kept within the body. Hussein commits totally to that moment of dance. One theme that makes this dance very unique is the use of break gestures in the arm. As we know, Hussein's very first encounter with dance was through breakdance and hip-hop. Now he is speaking manifold languages including contemporary dance and ballet, all the while opening himself up to other movement languages. But his mother tongue in dance is breakdance and hip-hop. Through breaks in the arms Smko closes and opens the movement toward the audience. It is through those arm breaks that he performs that tension between vulnerability and his power to overcome it, as well as giving the audience glimpses of where he sees his *home*.

The piece has two strong choreographic characteristics that frame its narrative. Hussein Smko mobilizes his arms in an extraordinary way. Throughout the piece we, the audience, feel that the hand, the arm, acts as a mirror; but this is not just a superficial mirror, allowing Smko to look at his appearance; this is a mirror that allows him to bare his soul on stage. His playful gestures utilizing his arms allows for moments of tenderness and vulnerability to shine through the narrative; in these moments in which he stares into his hand, we, as audience members, gain a glimpse into his soul. The second strand in this work is the extensive use of hip-hop and breakdance throughout the contemporary piece—exhibited mainly in breaks and fractures of movement, shifting between legato and staccato as movement textures and rhythms. The movement shifts between fluidity and gestures borrowed from the lexicon of hip-hop and breakdance. We know that Smko feels most at home in these languages; thus those moments of incorporating two languages together choreographically give us a glimpse into the languages occupying Smko's soul and where he feels at home. Here he shows us, in movement, that the false dichotomy between different movement languages, in this case, hip-hop and breakdance and contemporary dance, doesn't hold. Isaak Dinesen said that all sorrows can be born when a story is told about them. This piece is Smko's story told in manifold ways of expression, transcending division between them. The initial transmission of movement expands and takes many forms. From watching one video on a soldier's YouTube, Smko has made dance his world and is now transmitting the porous boundaries between forms as well as methods of transmission to a vast audience.

Smko exposes through his movement the coming to terms with his own humanity, his past, and looking into his future. But at the same time let us think of the breaks in movement and breaks in narrative as acts of sharing. Those are the moments in which Smko is opening himself up to solidarity, to compassion, and understanding from his spectator. We are, with Smko, considering what it means to be human and to tell one's own story in one's own way of expression. By sharing in his story we are all less alone. It is not only war and conflict that are themes for political reflections upon the darker side of humanity. The true bravery is exploring how those events leave their mark internally, upon the human soul. There are no safeguards, there; no protective shields, no methods of guarding the self. But the act of exposure itself is forceful. Looking into the scarier, darker sides of what it means to be human allows us, as spectators, to unravel our own souls; to shed our own protective shields, to explode with the movement of arm and wrist. Smko's breaks allow us to break with the narrative of ourselves. We share our conceptions of echoes, landscapes, hinterlands, childhood, memories; the theme of this work may now be rephrased as *what does it mean to be human?*

There are times, in a human being's life, in which the soul has a twilight, a time of change and profound transformation. And yet sharing that special light, that moment of twilight, opens up possibilities for reflection for the audience as well as the performer. The twilight of the soul is a very special time because it is an opportunity for solidarity. It is an opportunity to share fear, sadness, anger and sorrow by telling a story and making them easier to bear. The breaks in the wrists and arms of Hussein Smko are not only a reference to a dance move showed to him in his past, in Erbil, by an American soldier. Those breaks open his soul to us, as his spectators. They enable us to share the twilight of his soul, in the awakening of a new dawn in a new country that is now his home.[16]

Ballade of Belonging

Since arriving, Hussein has been consistently and patiently setting his roots in NYC. Performance after performance he is examining the boundaries of here/elsewhere, native/alien, someone who is part of a collective and a lone voice that has travelled across the oceans. Against the backdrop of exquisite skies and passing boats, Smko moves on a stage. The stage in the work "Ballade: Rain Song" is empty apart from a few scattered blocks. Smko moves the blocks carefully. There is intent and concentration in his motion. The audience is following him along. There is something very revealing about performing outdoors, where there are no wings; the audience constantly peering into the process of the dancer becoming the dance; the performer has no indulgence of being "offstage."

98   DANCE AND ACTIVISM

But this performer, once again Hussein Smko, does not seem to mind that. The energy in his movement is transfixing, and the audience is following him. He does not need music or rhythm; there is an internal rhythm that pushes him along. Behind him a boat passes but that does not take his concentration away from his task. The spatial arrangement of the stage begins to take shape. We see a parallel between the stone, and the stage, and the horizon. All draw lines parallel to the ground; multiple horizons that frame the movement but are also transcended by its shifts. The sun is setting slowly, changing the spatial relationship between those lines. Smko is the antithetical spatial configuration to those horizons, constantly shifting between them but also shifting them. He lies horizontally behind the stones. He is focused on the floor; the movement is slow, feline-like; far more fluid than in the previous piece we saw. His arms extend; open up toward the audience and the sky. A poem is being read but Smko moves to his own rhythm at the same time; and yet here the tempo of his movement is picking up. Here too we see some of his signature arm and wrist breaks; we remember his beginnings in dance and the echoes of Erbil. It is the movement of the arm that gives us a glimpse inside, into Smko's soul. The speeding up of the movement of the arms opens Smko toward the sky and toward the audience. This tension also reveals another rupture; the break between the horizon behind Smko, and the horizon he left behind, that of the echoes of Erbil. Quick jumps alter the relationship between Smko and the horizon; his leg raises, echoing the skyline. Echoes of the skyline become inscribed in the movement. The body shifts inward and outward; looking into the self and then extending out toward the audience. The poem has ceased, and the movement becomes more frantic, self-enclosed; Smko stands up, and from the book he holds above his head he pours water. This gesture seems like an act of grief, yet at the same time a beginning, an opening of a new horizon. The work culminates on this open-ended gesture, quite literally, in flow, in flux.

In conversation about this piece Smko says: "My favorite dance style is contemporary and I still love hip hop . . . it's my roots of dancing; when I started 2005. Officially when I dance hip hop is [sic] different from contemporary; when hip hop, it's more for me of [sic] expressing anger and careless [sic]. Contemporary is a life story telling and explaining different points of view in each dancer."[17] Smko has changed several homes; not only moving from Erbil to New York City, but changing his movement language—one of the most intimate, profound levels of engagement with himself—and incorporating contemporary dance into it. This piece, choreographed only months after "Echoes of Erbil," is far more fluid in its gestures and movement languages. There still are breaks, and gestures echoing hip-hop and breakdance, but the movement as a whole is far more legato than staccato. Smko is open to the audience. The hand no longer mirrors the soul; the audience suffices to be Smko's mirror. It is not that Smko abandoned his "mother tongue," hip-hop, but rather that this language is now incorporated into the new way he is telling stories about himself—through contemporary dance. The momentary fractures in movement are a reminder to the audience of the moment in which he was introduced into the world of dance, through that chance meeting with an American soldier. The incorporation of two languages into one is a testimony to the power of dance to bring people together, to create solidarity, and to allow human beings to make new homes for themselves literally and metaphorically. Hussein Smko's unique style is testimony to the solidarity of two danced movement languages. They are also a testimony to Hussein Smko's conversations translated into movement; his actions with others that are always aimed toward others, too; his own take on solidarity. The dialectic of transmission here is not only between different modes of technology and performance but between different forms of dance.

When Smko talks about this project, before the work was premiered, he says, "At the moment I'm working on a project about the islamophobia, that's happening in our time of living." The piece we are watching is reaching out to audiences in more than one way; the piece asks the audience members to go through the journey Smko has been through, and to open their eyes to the structures of love and hate that underpin our reality as human beings who all share the same earth. Smko continues: "it's something worth working for as for changing people's mentality; that is so easy to manipulate for the wrong choices of life."[18] The work is aimed at—and dedicated to— countering prejudice and hate in all the landscapes that Hussein Smko has seen and that have molded his hinterlands and horizons.

The spectator's heart opens when Smko switches on stage between the horizons of his home, Erbil, echoed in his movement, and the skyline of his new home, New York City, providing a backdrop for this merging of horizons. The shifts between the fluid, continuous movement, indebted to his new home in New York and contemporary dance, and breakdance, echoing Erbil, and echoing the first movement language he learnt, the first dance that filled his heart with love, show us that he is always at home in two homes. Through that, the audience, too, learns how to be at home in Erbil and New York City; how to break between two homes; and how to open the human heart to be filled with the love of dance.

Hussein Smko never just investigates the horizons of his own soul; he always reaches out to others. He concludes our conversation: "Last I just want to say that in life we choose sides and vision things and accomplish but the way you reach for it matters, because it's not just for you, but the rest of this earth, as we come from it!" The audience learns about the power of solidarity, or working together and sharing in praxis, through dance that has been grounded in manifold communities and gave rise to a dance work directly aimed at countering hate and strengthening solidarity. The landscapes of our childhood are never far away from us, but do not determine the way we will approach the world.[19]

At the Still Point of the Turning World

A year later, in 2019, Hussein once again takes to the Battery Festival against the gorgeous skyline, with once again a different work. This time he dances a duet with Amanita Jean under the title "Antoinette." This is an intimate work, full of soul searching and anger, the couple coming toward and withdrawing from each other, yet it is never completely clear whether we are indeed watching a work about a relationship or perhaps an articulation of ongoing inner struggle.

The piece shifts: from movement orientated up, toward higher tiers of the body, to crashing on the floor, from the dancers coming together to their separating, between different movement languages, different musical genres, different modes of expressiveness. Certain scenes within this short dance, less than eight minutes, can be assumed to be taken from remarkably different dances. The choreographic versatility is relentless. There is never a moment of purity and yet the mix of all these elements: high, low, still, moving, angry, loving makes toward many moments of pause that feel sublime. It is the ceaseless nature of the work that pushes the spectator toward feeling moments of the sublime. The harmony between Smko and Jean is flawless, which makes their movement appear like two narratives within the same psyche. Or perhaps this transitivity between inner and outer shows the fact that our humanity is rooted in the outer conversations, that we are never really alone, never dancing a solo,

Hussein Smko and Amanita Jean in the duet "Antoinette," Battery Dance Festival 2019. Photography by Julianna Crawford, courtesy of Julianna Crawford.

yet even when we are dancing a duet we are also dancing a duet within ourselves.

Perhaps this choreographic strategy and articulation of the sublime is most significant when juxtaposed to another feature of this work: the interplay between intimacy and violence. The passion in the work can be seen as anger; the dancers coming together can be seen as being drawn to each other, either through attraction or violence. The movements are forcefully executed, never easily reconciled, thus the fact that the spectator is drawn through the duality enacted on stage into their own duality means that they experience—sometimes in a hard and challenging way—the boundary between violence and passion within their own psyche. This is a work from which the spectator cannot draw away; it is a work about being human and all the glory and the downfalls that being human entails. Smko continues to tell his story forcefully, never conforming to limitations set on him by genre or style. And this story is always shared and reconfigures futures for others, through emerging solidarity.

Another feature of the work is the interplay between stillness and motion. When the dancers are still they are still moving. The moments of stillness are unforgiving, anything but a pause; they rather give the audience member the impression of a struggle by other means. "At the still point of the turning world. Neither flesh nor fleshless; Neither from nor towards; at the still point, there the dance is,"[20] wrote T. S. Eliot, and at the still point Hussein Smko and Amanita Jean are still, and are dancing.

Amanita Jean, an Alvin Ailey school alumna and Smko's collaborator and co-performer, gives further context for her meeting with Hussein, the development of the work, and her position toward it:

> The first time Hussein and I met was at my birthday party actually through a mutual friend. We were introduced as he was looking for dancers for his project and I was an actively working dancer/ choreographer at that time. His friend had shown Hussein my first choreographic work that was presented at the Actors Fund Theater in Brooklyn. He was intrigued by the spoken word poem I wrote "Home Away from Home" and presented accompanied by a violinist and six beautiful dancers. Hussein gave me his business card and asked me to email him. So I did, and we met about a week later at the Think cafe in Tribeca. . . . After listening to his words, observing his body language and reading the passion from his eyes I was open to get into the studio together. Hussein had told me about his Martial Arts, Breakdancing and Acting background and I could tell from our first rehearsal there was a lot we could learn from each other. My development in the arts started with dancing to the scores of my dad's drums, as he is a percussionist, and continued at age seven with strict training in ballet, modern, jazz, musical theater, tap, gymnastics and piano.[21]

Chance meetings can change lives and careers, and the arts are a powerful meeting point. Reflecting on the process of rehearsals as part of the dancers' praxis Jean says:

> In one week Hussein and I rehearsed for about 10 hours and got to know each other better through conversations after each rehearsal. He told me stories about the Middle East, Iraq and his family, I told him about my family from Latin America, the culture differences in Europe and how that affected me artistically. Eventually I told him about my first name: *Antoinette*. A name I only use for formal situations as it is my official first name. The name I normally go by is Melissa. Antoinette is my grandmother's name. A diminutive feminine form of Antoine and Antonia (from Latin Antonius), meaning beyond praise or highly

praiseworthy. He liked that name so much that he decided to name the piece "Antoinette" as it stood for female empowerment.[22]

Process cannot be discerned from performance, and many layers of the human life feed into a dance work as it is presented to an audience. The human life as a whole provides inspiration, a galvanizing force, and the layers of meaning of the dancing body that performs it. This is a forceful articulation of the relationship between temporality and praxis:

> At first this piece was a choreography that we had to finish within a week. We had both experienced harmful situations in our lives and as this piece had a theatrical feel to it, we used those experiences to express through our movement. After our first presentation of "Antoinette" succeeded, the piece became more than just an 8 minute dance routine. We started living the story that we were trying to tell the audience. For me it got so deep that after running the piece fully at the end of rehearsals I just couldn't look Hussein in the eyes without feeling the rage of how women are being treated in this world. Personally I was battling my inner demons, bad habits, shame, weaknesses, horrible memories and unspeakable situations that were all trapped in my mind. We would start our rehearsals with gaga movement improvisation, letting go, listening to our bodies, connecting the breath to the movement and touching our own bodies, this was for me the hardest part, as if I didn't want to connect to the person I was touching. As beautiful as our bodies are, all of those feelings would show if I didn't allow them to be what they are in our rehearsal process. The ability to see the world from another's point of view means that no meeting can be without change to those who have met, and the intensity of working on a danced creation that explores these shifting of perspectives changes both interlocutors profoundly.
>
> Hussein told me about his insecurities within this work as this would be the first time he presented his own choreography danced by two instead of one. This piece has connected us strongly through the vulnerability we showed each other … As love is the purest form of connection there is in this world. Hussein had told me afterwards that his intention for this piece was to present the power that lives inside of me. For that, I had to dig way deeper than my professional training. My artistic views were celebrated and nurtured in this process. At the moment I feel relieved having been able to go through that process in

104 DANCE AND ACTIVISM

a safe environment and with someone I naturally trusted. I truly feel more in tune with the meaning of my art after we created and performed "Antoinette" together.[23]

Jean concludes, reflecting on the transmission of the work into her own narrative, through this newfound solidarity:

I have been fortunate to work with inspiring artists who all had their unique share in this world. The difference Hussein makes is being so open to listen to other people's voices. He wanted to collaborate because he saw strengths in me that he didn't have and vice versa. We truly changed each other's lives since our first meeting. Now I look back at that time with a smile, the rush of accomplishing all the things we talked about reassures for anyone in the arts that technique and training are half of what makes an artist an artist. Passion prevails.[24]

Chance meetings, parties, and encounters in New York have been the source for radical dancing and activist praxis from the days of Emma Goldman to the second decade of the twenty-first century. The life of dancers extends beyond formal performances in theaters and even spending time in the studio; "Antoinette" is a crossroads of many lives around the world that gave rise to this multi-part collaboration. Alienation can be countered through always developing solidarities. And this occurs in shared praxis.

One central reason that Hussein Smko's work is a fascinating case study for a book on the connection between dance and activism is his ability to switch genres effortlessly and combine different movement languages without forgoing a deep rooting in his own background. He never appears as anyone but himself, no matter what movement language the audience sees on stage. The open endlessness of this work is an inspiring experience for the spectator. One can stop and reflect: is this breakdance? Is this contemporary dance? Maybe it is both, combined, and that is fine. Smko grasps the essence of several movement languages and mixes them so that they become one, and so we forget about the need to trace their origins. This is a challenging experience for anyone invested in taxonomy, which perhaps also challenges our own categories and attitude toward what radical action is. Perhaps, if one watches this work attentively, we can see how beginnings become new beginnings in mixing and swaying and transcending lines drawn in writing between moving bodies utilizing different languages. This is a theoretical challenge that comes from lived experience, bringing the core of the argument of this book to the forefront: that radical dance starts from a lived experience and in part always transcends theory. Perhaps the fact that the spectator is not sure exactly what they are seeing is part of the challenge of a radically new type of dance that brings together several forms. Radical dance can transcend classification and taxonomies. And so writing on radical dance should enable the open-endlessness that the work invokes in the spectator.

The work ends with the two dancers parting, walking to different sides of the stage. It is unclear when exactly the dance ends, or maybe it does not end at all. Perhaps the struggle and the tensions are continuing in the dancers' psyches as they take their bows; they certainly do continue in the spectators' psyches. There is a feeling that this could go on forever; the dance could continue and bring many other facets of movement to the spectator. Thus the last tension in this work is articulated in the overarching structure: that of beginning and end. There is no clear beginning and no clear end, just opening up to another level of action. Radical dance allows for the next layer to emerge, without knowing and without a physical place holder for it to begin from.[25] This is where the radical force of dance emerges: from its spilling over into an unknown future (articulated by Eleanor Marx as "the sequel").

This book looks at the interplay of solidarity and alienation, and in Hussein Smko's work we see them clashing profoundly without resolution. Perhaps the complexity of the interplay is one that can provide a different kind of solidarity: always in the now, without conclusion, always transmitted onward, opening up to the next stage, to the next horizon, to the next sunset.

Break/Dance: Echoing Further: Erbil

This is a unique story but it is also telling of other elements of its unraveling that are far from unique. A young man, Adel Euro, who lost his life to a terror attack, supported by the incomparable and visionary generosity in the solidarity of Jonathan Hollander and Battery Dance, opened the door for another young man, Hussein Smko, to make a new home for himself and to create a new home in dance that keeps expanding, with new collaborations such as "Antoinette." Coming from a war-ridden region that challenges one's ability to create a nourishing, harmonious life, brought Smko to a new home, which had its own challenges but sparked a flourishing that is ceaselessly expanding. From the American soldier who was to change the course of his life forever by showing him a video clip on a phone, to Jonathan Hollander who provided him with a new beginning, new interactions were sparked with people from across the globe. In his work Smko transcends divisions of genre; he transcends divisions of place, and he pushes spectators as well as his collaborators to question how they perceive the term "home." This is the story of one form of solidarity spilling into another.

This book started from a moment in history when modern dance exploded into the world of art, from a background of immigrant radical action on the Lower East Side. This moment, so it seems, continues in different guises, in new generations that bring unlikely partnerships to create cutting-edge dance. Modern dance, as we have seen in the first chapter of this book, is now taught as a tradition; now other forms of dance diverge and intervene and create new modes of being together.

The story of Hussein Smko's work is a story of the triumph of humanity and solidarity in the face of raging impulses of alienation, both within his homeland of Erbil and in his now adopted home of New York City. Hussein Smko's work continues to bring chances and introductions to his life. As part of his project TAG, Smko works in intersections of dance, theater, and performances, exploring themes of religion, politics, and war as a lived experience, presenting performances in prestigious venues in New York City.[26] TAG will also see Hussein's return to Erbil, for the first time since he left and his family fled the violence six years previously. The sunsets of New York will be replaced by echoes of Erbil; the dance continues. Others around the world continue to raise their voices against global injustice. The next chapter looks at solidarity on the streets; in protest and on the march.

5 STEPS IN THE STREET: REVOLUTION DJ

Dance on the March

The history of dance is bound in the history of revolution, as practice, ethos, and concept. The belief that another world is possible allowed for a radical reinterpretation of what is possible for the moving body. The French and Russian revolutions were, of course, crucial for the history of ballet;[1] yet the intersection of dance and revolution is broad and rich. The closing of the century that commenced in 1920 is undeniably a revolutionary time. People are taking to the streets en masse, all over the world. Strikes, marches, demonstrations, and sit-ins are staged to demand more voices being heard and more bodies being taken into account. Human beings are contesting the limits of the scope of representation of their voices and reclaiming their agency. This chapter seeks to understand what role dance plays "on the march," as part of activists' praxis, particularly in the twenty-first century and particularly in reconfigured or emerging solidarities. Why do people dance in public assemblies demanding a better future? What creates moments of dance within large political demonstrations and events? And what is the relationship between dance performed as public protest as part of a march and dance in theaters?

Martha Graham choreographed "Steps in the Street," part of her work "Chronicle," in 1936, against the backdrop of unrest, anti-war feeling, and socialist and feminist direct action on the lower East Side of New York City. But steps in the street—manifold steps in manifold streets, have been pounding the world ever since. Steps in the Street, or more precisely *dancing* Steps in the Street, have been part and parcel of waves of uprising for many epochs, yet new technologies show how central this part of action is to radical action today. New technologies and social media mean that we can see many dances across many causes, and enable us to see the similarities as well as differences between different dances on the march. Thus far the book has looked at the praxis of the dancer-activist; here, conversely, the focus shifts to the activist- dancer. Looking at the prevalence of dance within protest, the chapter seeks to find everyday dancing—not dance for stage; dance for performance in large public spaces.

A proviso for this chapter, which is a proviso for the entire book, should be clearly stated. This chapter does not attempt to chronicle an exhaustive survey of how dance is utilized in public demonstrations and radical actions. It would be near impossible—even in an entire book devoted to this theme solely—to present a comprehensive account of all performances. This chapter, instead, aims to disrupt the argument and the expectations of the reader, by showing a wide range of forms of dance and conditions of performance as well as a wide range of causes for which dance was used as an expression of solidarity. There is one running thread across these very different cases. They all represent people fighting together against growing alienation and taking to the streets in new forms of solidarity. The dialectic sitting at the heart of this chapter is that of march and dance. The following focus expounds this dialectic tension.

There are undeniable similarities between dance created for the theater and dance as protest. Bodies moving together in front of other bodies, both marches and performances are underpinned by the same organizing principles. Yet the politics of dance world (which have been a large part of the analysis thus far) are different to a set of bodies assembled in the city-square, claiming a better future for all. This is also, then, a phenomenological inquiry into the experience of activism through movement. What does it feel like to be in a collective of bodies moving together? How does this experience alter our human experience and our relationship to others? The core dialectic of this book is between alienation and solidarity reconfigured in praxis. The question presented in this chapter is how the balance between them changes when the body becomes part of many moving together, in an act of solidarity demanding a better future for all.

The People (Dancing) United Can Never be Defeated

Political theory is rife with theories of the dangers of the "masses," in overpowering individual voices as well as threatening the political process.[2] Masses taking over city squares have by and large been seen as a menace. They are seen as escaping a more heightened sense of alienation, the disengagement from the self, rather than solidarity, unraveling a sphere of collective action. Looking at the turn-of-the-decade protests with a focus on dance can generate a specific research question: can dance on the march open a vista for a theory of mass movement as a method of change making that is attentive to the bodies of which it is comprised? This is also a moment of taking stock of where activism is at this moment in time.

The #MeToo movement,[3] originally founded by an African American woman, Tarana Burke, spurred a cultural revolution when (primarily white) actors accused powerful men in Hollywood of sexual exploitation and abuse. The movement has since flooded into other areas of life and has had substantially divergent responses, yet undoubtedly is a major event in the twenty-first century. This movement has showed the deep divides underpinning the contemporary feminist movement.

A rupture that spurred a wave of activism commenced in Chile in 2019.[4] Arising out of a mass movement against inequality, Chilean women started a feminist flash-mob that carried through around the world. The flash-mob begins with marching on the spot, eyes blindfolded. Then hands go behind the head, in a posture that women should assume when arrested. Who is the oppressor? They ask with a charged use of body language. The survivor becomes the accuser. The flash-mob then continues to run in place, to a moment of stark accusation. *The rapist is you!* The patriarchy is everywhere, and we can only overcome it with collective action. Pointing continues everywhere. "The rapist is you," they chant. Patriarchy is the culprit. And we are all part of it. Only 8 percent of rape cases in Chile lead to conviction. Since being performed in Chile the flash-mob has been performed—mostly using the lyrics in Spanish—in multiple locations including Paris and New York. The latter has served as the location of its own feminist spontaneous flash-mob—against the Hollywood producer Harvey Weinstein who has become a symbol of the #MeToo movement.[5] This flash-mob referred to the body language as well as blindfolds of the Chilean precedent. The movement and dramaturgy had moved from a small Chilean collective to Hollywood and Fifth Avenue. The power of feminist solidarity here has transcended many obstacles, many elements of alienated lives, prohibiting them from telling their story.

The statement "Y la culpa no era mía, ni dónde estaba, ni cómo vestía" is the driving force of the flash-mob. The flash-mob sees its goal as unraveling a world in which women do not fear for their selves, for their bodies, and their lives. By taking up public space, by their collective movement, they are nudging history along, pushing it toward the sequel, a world in which all are equal regardless of sex. Millions of people around the world performed this flash-mob in solidarity with survivors they know and do not know. The accusation is both personal and collective. Every human being who is an accomplice to gender injustice is part of the problem. Yet the solution in the flash-mob is never individual. The focus is not only on #MeToo, but, in this flash-mob, on #UsToo.

The practice of blindfolding, highly charged (between sexual references and symbolizing blindness), means that the collective becomes deindividuated. It is harder to recognize the blindfolded protesters, thus #MeToo becomes a far more collective experience than individual columns, monologues, or accusations. Troubling perhaps for some, also emancipating for others, the horrors and violence of the patriarchy are protested without disclosing individual bodies. And yet, the protest is founded and motivated by the need to restore respect for individual bodies. The flash-mob is non-violent and asks for a non-violent society we do not yet know. This emotive dialectic is the power of these flash-mobs, which drew more responses than those women who started them could imagine.

At the same time, a new wave of protest in defense of abortion rights, a core cause for the feminist struggle since its earliest years, has been sweeping the globe. In addition to placing the rights of women to control their bodies at the core in the Women's Marches in the USA, two key locations for these uprisings have been Poland and Argentina. Mass marches and demonstrations have been—and still are—taking place defending women's rights to control their bodies. Like many of the mass marches discussed in this chapter, collective movement was part and parcel of these gatherings.[6] The rise of a new wave of feminist protests and especially the #NiUnaMenos (Not One Less) movement influenced many areas of life in Argentina, including one of its most famous staples, the tango. There have been long debates about the power and gender dynamics of the tango,[7] yet a crucial moment in the context of this chapter was the foundation of a tango festival against the machismo culture in tango, set up to directly address the issue of violence against women and girls. Tango Hembra, Argentine's first female-only international tango event, occurred against the backdrop of these protests, and was galvanized by the spirit of the resistance they exemplified;

112 DANCE AND ACTIVISM

Claudia Levy, a pianist and composer, notes how eight years ago she was not able to sing a tango about an abused woman. "I had to stop singing it, as it made people uncomfortable. That was when feminism was a bad word, and when people hushed issues of domestic violence. But now, feminism is touching everything, so I began to sing it again."[8] This is a clear articulation of solidarity and an example of the porous boundaries between dance on the march, flash-mobs, and collective movement, with festivals as another site of collective movement that can be transformed and altered. Marisa Vasquez, founder of the Tango Hembra festival, elucidates this point clearly: "'I used to do this alone, I would call radio and festival executives and ask why they didn't include women,' she said. "But now, the feminist movement has awoken here. It was the ideal moment to do this." Dance on the march pours from mass rallies into festivals, equal spaces for resistance and reconfiguration of public life, generating new solidarities and new spaces for dancer-activists to explore their praxis.

Flash-mobs, though, are far from being only the property of feminist (and mostly woman's, transgender and non-binary people's) protest. The Gilets Jaunes (Yellow Vests) movement took over France in fall 2018. Originally motivated by rising fuel prices and the heavy burden of the cost of living, the movement spans the political spectrum and uses the high visibility vest as its symbol. Arising out of protest in solidarity with those most vulnerable to fuel tax, truck drivers, the movement spun far beyond its initial claim and has encompassed many actions from road blockages to demonstrations. The French police tried to constrain the Gilets Jaunes movement and the violence sparked in these clashes was compared to that which burst out in May 1968.

Much is debated around the Gilets Jaunes and their ability to counter the policies of Emmanuel Macron, bringing liberal and neoliberal policies in full swing into the French state, but it is clear that one cannot ignore this phenomenon in the history of French protest.

Dance made its surprising but also consistent appearances in the Gilet Jaunes protests, in various contexts and iterations. Many of the participants in the flash-mob danced to the sound of the darbuukah,[9] a traditional Arabic instrument. Many are men; they are fairly evidently not very coordinated, and yet movement brings them all together and attracts attention from passersby. On the other hand, a collection of clips showing dance and the Gilets Jaunes presents everything from a skilled hip-hop dancer enthusing her onlookers, to two nuns dancing among cheering

Women wearing a yellow vest (*gilet jaune*) dance and hold banners reading "angry women, fight for the purchasing power," "resignation of Macron and the government," as they walk toward the new police station in Le Mans, on January 13, 2019, to protest against the government and the police violence during the nationwide demonstrations of the Gilets Jaunes movement. Photo by JEAN-FRANCOIS MONIER / AFP via Getty Images.

Gilets Jaunes yelling at them: "alles! alles!" The next clips show a variety of protesters moving together on the march itself. Then, we see dancers wearing masks characteristic of the anonymous movement, reminding us that to protest is still dangerous, still taking a risk, and from the days of Emma Goldman to our own times people pay a heavy price for activism and may wish to do so anonymously.

Another part of the clip shows dancers going into a full rave, abandoning and letting loose of constraints. Both in dance and in protest there is a break from everyday life. Order is being negotiated and opens up possibilities of a different order. But in order to attain that, experiencing disorder allows a phenomenological experience of living without the previous order. Perhaps surprisingly, another iteration of the Gilets Jaunes flash-mob is a performance of the ever popular dance the "Macarena." The iteration of collective joy in this dance becomes a means of resistance when performed in the context of this movement. Even what seems like an iteration of folk dance in a circle is part of one flash-mob.[10]

The different example of dance in the context of Gilets Jaunes show the wide array of avenues the movement took, and the fact that it encompassed so much of French society. There is one uniting feature of all these clips: they show immense joy in togetherness and in being visible in movement—the entire ethos behind wearing yellow vests as a protest symbol—and there is nothing predictable about any of them. This variety of performances shows there is nothing gendered about a flash-mob in and of itself, an iteration of solidarity in motion, different ways to live one's beautiful ideal, to generate praxis in movement. Moreover, it is living testament that the French tradition of protest and subversion from the revolution through the commune of 1871, is alive and well in the dancing Gilets Jaunes. [11]

The sex/gender debate and its connections to dance have a long shared history. The film *Paris is Burning*, documenting the voguing/ball scene, led to much controversy alleging that the director exploited the Latino and African American queer subjects of her film, many of whom met harrowing deaths in poverty. This controversy hovered at the background of recent shows such as *RuPaul's Drag Race* and *Pose*, which brought much of the ball and drag subculture to mainstream media. And alongside this have been everyday attacks on transgender rights and the denial of bodily and identity autonomy of transgender activists. Thus, visibility of transgender people is in itself an act of protest, an affirmation that no one can deny human rights for all, and that human rights are never a zero-sum game. On 20 November, Transgender Day of Remembrance, trans activists (both transgender and cisgender bodied)[12] took to Washington Square Park, site of many revolutionary movements that were at the heart of Chapter 2 of this book, to perform the flash-mob "Esprit Yourself." Text accompanying the video cites: "This song 'Esprit Yourself' was inspired by a transgender conference called The Esprit Gala, and is dedicated to the transgender community. May we all be free to celebrate who we are. The shrine decorated with flowers that you see in this video lists the names of those who have been murdered in the past year as a result of transphobia. The shrine includes each person's name, age, and cause and date of death. For more information on the Transgender Day of Remembrance please visit: TGOR.info ~ Better To Light a Candle Than Curse the Darkness."[13]

For transgender people contesting violence that disputes their actual right to appear as who they are in public means that appearing as they are is subversive. Alienation, the inability to tell their own story in their own way, is first and foremost a risk to their lives posed for their very attempt to challenge the conditions of their alienation. The dance performed here is full of joy, and moreover as one onlooker joins in, the dance is greeted by applause and cheer. Much like the logic that underpins feminist flash-mobs, which are there to protest the disappearing of women from public spaces, this transgender flash-mob contests the inability to appear as who trans people are, and the fear of violence from various sources due to the rise in transphobia. Adding a joyful dance to appearing transforms the site of performance as well as onlookers' perceptions of what remembering and resisting may look like.

In the same year, in a different part of the globe, another flash-mob provided affirmation for LGBTI+ rights. Under the premiership of Narendra Modi and the BJP, attacks on minorities and the normalization of violence in India has become mainstream (while Modi's allies such as Boris Johnson, Donald Trump, and Benjamin Netanyahu in Israel and others globally go suspiciously silent). The attack on religious minorities is harsh and ongoing, under the façade of so-called "Hindu-nationalism," and the latest developments have seen the annexation of Kashmir and deployment of Indian troops, as well as the cutting down of communication and access to internet, and the widespread normalization of violence.

The fight for progressive politics in India is ongoing and strong. This flash-mob is multi-dimensional in its choreographic language. It is both joyful and powerful, showing many gendered identities performed by all (thus transcending their gendering), and shifts from group dance to loving duets to give a cohesive, almost full-performance-like quality. Some statements from activists after the flash-mob illuminate both the force of the dance and its intention, one claiming that, "dance is one medium with which everyone can connect," another, "[the] only way we can accommodate every kind of expression," and finally, "if loving someone is a crime then we want to be criminals in this world."[14] It would be wrong, however, to categorize all flash-mobs as joyful intervention. Indeed, for many for whom existing and appearing is in itself a subversive act, flash-mobs act as a register above; showing that occupying space and a body is always within one's freedom. Protesting that "love is love" when homophobia is normalized is a brave step forward on the march, as this inaugural flash-mob shows. This is an articulation of love qua love as part of the dancer activists' praxis.

In all these case studies the dance becomes a march itself; the phenomenological experience of demonstration, the transformation of

116   DANCE AND ACTIVISM

its bodies in the course of its action is experienced through moving bodies together. As argued when reading the ballet class as an act of solidarity, here dance on the march allows moving bodies to transform their presence in the world through the act of protest itself. The #MeToo movement may be the newest iteration of the longstanding history of the feminist movement, just as the Gilets Jaunes encapsulates a long struggle against neo-liberal reforms in France and beyond; thus, the march of return is the newest iteration of the Palestinian struggle against Israeli occupation.

On March 30, 2018, a series of protests on the Israel/Gaza border demanding the right of return of Palestinian refugees and displaced people escalated into a wave of violent protest, perhaps a popular uprising. Coinciding with celebration of seventy years of what is termed "the Nakba," the disaster, seventy years of displacement and uprooting, which is seen on the other side of the border as seventy years of independence for the state of Israel, the march of return attracted international attention and showed that the precarious but never settled status quo can change quickly. The cost in life was immense; 183 Palestinians were shot dead and over 9,000 injured in multiple ways.[15] This context, of escalating anger and seemingly irresolvable readings of history, hardly appear as a context for dance, yet dance, just as in flash-mobs against sexual violence, is not only an expression of happiness and joy; dance can be a powerful mechanism with which to express anger.

During the march of return, several performances of the dabke took place as part of the wave of protest. The dabke is a dance with a long and radical history that is educational of the complexity of the Palestinian struggle as well as its ongoing radical essence. The dabke is a participatory dance in which people form a line that can be expanded as new dancers join the moving chorus. The movements of the line are led by a *lawith*, a dancer who leads and initiates changes in the line formation, and who is followed by a chorus. There are breaks created by individual dancers performing solos and the group response to them.

The use of the dabke in political contexts is hardly new. During the British Mandate, Palestinians danced the dabke as a statement of resistance to Jewish immigration to Palestine before 1948 (there is evidence of performance of the dabke in 1923 in the village of Nebi Musa during a protest against the arrival in large numbers of Jews), as well as the growing international support for Zionism. After 1948, dabke dances were choreographed into stories of the villages destroyed in the Nakba.

Like many other elements of Palestinian life, dance has always been connected to politics. The dabke's subversive potential was soon recognized across the borders of Palestine. Palestinian culture had already been subjected to censorship through increasing military and political presence in everyday life, but after 1967 the interventions became starker and harsher. Israeli authorities regularly delayed permission for West Bank performances honoring indigenous heritage and folklore to travel to perform abroad.

After Israel and the Palestinian Authority signed the Oslo Accords in 1993, Palestinian society began to open up more to the international community. El Fanoun, a famous Palestinian dance troupe, was provided funding for the first time, dance facilities were built, and international sponsorship enabled the founding of dance troupes for children in refugee camps. International choreography was introduced into dance curricula across Palestine, from classical ballet to the Martha Graham technique, changing the performance style of the dabke in Palestine.[16]

And so, coming back to the march of return, it was both surprising and apt that the dabke was danced through tear gas and rubber bullets shot by the Israeli army. The dabke circle was composed of old and young, men and women, some wearing keffiyehs. What can the dabke serve those people, in the harsh conditions under which they protest? The march of return was highly charged in its practice as well as its ethos. The quest to return to a land from which those dancers were exiled is grounded in anger and longing. This dance, as angry and joyless as it is, is expressive of this longing and its call for action.[17] Dance here is part of a march of return, allowing anger for loss to be recorded in manifold ways. The stories held within the dabke, now danced on the border, are held within the bodies dancing and then transmitted to the world. History cannot be undone, and bodies hold possibilities for telling their stories against many odds.[18] Praxis as chronicling a history denied elsewhere can in turn open up new solidarities.

Meanwhile, another country that had managed to overcome its regime of Apartheid, providing an example for the Palestinian people (and many others), South Africa, was battling its own challenges. Since the days of Nelson Mandela, the African National Congress (ANC), the party of which he was a longstanding member since 1943 and co-founder of its youth league in 1944, had come into new difficulties. In 2008, Jacob Zuma was elected as the fourth president of South Africa. Initially hailed as "the people's president," he finally succumbed to a ninth vote of no confidence

Palestinians perform a traditional folk dance called "dabke" at the "Great March of Return" demonstration area during an event, based on Palestinian cultural legacy, organized by a Palestinian committee in Khan Yunis, Gaza on October 10, 2018. Photo by Mustafa Hassona/Anadolu Agency/Getty Images.

by his own party, the ANC. Against a backdrop of increasing charges of corruption, building one on top of the other, the people of South Africa had taken to the streets in their masses. The proud tradition of dance as protest within South Africa appeared in these waves of protest, too. In the "Zuma must go" protests, dances that had been part of the struggle against apartheid, such as the Pantsula, were once again performed on the streets. The Pantsula is a dance that arose from the early 1950s, from financial hardship in townships. Combining tap, gumboot dance, tribal dance, and everyday gestures, the Pantsula always carried political significance. However, the new circumstances of life in post-apartheid South Africa, with its new challenges, brought new weight and contents to the dance. Alongside the mass marches that did indeed bring about the vote of no confidence for Zuma, Gregory Maquoma, a contemporary choreographer, created a dance about corruption. One of the dancers said: "You know, my grandmother still lives in a shack, and I live in a shack, and it's 24 years after apartheid: what has the fight really been for? Why are things still the same? Why are things worse?" Maquoma sees dance as a way to counter the frustration of these ongoing battles. "Dance and Music is what we own and it gives us life." As in the example of the tango in Argentina, this is a case in which a dance performed as protest under the auspices of a sweeping political movement can be performed on stage while still encapsulating the spirit of "dance on the march." [19]

As South Africa saw a triumph in the battle against corruption, another battle was just emerging elsewhere. Marches often spill over from their intended cause to many agendas that may or may not overlap with it. Between 2019 and the start of 2020, Lebanon saw unrest that brought thousands onto the streets in a call to end pulling political elites, and protesting planned taxes on gasoline, tobacco, and online phone calls using programs such as WhatsApp. Banks had imposed controls on US and local currency, preventing people from taking out more than $300 per week, leading to anger against the banks and proving the age old connection between capital and power. Thus, thousands who have been occupying the streets are not only demanding a change to government but rather a systemic change. Art—of all sorts, including dance—has become a staple of this mass protest movement. Dance teacher Mazen Tannous says: "The most artistic places come from pain and suffering, because when you don't have much to do, there is nothing else but to be creative. So, we try to explore our emotions in an artistic way, not in an angry way."[20] This is a robust articulation of alienation as the force toward creating new solidarities.

In Tripoli, the popular Lebanese DJ Madi Karimeh leads nightly dance parties for thousands of protesters as a self-styled "Revolution DJ." He believes that when Lebanon's youth comes together creatively, they can create a new country that will take all their voices into account. A rather unique instance of solidarity that is worthy of a pause emerged from the Lebanon protests. One historical argument against the freedom to protest has been the effect it may have on onlookers and passersby. Yes, you may think your protest is crucial and burning, but by taking to the streets you are obstructing the rights of free movement of those who are not part of the protest, the argument follows. Moreover, protesters can erupt in violence toward those who are not part of their movement; ideas about "the angry mob" attacking passersby has been haunting protest literature for centuries, from Gustav le Bon to our times.

Lebanon in 2019 provided a unique case study that is also a counter-argument to the idea of demonstrations being facilitated by "angry mobs." A mother, Eliane, and her toddler Robin were accidentally caught in the midst of lively protests, in this case noticeably populated mostly by men. The clash between the protesters and mother and son ended in a surprising way: the protesters sang and danced the globally popular "Baby Shark" to the boy (with mass performance of accompanying hand gestures).[21] The video showing the instance is surprising to the viewer, too; one may have thought that Robin, caught completely against his mother's wish in the midst of these events, would show some concern or worry, but he does not utter a single sound and in fact looks relaxed. Moreover, the scene of a mass of young men performing a children's song and dance together, just to ensure that the toddler and his mother were not worried by the situation in which they found themselves, is heartwarming. Beyond the impossibility of not smiling at this instance of dance and protest there is a deeper message. The discussion of alienation that sits at the crux of this book's argument, and consequently positions solidarity as its counter concept, centralizing the action of multitudes in concert, works from a specific premise. This premise is that action in concert does not come at the expense of an individual—that we are always entrenched in our communities, thus coming together as collectives can be practiced in a way that does not make the individuals who are part of this collective vulnerable. Here we see an interruption of a mass movement in order to protect an individual who has wandered into its midst unintentionally, breaking its own plan of protest. There are no parts of this book that are deterministic or prescriptive, but this rather rare instance is used here to highlight an opportunity; a moment of rupture in which the crowd has focused on an individual and disturbed its own actions in order to protect them.

A case study of an exceptional singular moment that expanded beyond its intention can be found in another part of the world, Sudan, where a wave of popular protest took over the country. In Sudan protests have taken multiple turns and many of them involved dance. Most notably, a 22-year-old student from Khartoum became an unlikely heroine of mass protest, sparked by cuts to bread and fuel subsidies but developing into a mass protest over the issues of austerity and the ruthlessness of the reign of Omar al-Bashir, who had been the president of Sudan for the past thirty years. Tens of thousands of people have taken to the streets in what is now termed "the Sudanese Revolution," and which has gained a symbol in the figurehead of Alaa Saleh. Nicknamed the Nubian Queen, Ms. Saleh was portrayed in a video that has gone viral, in which she is depicted performing in a graceful dance. Ms. Saleh chanted: "they burned us in the name of religion, jailed us in the name of religion." Her *tob*, or gown, wrote activist Hind Makki, is a "callback" to the Sudanese women of the 1960s, 1970s, and 1980s who took to the streets to demand the end of dictatorships. The image and video are striking in the contrast between a graceful, composed dance, and the ease with which she commands her audience and the masses who are attending the protest. "That image means so much to me," said Sara Abdul-Jaleel, spokeswoman for the Association of Professional Unions, one of the driving forces behind the protests. "I commend her for her courage. She has exposed herself to great dangers and she will be pursued by authorities."[22]

The image of "The Nubian Queen" was juxtaposed to that of Bashir. The dialectic between both kinds of authority have created a new form of solidarity, a new togetherness that has started through movement. Moreover, much like in the "Baby Shark" instance, here the interruption of protest into a moment of stillness and stoppage of movement dispels myths about crowds and marches, and the use of movement within them. Dance on the march, just like dance in theaters, is not just a way to bring people together in anger and hot emotions but can galvanize and create a response to other forces through grace, humor, stillness, and calm. Dance on the march can bring people together in collective action and yet it can also create moments of calm within collective motion. Dance can be used as unison movement or in distilled solos. Dance can be slow or fast, quiet or rowdy. Dance on the march can be planned or spontaneous. Dance on the march mirrors everything that dance on stage, or theatrical dance, can become. Surveying the range of examples from around the world allows theorists to shed preconceptions and to understand that dance— of any kind—is crucial for the work of contemporary activism, and although it is not always taken to be crucial for solidarity, this brief survey has already proved it is.

Together with #MeToo, a major phenomenon of the last decade of the twenty-first century is the uprising for environmental justice. Greta Thunberg, a teenager who rose to unexpected stardom as a new iteration of a prototype of activist, has been equally revered and vilified.[23] The Fridays for Future wave of mass strikes took over the world unexpectedly, surprising cynics and those who argue that the spirit of activism has died, that teenagers are too engrossed in their phones and do not care about the world. Major cities in the world had been brought to a standstill, and millions of young people joined an international march demanding better care of the planet as a whole. Extinction Rebellion arose as a movement that draws on non-violent civil disobedience to compel government action; agitating against tipping points in the climate system, biodiversity loss, and the risk of social and ecological collapse.

An Australian activist provided her own variation on the dance while she performed it in elegant clothes to the sound of the Bee Gees' "Staying Alive," showcasing a clearly amateur effort but much passion for the cause and a love for disco. Meanwhile, a flash-mob in London's Trafalgar Square,[24] one of the main sites brought to a halt, featured activists reenacting lyrics of a pop song agitating to call for action in the face of indifference. Flash-mobs are a highly useful and effective way to generate attention from bystanders, here by running and raising voices together with movement.[25] They are a way for people to reconfigure new solidarities.

Meanwhile, another flash-mob, this time in Sydney, calls for a rising to the music of protest classic "Bella Ciao."[26] This song, with a long and illustrious history of anti-fascist struggles, is being updated for the urgent causes of this movement, calling on people to "start right now." The participants here come from various ages and the flash-mob performs fairly simple arm gestures.[27]

Another useful element for flash-mobs in activism is the ability to draw in people and allow them to be active participants even if they do not feel comfortable speaking up from a platform. Extinction Rebellion has been widely critiqued for its surpassing of voices of people of color and its utilizing protest techniques that are exclusionary.[28] (One of the main vehicles by which Extinction Rebellion disrupts is by aiming for mass arrests, through sit-ins and blocking public paths. In a world in which police brutality is discriminatory toward people of color it is a big ask for "everyone to join"—where persons of color are in much more danger of being attacked by the police than are white protesters. This premise is hugely problematic.) Nevertheless, the diversity of both the choice of flash-mobs and the modes of utilizing them, within the same movement, and within a broadly white and Western context is surprising. No two flash-mobs surveyed above are identical and neither are their participants.

Extinction Rebellion signaled a mass uprising, mainly across the global north, but is anything but the most substantial revolution the past decade has brought to the world. The so-called Arab Spring has shifted the way the Middle East is seen both internally and externally. A series of anti-government protests, uprisings, and armed rebellions that spread from the early 2010, began as a response to oppressive regimes as well as a low standard of living, and erupted from Tunisia to many locations where power was contested. Also generated were mass performances of solidarity. These events catalyzed a change in how public life and engagement with spaces were negotiated within the Arab world. And within this radical context, dance occupied an interesting place. Whereas the focus of the second chapter of this book engaged with ballet—showing that it holds radical potential beyond its beginnings (which were essentially conservative)—here the radical power of ballet transcends the theater and the studio and spilled over to the street.

Egypt has been a hub of radical action for many years, but particular events in Tahrir Square formed a significant marker within the Arab Spring and caused a shockwave worldwide. At the same time, protests in Egypt took manifold forms and via many mediums. The relationship between technology and activism was queried in the previous chapter—where connections between New York and Iraq enabled a truly unique career in dance activism to unravel—yet in this case study of dance on the march, the virtual sphere provided other spaces of action.

The Ballerina Project is an online project placing ballet dancers in urban settings, generating multiple reactions on social media. This galvanized Cairo-based photographer Mohammed Taher to start the Ballerinas of Cairo project. But here he was confronted with the duality of public spaces for women. "There's a huge problem for women in Egypt streets," Taher said as part of a piece surveying the project, "There's a lot of sexual harassment . . . so now this was a layer of the project." Making bodies visible in their own terms acts as a pushback to a culture of violence against women. As much as 99.3 percent of Egyptian women, according to a UN report, experienced street harassment. Public protest may not always be safe for women, but the online world provides new dangers, with harassment and violence a constant spectre for women who make themselves visible online. The Ballerinas of Cairo project is an embodied resistance to various forces creating oppressive lives for women on several layers. "We got a lot of comments from girls saying they want to do this, and they were very enthused about it," Taher said. "They want to dance on the street. They want to feel free. They want to have this feeling of being on the streets again, just walking the street."[29] The freedom presented in the photographs—utterly stunning and hard to ignore, and uniquely divergent from the Ballerina Project that catalyzed them—is not an unequivocal freedom. It does not get rid of the culture of violence that was the galvanizing force for its emergence. Yet the ability to claim the space, once again, like in the Chilean flash-mob, extends solidarity and spills it over through the use of technology. Centering the female body as a powerful claimant of space enables new solidarities to unravel. The men who appreciate and admire the Ballerinas of Cairo's reclaiming of the streets will perhaps be able to look at the women around them in a different way—to look into their hearts and eyes with more sincerity—while laws of equality inch closer.

The breadlines that were part and parcel of Martha Graham's social landscapes as she choreographed "Chronicle" were also the hub of labor organizing and strikes. Once again, in the twenty-first century, strikes are returning to the forefront of our news as a powerful mechanism to show the power of the masses. France was brought to a halt in a wave of strikes against Emmanuel Macron's neoliberal policies, and specifically his attack on pensions from December 5, 2019. The Paris Opera Ballet cancelled more than sixty-three performances. Stagehands' strikes are fairly common, and yet artists joining this national wave of strikes and protests made history. One occurrence of this contemporary mass strike action circulated widely on social media and aroused the attention of many outside the world of dance, once again bringing ballet to the forefront of struggles in unexpected ways. For the first time in its 350-year history, the Paris Opera Ballet went on a month-long strike, over the most financially generative season for ballet companies worldwide: Nutcracker Season.[30]

On a cold December day, musicians and dancers of the Paris Opera Ballet performed, outside the historic Opera Garnier, fifteen minutes of *Swan Lake*. In full performance dress, tutus, and a few over garments (which were perhaps one of the only reminders that this performance is part of a strike, in an unusual setting, rather than a theatrical rendition of one of the most loved ballets in the canon), the dancers performed one of the most loved and admired pieces in classical canon to a huge and enthusiastic audience. One of the dancers, Heloise Jacqueviel, commented that "it is to show that we are against the reforms ... but it's also a gesture towards spectators, because we as artists are sorry for what is happening to thousands of people who are deprived of seeing Christmas shows ....."[31] This extraordinary performance is disruptive in many ways; first, it is disruptive to how dance on the march can be perceived, including the perceptions analyzed in this chapter. Raves, folk dancing, dancing to "Baby Shark," flash-mobs, and the online presence of ballet dancers have all contributed to understanding the power of dance on the march. Here, an outdoors performance of a classical, canonical work adds another layer to what can be understood as dance on the march. The context of a performance can change its efficacy as well as its radical power. Ballet, it has been argued throughout, can be utilized as a radical form of expression to many. Here the context of the performance allows the dancers to be in solidarity with many others who are taking radical action.

Second, this performance, especially when narrated with the dancers' commentary, disrupts the perception of strikes as dangerous and inconsiderate. Strikes are disruptive by their very nature, but that does not mean they are harmful. Extending the beauty of ballet to hundreds of strikers (who may well not be in the financial position to purchase a ticket for the ballet otherwise) is a way to extend solidarity and empathy. The image of the violent mob with which this discussion started is replaced with a ballet performance, entrancing hundreds of spectators, and allowing the dancers to keep performing their art for the public good.

Dancing Onwards!

As with the book overall, this chapter offers not a conclusive ending but an exploration of tensions between various forms of dance and various forms of activism. The discussion has shown that there is not one arc to being an activist dancer, not one way to counter alienation through solidarity, and not one way to live one's beautiful ideal, in praxis.

The discussion, which has surveyed global phenomena as well as global waves of activism, pushes the argument toward its next chapter, which will try to transcend borders as categories separating nation-states and creating new forms of movement, those of migration. This chapter will also push beyond the activists whose praxis inspired and galvanized the discussion in the book, who are still—even if participating in global movements—appealing to nation-states.

At the same time, this chapter, elucidating the various iterations and forms that the activist dancer can take, is an important layer in understanding the praxis of dance as activism. Dance on the march, dancing steps in the street, have appeared in manifold movements of social justice across the globe. If we can't dance, our praxis won't be part of our revolution for many activists, this (very partial) survey has shown.

Dance happens in many iterations on the march and transforms its experience for dancers as well as onlookers.

This book is written in an attempt to understand dance as activism, a praxis, a mode of being in the world. This mode can be part of an ongoing struggle, or an intervention, or, most substantially, as an offering of different ways to experience solidarity within the moving human body. It would be hard to imagine anyone partaking in any of the events discussed above remaining unchanged by their force. The next chapter presents an exploration of solidarities arising on other global stages, those organized around seas and oceans, and those whose praxis entails risking their lives while boarding boats to start a new, unknown tomorrow.

6 DANCE AS A HOME

Our country is a country of words.
Speak, speak,
that I might lay a trail, stone by stone.
Our country is a country of words.
Speak, speak,
that we may know an end to traveling.

MAHMOUD DARWISH

The question of migration and how migrants are treated have been in the headlines from Karl and Eleanor Marx's time, when German-Jewish and other immigrants inhabited Victorian London, to our present day, and necessitates that we shift our own thinking forward and ask about our present solidarities. "In the first place, we do not like to be called 'refugees'. We ourselves call each other 'newcomers' or 'immigrants',"[1] starts political theorist Hannah Arendt in her 1943 text *We Refugees*. On the cusp of the end of the Second World War, before Anna Sokolow premiered her groundbreaking work "Kaddish," remembering the atrocities of concentration and death camps of the Second World War, Arendt, herself a young woman who fled Nazi Germany and arrived for a new life in America, was to witness how many people would join her in the fate of being named refugees while preferring to be named newcomers. At the same time, the end of the Second World War also spurred the development of international law and especially the doctrine of human rights, which arose from the hope of ending atrocities of the kind that Arendt fled, and to create a system of accountability across borders for violations against human dignity. In this book, the focus has been on those people who live in the midst of political upheavals, not only formally, as law makers or lawyers, but as those bringing meaning into the law through their praxis. This focus became heightened in the last decade of our century. In the

2010s our media was swamped—sporadically, depending on what else was chosen to cultivate our consciousness—with images of people in rubber boats, and other hazardous methods of transport, crossing seas in order to escape wrongs and strife around the world and attempting to arrive in Europe. What is commonly referred to as the "refugee crisis" (which is, in fact, not a crisis but an ongoing phenomenon) was a pulse of consciousness about the fact that eighty years after the end of the Second World War we are far from creating a stable solution for those escaping their homeland and finding a new tomorrow. The challenge here is twofold. At first, how can we all enable more people to feel at home? And second, what can we do for the system that clearly is not working to save the lives of those fleeing persecution globally? Which solidarity may emerge through dance to all those who are in motion to create a new home for themselves, and what does this mean to our current political configuration, the global system of nation-states?

This chapter focuses on danced responses to refugees arriving on our shores. It is a step toward the conclusion for the book in two ways. First, it is an attempt to reflect on structural challenges within international law and politics as a whole, and how they still fail those most vulnerable in our world. Second, the chapter presents an embodied exercise that might expand our consciousness and help us become activist-dancers, or at least activist-dance-spectators, drawing on a particular case study (which, it will be argued, is not an example but an exemplar). Thus, it is not only a discussion but a call for action, a suggestion to the reader of this book on what they may learn from this galvanizing occurrence. The chapter works within the dialectic of home and homelessness, thinking about what a loss of one's world through forced migration, intimately related to experience of alienation, and being prohibited from telling one's own story in one's own world, teaches us about this particular experience of alienation. At the same time, the chapter exposes new solidarities acting in dialectical tension to this alienation haunting those migrating and seeking refuge.

The chapter, in the spirit of the dialectical thinking that has underpinned this book, flips the points of view discussed thus far. While up to now the focus was on dancer-activists telling their own stories, the book now shifts to our responsibility—as a global community—toward those at the frontline, those experiencing the challenge and strife of migration in the twenty-first century. The question now is: How can we, non-migrants, understand migrants better? How can we make a world in which they feel less like those on the margins of society? Thus, the chapter looks at three works of art and movement that aim to engage migration and refugees by those who are not seeking refuge themselves. Dialectally, this expands the range of who may be able to act or respond. Ethically, the chapter asks, what do we owe refugees?[2] Politically, the chapter asks us to focus on the refugee crisis as a test case of the challenges of our post-world-war world that has failed many people after Arendt and her generation arrived in a new home, and the doctrine of human rights were legislated and became a hope for a better world, still in becoming. Last, this chapter, arriving toward the end of the argument of the book, revisits the underlying problematic and catalyst for action, that of alienation, and examines it in relation to the concept of exile. What do we learn about alienation from those who are negotiating the concept of home in their everyday life?

Transitions

It is an unusually warm day in Oxford, UK. The sun is shining brightly through the windows of a building usually used for dormitories and office buildings. All the chairs have been moved aside and, on the floor, sitting, are a large group of young refugees who are being invited to tell their stories by two other refugees who are leading the activity. Among the people sitting in the room is one of the United Kingdom's most remarkable and admired literary personalities, Dame Professor Marina Warner. The mind and heart behind the Stories in Transit project, Warner narrates the idea and praxis that pushed her to throw herself into this unique and inspiring project:

> In April 2018, around eighty young refugees and asylum seekers (*minorenni*, or minors, aged 18 and under) were taking part in the project Stories in Transit in Palermo. The plan was to set out from Ballarò, the old multicultural part of the city, and go for a walk through the historic centre, where many of them hadn't been before—not because it is forbidden to them, but for other reasons arising from their situation: they don't want to run any more risks now that they have crossed the Mediterranean and found shelter (temporarily) in Italy.[3]

Warner brings her organizing work to a reflection on the process of mapping and its consequences of twenty-first-century lives: "The idea

DANCE AS A HOME   131

was to gather sights and sounds towards making story maps and thereby forge a sense of ownership for young people who mostly arrived alone and left behind everything they know."[4] However, maps carry with them manifold possibilities, and in order to generate activism from them specific actions should be allowed to unravel: "[I]t is amazing what a difference it makes to carry a drawing pad and start looking carefully at everything around, noting things down. People were curious, in a friendly way, and admiring of the results."[5] For some people, re-drawing and drawing maps can be an act of tremendous empowerment, as it allows them to relate differently to the physical spaces they inhabit. This act occurs in the context of an elaborate and complex rationale:

> Stories in Transit began in 2016, and the project proceeds on the principle that arrivants have a right to cultural expression (arrivant is the more open, factual, and welcoming term Kamau Brathwaite adopted in his epic, *The Arrivants: A New World Trilogy*—it embraces immigrant, émigré, migrant, refugee, asylum seeker etc.). Such new arrivals are often severed from families and friends and from their geography of home, and one of their needs that must command attention is the need for culture. It will develop spontaneously, of course; music, confabulation, art, and so on cannot be altogether stifled. Yet creating conditions for expressions and exchanges to happen remains vital, even when other resources are extremely stretched. Stories in Transit encourages displaced individuals to tell stories, drawing on their own traditions and their faculty of imagination. We then workshop the material together, in combinations of media—puppetry, animation, performance—with movement and music, without relying too deeply on language (we can't yet all communicate with one another, since their Italian is in its early stages, and they come from all over Africa and the Middle East).[6]

Performance and non-lingual conversations are key to Stories in Transit, as a project that aims to transcend borders and to challenge divisions.

> We listen helplessly, trying to feel—to *empathize*—and sometimes feeling that the emotions that the stories stir are helping us to do something. However, in relation to the well-being of the individuals caught up in these massive upheavals and dislocations, these forms of narrative restrict the human spirit to a single genre of narrative and, I

believe, narrow the potential for flourishing through imaginative engagement with the world.[7]

There is a key process here, which is opening up a possibility of alternative narration and empowerment to the narrator. To many who cross borders, the process entails being engrossed in never-ending process of administrative storytelling: Where are you from? Why are you here? What is your financial situation? How long will you stay? "A refugee today must tell it again and again and never deviate from the circumstances as given from the first moment. The story can become a mark of identity that becomes a yoke, an insurmountable border in itself: you must not change your story."[8] Storytelling, chronicling as part of this praxis, is key to the process of migration yet is hardly empowering in these circumstances.

However, answering the questions at the border does not allow for a life story to unravel; thus, Stories in Transit aims to open up an alternative space, perhaps to act in dialectic to those endless procedures at the border. This is also an opportunity to create new solidarities where they otherwise would not exist:

> With regard to people on the move, their stories are key to their success as asylum seekers, but this can add to another loss: the loss of a shared culture, both from the past place of belonging and in the new places of arrival. The dominant form of storytelling that arrivants are encouraged to adopt is autobiographical, and their legal situation requires them to tell this story in a way that will meet the regulations for asylum; this *récit*, or account, resembles the pardon tales that past condemned criminals were permitted to write to the king in France to sue for grace.[9]

Moreover, listening to a new story is crucial for all sides implicated in transitioning or migrating, Warner explains: "For both the host communities where the displaced people arrive and for the arrivants themselves, a space for other ways of telling the story can inaugurate and stitch and invigorate relations between them. Secondly, the witness statement, the confession, the traumatic utterance of memory all depends on the subject's own lived experience, not on dreamed or imagined possibilities."[10] Warner reflects on the urgency of the project, which becomes exacerbated with the tightening of migration laws and policies,

DANCE AS A HOME   133

rise of xenophobia and retreat into the ideational and geographical constraints of the nation-state:

> As I write, the Minister of the Interior,[11] from the right-wing Lega party who are part of the new government in Italy, have closed the ports and a rescue boat with over 600 refugees on board is stranded in the Mediterranean. The atmosphere will have changed, and the mood will be more somber, to say the least. We shall be returning for a workshop from Sept 26–30, and we were expecting there to be a new group of arrivants entering the refugee schools. But if those who have fled their homes can't enter Italy, they will find somewhere, and political promises to deport them back are just so much wasted breath—like Trump's Mexican wall. The movement of peoples is a modern reality and realistic modes need to develop to allow its potential to flower (the past gives us many examples—the USA's own history, above all).[12]

The connections between Stories in Transit and the beginnings of modern dance, narrated in Chapter 2 of this book, can be drawn explicitly. Anna Sokolow's parents arrived in Ellis Island; Pearl Primus's family came from Trinidad to New York; Hussein Smko came to New York from Erbil. Modern dance would not be what it is today without these people. Warner gives her own narrative and understanding of home and homelessness, two concepts encircling the argument of this book and acting as core concepts in this chapter:

> In my own fiction and essays, I have written about flight, about the loss of home and the loss of bearings, and the recent intensity of the refugee situation made me feel quite helpless to do anything, as it does us all. I was looking at images of camps with their endless rows of tents or huts, and no focal points or gathering places, and wondering how these new cities—many of the inhabitants spend decades living there—could be given some qualities of home. In my 2015 Holberg lecture I explored the question of literature as an alternative shelter. Then I noticed, from a drawing published by Save the Children, that a refugee child named Farah had drawn a crowd around ... the lorry delivering water.[13]

Palestinian poet Mahmoud Darwish's poem, "We travel like other people . . ." includes the line, "We live in a country of words."[14] In her essay, Warner invokes Darwish, whose poem contemplating the concept and praxis of an exile was inspiring and galvanizing to many. Warner's work and reading of Darwish allows us to progress to one of the most critical thinkers and activists to bring displacement—his own as well as his people's—to the forefront of his work: Edward Said. For Darwish, Said, and Warner, culture—words, stories, literature—can become ersatz homes. Moving to Said allows us to move to the question: Can dance become a substitute home for those who are homeless?

Home, Exile, Words, Movement

For Palestinian intellectual Edward Said, exile was never a theoretical question. His loss of home was tangible and one of the main arcs of his biography as well as his work. Jeanne Morefield, in a much needed and overdue forthcoming intervention, brings Said's thinking back to political theory (in illuminating the centrality of exile as a central pillar of his work; perhaps unsurprising for a Palestinian who lost his childhood home in Jerusalem when Israel was declared a sovereign state). The shift to Edward Said is a quest for a resolution outside of our current time and nation-state system. Internationalism necessitates thinking not only beyond borders but about the borders themselves. Said's groundbreaking work on empire, which created a counter-canon to a world marred by division through maps and borders, allowed for a horizon transcending our present time, not only in legal amelioration within the nation-state system but by overhauling it, by listening to those affected the most by it, those exiled by its methodical, ontological, and theoretical boundaries.

In 2002 Said stated that:

> The greatest single fact of the past three decades has been, I believe, the vast human migration attendant upon war, colonialism, and decolonization, economic and political revolution, and such devastating occurrences as famine, ethnic cleansing, and great power machinations ... Exiles, émigrés, refugees, and expatriates uprooted from their lands must make do in new surroundings, and the creativity as well as the sadness that can be seen in what they do is one of the experiences that has still to find its chroniclers, even though a splendid cohort of writers that includes such different figures as Salman

DANCE AS A HOME **135**

Rushdie and V.S Naipaul has already opened further the door first tried by Conrad.[15]

The question of exile—as a concept, an organizing pillar, a phenomenon—is never theoretical for Said, as well as the question of how it is chronicled and by whom: these are tangible and life changing questions. It is inextricable from his praxis. "The pathos of exile is the loss of contact with the solidity and all the satisfaction of earth: homecoming is out of the question."[16] Exiles are expelled from their existential home to which they can never return; this is always already an embodied experience, engrained in pathos. There is a conceptual difference between refugees and exiles, as Said elucidates: "Refugees, on the other hand, are a creation of the twentieth century state. The word refugee has become a political one, suggesting large herds of innocent and bewildered people requiring urgent international assistance, whereas 'exile' carries with it, I think, a touch of solitude and spirituality."[17] But when considering both categories, and especially in light of the pathos of refugees in the twenty-first century, there is much that can be derived from Said's work on exile to understand the refugee experience. Moreover, as this chapter will proceed to show, Said's understanding of the position of the non-exile toward the exile will be used here to forward the understanding of the non-refugee toward the refugee, and an underlying argument about solidarity and the ability to raise one's voice for justice regardless of who you are. Radakrishnan offers further explanation: "Said is asking, in other words, for a 'contrapuntal' reading of literature and cultural texts, i.e., a reading that will acknowledge the complicity of culture in matters of empire and political power without at the same time reducing the aesthetic to the political."[18] The ability to see the world from another's point of view and, moreover, to see how empire as a historical and political fact had given many the illusion that their world and way of was the only possible one, allows us all to understand exiles—as a political and existential category. This is a key point on the way to forming solidarity, allowing more people to tell their own stories and sharing them collectively.

Said writes: "Exiles look at non-exiles with resentment. *They* belong in their surroundings, you feel, whereas an exile is always out of place. What is it like to be born in a place, to stay and live there, to know that you are of it, more or less, forever?"[19] And here lies the crux of Said's work, which transcends the distinction between theory and action, much like the

136 DANCE AND ACTIVISM

work of many dancer-activists whose work is discussed in this book. Said elucidates relationality between those who are exiled and those who are not. The twenty-first century divides humanity between those who feel existential threat to their being by the forever loss of home and those who are shielded from this anxiety.

It is harrowing that since Said left the earth, as well as Arendt, so many more people have been exiled from their homes. Said is helpful for this thinking as he provides an overarching and revolutionary critique of the world that allows for exile, not only reforms that would allow some wrongs to persist. "Necessarily, then, I speak of exile not as a privilege but as an alternative to the mass institutions that dominate modern life."[20] The institutional failure yields a shift in consciousness that is experienced in the individual. It is important to pause and clarify here that the focus on exile is not on the romantic notion of exile, but on the tangible, raw, lived experience of many millions of people. Much as in the spirit of this book, far away from "great man" or even "great woman" narratives of history, the focus is on those collectives whose daily lived strife pushes them to work toward a better world, creating shared visions and through that emerging new solidarities. There is something crucial and fundamental we can learn from exiles. "Exiles cross borders, break barriers of thoughts and experience."[21] In their very being exiles traverse known categories of home/away, nation-state/borders, thus they force all those who listen to their stories to reconsider their own categories.

Said notes that most people are principally aware of one culture, one setting, one home; exiles are aware of at least two, and this plurality of vision gives rise to an awareness of simultaneous dimensions, an awareness that—to borrow a phrase from music—is contrapuntal.[22] Thinking with Said of the idea of exile as counterpoint, makes the exilic experience heterocultural and heteronormative. "Without choosing the exiles understand that another world is possible— because they are living more than one world daily. This however bears a high price. It is not a pleasurable heteronomy, indulgence in multitude."[23] Asking one to take on exilic thinking proposes thinking with those dispossessed of their physical as well as their emotional homes, who are forced to live with multitudes, often in tensions with conflicted narratives. "Perhaps this is another way of saying that a life of exile moves according to a different calendar and is less seasonal and settled than life at home. Exile is life lived outside habitual order. It is nomadic, decentered, contrapuntal: but no sooner does one get accustomed to it than its unsettling force erupts anew."[24] In his own words, Said elucidates exilic relationality as an imaginative, emotive connection: "The third point I want to make is that I never said anything about the rootless and exilic marginality as excluding the possibility of, shall we say, sympathetic—I'm using a simple word—sympathetic—identification with a people suffering oppression. Especially when the oppression is caused by one's own community or one's own polity."[25] Building solidarity out of emotive relationship has to be an intentional, examined process, especially in the context of structural silencing as in the case of the Palestinian struggle that was the backdrop to Said's life and thought.[26] Addressing the question of whether those on the "inside," those comfortably within a home, can adopt the identity of those on the outside, an exiled Palestinian, Said remarks clearly: "The major task—I say this actually without a qualification whatever—the major task of the American or the Palestinian or Israeli intellectual of the left is to reveal the disparity between the so-called 'sides,' which appear rhetorically and ideologically to be in perfect balance but are not in fact."[27] The insider is always able to adopt the position of the outsider but this is not true in the counter juxtaposition. The concept of exile becomes a complex and generative concept in Said's framework:

> Exile is both a choice and a dictate. Leaving one's own country to live abroad may be either voluntary or imposed by circumstances. Either way, the sense of being exiled results in an acute awareness of territorial relationality, of a sense of being inside and outside, of inclusion and exclusion. It is not necessarily a case of distinguishing one from the other, but of learning to live with each within the other.[28]

"The exile can never feel 'at home,'" Said argues, because they cannot sever their ties to a "home" to which they can or may never return.[29] Said argues further:

> The exile sees things both in terms of what has been left behind and what is actually here and now, there is a double perspective that never sees things in isolation. Every scene or situation in the new country necessarily draws on its counterpart in the old country. Intellectually this means that an idea or experience is always counter posed with another, therefore making them both appear in a sometimes new and unpredictable light."[30]

The life of the exile means that there is always more than one point of view that one is forced to take. This is a vast step away from alienation as it has been discussed in this book; it forces us to think of more than one story, to listen to more points of view and understand the relative position of our own in larger configurations.

This experience may generate a methodological insight, as in Jeanne Morefield's study of Said as a thinker-activist outside the hegemony, or supremacy, of white middle-class intellectuals, in the political thought of our times:

> By contrast, Said took inspiration from the experience of exile, arguing in a 1992 interview that, as an exile, "you always bear within yourself a recollection of what you've left behind and what you can remember, and you play it against the current experience." From this perspective, he continued, "the notion of a *single* identity" becomes especially fraught because it mutes the tensions and contradictions of the exilic experience, demanding "simple reconciliation" between competing visions of home and identity that, from the perspective of exile, can never be made to cohere. Said's own exilic and generous understanding of identity rejected simple reconciliation and embraced the "many voices playing off against each other," insisting on the need "just to hold them together"[31]

Morefield argues that Said's own experience of exile and its place in his thinking is part and parcel of his critique of Eurocentric thinking, put forth in his most famous work, *Orientalism*. His positioning of multitude of voices and experiences becomes an alternative arc to that of a single linear narrative or Eurocentrism. The chapter that chronicles the experience of a multitude of voices trying to arrive in Europe and yet never molded to be part of its chorus, pushes those from within Europe— the continent and the idea—to listen to this heteronomy.

Accompanying the notion of the enabling intellectual consequences of an exilic position, Said therefore also suggested the idea of the traveler as desirable for critical thinkers. Thus, engaging in what may be termed "exilic thinking" pushes us to examine the singularity of narratives within which we are entrenched and the idea of an inevitability of a singular narrative that triumphs. Non-exiles, engaging in "exilic thinking," may, too, be able to witness the world from another's point of view, even if their own experience will never be identical to that of an exile. The quest for

DANCE AS A HOME   **139**

suspension of custom and away from understanding the world as inevitable pushes the non-exile engaging in exilic thinking into a critical new mode of being. This chapter now moves to examine three dance works that focused on the experience of migration while engaging in a method of exilic thinking. What can dance do to bridge the gap between the native and the refugee, the exile and those who have never experienced exile?

Edward Said was inspired by Glen Gould and Bach when thinking of counterpoint, the ability to hold tension, to reflect on more than one identity. This is not appropriation of another's body, or appropriating their story, but a plea from an exile to think from more than one narrative. Taking this method of critical thinking on board the argument can shift to the core of this book and look at how three different works sought to provide contrapuntal or exilic thinking through dance. How does telling the stories of exiles enable us to have an enlarged mentality, to hold more than one story, and allow others to counter their alienation? And moreover, how does this form of thinking shift us to think beyond the current political system—reflecting maps and nation-states divided by random lines and making people exiles by so doing—and progress to work toward a world without borders?

Arriving

Simon Birch's "Shoreline" is extraordinary in form and content. Premiered in 2016 and performed on a beach in Cornwall with a live choir, the work presents the duality of the shore, which is also a border. The landscape provides multiple viewpoints, never presenting a singular narrative; the work addresses key themes of both migration and boundaries explicitly. In a section called "Islands" the lyrics enunciate:

Most refugees come in rickety boats
Risking their lives to flee war and terror
They were received scared soaked helped by teachers,
Pensioners and students.

On the Greek islands in the Aegean
Grandmothers have sung terrified babies
To sleep, teachers, pensioners and students are
Trying to give comfort.

I will never forget seeing young girls
Being rescued, they were smiling they had
No possessions only their school certificates
Drying in the sun.

At least forty people drowned last Friday
In Greek waters most were women and children they were
Fleeing war and terror back at home.
There is a crisis.

Other references to the crisis and to people arriving by sea are spelled out
in the work, but beyond those direct verbal references, there is a forceful,
poignant message in the idea of creating a dance work focusing on
connectivity and responsibility to each other's bodies on the shore. What
does the shore symbolize? In Britain, as well as in the Greek islands
discussed above, the shore is also the first physical border separating the
small island from its oceanic surroundings. Arriving on a beach means
arriving in a new land. One of the singers, Dinah Master, said of the process:
"I felt an unbearable sense of desperation—on the one hand, of history
repeating itself over and over again, but on the other, a sense of collective
hope, by us all touching and supporting one another and in some way
making a stand to say 'never again.'"[32] This tension sits at the heart of the
work as well as the experience of the shore in our times. The movement in
this work is collective, often joyful, always interconnected, exploring
intimacy and group dynamics as part of the experience of the shore. This
creates a tension sitting at the heart of the work between human beings–
shore–sea. And yet their dialectic tensions generate a different kind of
togetherness, a collective feeling, that raises questions of responsibility.

The performers carry suitcases, alluding to a beginning of a new
narrative, the experience of arriving in a new place, not just a casual
visitor to the beach. Many people can arrive at the beach, but those who
carry possibilities for new beginnings also carry the urgency to catalyze
those beginnings. The movement in the piece is lush and generous,
connectivity creating an intensely moving choreographic experience.
Poet John Donne wrote in the sixteenth century, "no man is an island,
entire of itself,"[33] and shoreline seems to be a moving contemplation
about this statement. Dancers, singers, and audiences intertwined, each
approaching sand and water from a different position, but all united in
the sharing of an emerging solidarity.

DANCE AS A HOME   **141**

The dramaturgical decision to perform this work on the beach with live music, creating an overwhelming emotive and sensory experience, pushes this message forward. The work is ostensibly not only specifically about the refugee crisis; it is also about togetherness, collectivity, what it means to be human: experienced as a visceral, sensual overwhelming performance. The shore is a concept and a metaphor that resonate in many tales, beyond those who arrive at it seeking refuge from exile. By presenting that which is common, standing all together on a beach, water brushing against the soundtrack, movement moving between the dancers and the audience (who unlike in other performances are not still), the work throws at the spectator the question of what unites human beings; what unites those singing and dancing at the beach with those who watch them, and with those who may be arriving at other beaches asking for help. Questions of responsibility are key when contemplating migration and, as this work shows, need not be articulated in a disengaged, intellectualized manner. Being overwhelmed by beauty shared with other human beings invokes the question of what is owed to those with whom the experience is shared, and in turn what is owed to those who are absent from such an experience, whose stories are not told in the formation of our current solidarities.

The shore is the first place in which stories about migration enter into our psyches. It is the first physical articulation of a beginning. A shared physical space that is not a home for unified experience but allows for the sharing of different points of view; those just arrived and those already there; those carrying suitcases and those without; the exiled and those with homes.[34]

Storytelling

"Impronte" is a four-part multidisciplinary dance work by Spanish journalist and choreographer Isabel Cuesta Camacho. Based on her research on migration and the refugee crisis, each part adds a layer to the narrative as it unfolds, giving different dimensions of the migrants' perspectives. The work starts with the first segment, "Confine" (Border). Starting with a performer walking against a backdrop of speeches on migration, there is no doubt: there are borders within the body; the body is a border. More people entering the stage push the complexity of the movement to develop. The border is not only between migrant and nation-state but between moving bodies, wherever they are. The space, divided by moving bodies, is establishing its own imaginary borders, echoed by the words iterated as part of the soundtrack. The movement shifts from every day, casual movement to more elaborate gestures. The movement is angry, robust; there is little kept withdrawn within the dancers' bodies. Slowly into the soundtrack, the narrative of refugees' journeys is interleaved, and the audience is struck by a mix of narration and movement. The dancers are interconnected, and start holding hands. Yet they do not occupy the same place in space, nor within the narrative. Touch shifts between aggression and support, the boundaries permeating emotion. This piece goes toward its culmination with an invocation of President Trump's famous statement: "who's going to pay for the wall?" referring to his infamous attempts to build a wall between the USA and Mexico to prevent migration. The dancers keep shifting hands and moving on stage, while the question "who's going to pay for the wall?" echoes repeatedly. The work develops and works throughout via tension: between the dancers and materials around them (including a plastic bottle passed violently between the dancers), tensions between the dancers and each other, between theatrical movement and everyday movement, and, lastly, tensions between theater and dance. This section ends with a monologue on home and migration, and an intimate duet between two dancers.

The middle two sections recount in word and theatrical movement the dialectic position of refugees. The second section, "Identity," retells the real story of a Syrian refugee and actor who refused to collaborate with Assad's regime: a monologue about someone who reinvented himself in order to survive and doesn't know anymore who he is. The third section, "Inorcio" (Crossroads) retells the story of coping with the massive internal south-to-north migration during Italy's economic miracle: entire neighborhoods were built in the 1950s and 1960s. Today mainly external migrants live in those areas, and discrimination now has another face. A dance and video performance with the voices from the habitants of Pilastro, Bologna. And yet it is the fourth section that is perhaps the most surprising and that acts in the strongest dialectic tension to the first section, and the analysis henceforth moves to that.

The fourth section of "Impronte" is entitled "Incertezza" (Love in Times of Uncertainty). "There is this house that is your body, and if I enter, I will get lost in all minuscule places that hide your tears." A dance about three moments in a love relationship; about the fear of falling in

DANCE AS A HOME 143

love, about love in a society hit by fear. Continuing the question of home/love/where one resides in times of great uncertainty, this part of the work is intimate and forceful. It may be asked why a segment on love is part of a dance work that focuses on migration, and yet positioning this as the conclusion of the work gives a forceful response to the question "what do we owe to refugees?" The dialogue is around the themes of home and body. An imitate duet, delicate, passionate, sensual. This is dramatically different to the movement in other parts of the work, which is emotive but shows anger, resistance, a response to violence. Dramatic movement in this work, too, sustains the intensity of the entirety of "Impronte," but this is the drama of the everyday relationships. The dancers change positions, different perspectives in space. The dialectic between everyday movement and choreographed movement continues. Childhood games using a "catch" of the palms is completely different when performed in the context of intimacy/opening-up; belonging/not-belonging. The movement seems violent and affectionate at the same time. Bodies move toward and away from each other, always in tension, never, it seems, quite at home—on stage, with each other, in the world.

The monologue shifts to discussing a home, with a wooden floor, and a broken glass of water all in relation to a nameless body, while the dancers continue to come to and from each other in an intimate manner, caressing, pushing, desiring, refusing each other. The movement becomes more and more frantic, more and more tensions build between the dancers. The dancers frantically pass a bottle of water from one to another, drinking it, pouring it. The music fades, the dancers are left alone, with nothing but each other. Slowly they are left, motionless, on the floor.

Reflecting on this work, episodically the first and the last parts in tension to each other, brings to the forefront of the spectators' consciousness some core tensions lying at the heart of issues of migration and home. The border is enacted by human bodies, but so is love, that unruly emotion that is able to transcend and unsettle boundaries to which we all as human beings willingly succumb. Questions of borders are not only enacted by refugees coming on boats to seek shelter from wrongs in our lands; these are questions about how we relate to each other, generally, as human beings in the world, exemplified and pushed to the extreme by these conditions of homelessness and refuge-seeking.

Where are we at home?[35] Many of us, this work shows, are never really at home, depending on the mercy of our fellow woman and man to give us legal and political status allowing us to reside away from danger. And

144 DANCE AND ACTIVISM

yet homelessness can go beyond that condition. Returning to the question of alienation that started this discussion and, fittingly, also ends it, the exploration of love within questions of border shows bodies moving to and from each other, seeking refuge in each other and pushing each other simultaneously.

And yet, it would be disingenuous and ethically flawed to comment that "we are all refugees," because we clearly are not. There is a distinct amount of people seeking to flee danger and find a settled home, whose existence cannot be completely made tangible to those whose life is settled and fairly secure, even if facing other forms of alienation. Said's warnings against sympathy without political analysis resonate here: understanding structural power relations and how they shape our narratives is key. Yet the reading of the first part of "Impronte," dissecting the concept of the border as lived and enacted by many, and the last part, showing the most intimate lived experience of a border within love, allows for a glimpse of what may be termed "contrapuntal thinking." Through experiencing the work as a whole, stories of migrants and those who engage their narratives, the spectators and dancers are able to experience an issue from more than one point of view, expanding our collective imaginaries and creating new solidarities; not shedding their own identity but allowing another to enter their discourse. The positioning of a multitude of points of views and positions allows this contrapunt to unravel. Both works presented thus far problematize how we treat those who move lands and homelands. The third work, discussed next, allows us to push further, toward an alternative vision, not entirely founded in our present psyches. [36]

Unraveling

The next case study continues from where the two previous ones left off and yet provides a vital intervention. Sivan Rubinstein's "MAPS" is extraordinary in form and content yet its message is key to much of the writing and choreography discussed thus far. As the light comes on stage, three performers/laborers are already in action. What may seem at first sight to be spreading and organizing, a salt-like material in contingent patterns takes form as the action progresses, and those patterns become the stage's surface. The dancers put the material into place using their entire bodies, mold it, transfigure it into an entity that is now independent of the stage. Distinctly, it is the performers' work that has created the pattern, in front of the audience, where it did not exist beforehand. The performers' bodies, the surface on which they work, and the material that they use are intertwined and create a new entity in the world: the stage, which is becoming more clearly a very specific entity—a map. Even when the pattern, the map, emerges, the dialectic of the body and the material keeps shifting it; there is nothing fixed or stable about the map. Through feet, arms, chest, and performers' entire bodies the map is constantly reconfigured and reorganized. At the same time, the bodies of the performers, as they are perceived by the audience, are also transformed in the process of map-making through movement. There is intensity and focus in the map's creation. The dancers put thought and action into creating the pattern, and yet, it is evident that this pattern is contingent upon the situation in which the maps emerged. There is no obvious logic behind it, nor a rationale; yet the performers work intensely on allowing those patterns to emerge and then become a fact in their own right. The dancers then leave the stage and the pattern is left there, a physical entity created by labor but transcending it.

When the dancers return to the stage, they begin by examining the detail of the pattern that they had just created though intense labor. As if their bodies had not been immersed in the creative process just a few minutes ago, the performers now learn the entity that exists on stage, these curious maps that have emerged in front of the audience. Slowly, they start moving, and seemingly unintentionally re-draft the maps through their movement, and progressively the maps disappear from their neat formation. The movement in this part of the piece is less focused. The performers now revel in dismantling what they had carefully set. This re-drafting is incremental—first there are new patterns set within the "maps," and then, slowly, they begin to disappear from the audiences' eyes. The organization of space on stage that the audience had seen emerge now is undone, negotiated, slowly but with great passion. The soundtrack that up to this point consisted of a solo musician now moves to some spoken word, evoking names of places, shifting the audience between feelings of confusion and place. The movement escalates in volume and intensity. The careful laboring actions of the start of the piece are now joyous movement, encapsulating abandon. The performers test each other's boundaries; lean, push, shift each other, and in this process the maps become more and more dissolved. Dialectic of self and other, work and materials underpin both the start and progression of the piece,

146 DANCE AND ACTIVISM

showing contingent boundaries between these concepts. The performers now shift into purposeful walking, sliding, gliding across the stage, undoing the maps further inch by inch. The stage is now nothing but the material holding the performers' paths, as physical remains of the action witnessed thus far on stage. The maps are now a memory in the audiences' mind.

The performers' bodies, too, have pushes their boundaries in this process and the movement becomes more and more undone. There is *jouissance*, abandon in the approach to space and material. This is a sense of undoing, dismantling, and it is open-ended and free. The movement language throughout the piece is intense, though the focus of the piece shifts from dismantling to abandon to unraveling alongside the sound track of electronic rave-like music. The lights are now darker, a deep blue, and the music shifts into electronic rave-like music. There is a clear sense of letting-go, undoing, which the audience is immersed within. The feeling is of exploration of space, body, material; all acting in tension to each other. The light rises on the stage and the audience sees how bodies undo and redo patterns, unraveling paths in the salt on stage, while dismantling others. The music has now faded and the performers move in silence. The relationship between set–movement–music accentuates the contingency of these combinations. There is nothing necessary about each scene in this complex, hugely rich work; yet to the audience it seems complete within its own internal logic. A narrator now, in this part of the piece, discusses different kinds of maps, and proclaims: "this is a map of the world." The narrator discusses man and nature; never a simple, unidirectional process but always a dialectic. The narrator points out that the random lines made by men is the political map. The only sound audible for a few minutes is the sound of the salt swaying on stage. Soon, music returns, and the performers' movement shifts in register again; it is focused yet open; searching, perhaps, for a new connection to the new landscapes created by the act of undoing. The movement is a response to both the purposeful laboring as well as the cathartic reveling; abandon now inhabiting the body as a space, testing its boundaries in a space that no longer has boundaries. This is not a sense of resolution but of a new stage in the work, a stage we do not yet know, and yet we always inhabit a body poised to explore further facets of movement. Voice is added to music in a sense of wholeness and complete submission. A new pattern has emerged on stage, now; circles of feet that treaded it without any structure or pre-meditated form. That, too, feels like a map, but perhaps a map of another entity; a map of a body unconstrained, of human materiality when it lets go of its premeditated forms. All patterns are contingent, and all patterns are woman and man made. As the light comes down on stage there is a material history that the audience carries, of doing and undoing, of creating and annulling, but mostly of bodies, materials, and music that are never without relationship to each other and never act in a void.

The work "MAPS" encapsulates dialectic tensions; between the body and the world, the self and the material, doing and undoing, presence and absence, and being and not-being present. The work forcefully shows the contingency of creating maps that then attain a physical presence in the world, structuring behavior but can then be equally undone. In many of the protests discussed throughout the book, chants and placards such as "no walls, no borders" were essential to the dissent; however, this work goes beyond this negation of present constraints. "MAPS" opens up an imaginary that the audience may not yet possess, of a world beyond one demarcated by divisions between nation-states and borders. It is an unfolding of solidarity in becoming, beyond the world we know it today. The work shows how the presence is grounded in the audience's past imaginaries. Everything that we live between was once man-made; this in turn means it can be man-unmade.[37]

Homelessness–Devastation–Exile

Martha Graham choreographed her work "Chronicle" in 1936, and the middle section, "Steps in the Street," is divided into three sections: "homelessness," "devastation," and "exile." She looked at the embodied experience of exile through the prism of her times, as this was key to many of her dancers. Edward Said fought lifelong struggles against imperial gestures and fascism, which continue to resonate and inspire today. The centrality of the urgency to consider exile through dance prevails through changes in political-historical landscapes. The idea of exilic thinking—adopting especially those points of view most excluded by a world governed by nation-states, remainders of the old imperialistic order, is an opportunity to dismantle the nation-state-organized world. This opportunity offers a possibility to create solidarities, beyond amending our current wrongs, toward another world in which no exiles exist, without maps, without borders. Countering alienation as experienced

148   DANCE AND ACTIVISM

in this century requires opening new imaginaries and horizons, dismantling old orders, first and foremost, in our minds, and allowing ourselves to be open to others' point of view. Another world is possible, and another world is lived in manifold different experiences that are often not part of our psyche. Allowing ourselves to be attentive to those experiences allows for unraveling this world and its possibilities.

7 SPECTRE, HAUNTING

History repeats itself, first as tragedy, second as farce,[1] third as woman raising a rallying cry against injustice. Martha Graham's "Chronicle," created against the rise of fascism in Nazi Germany in 1936, has been performed countless times, changing manifold bodies, and creating different narratives of radical politics. A solitary woman wrapped in the wrath of a red cloth in "Spectre—1914" has given space to many women dancing steps in the street, marching in dissent against alienation from New York in the 1930s till now, and a call for action, leader and group together, in "Prelude to Action," galvanized many women who have chronicled their own radical path. "Chronicle," which generated praxis protesting the spectres of wars haunting America in 1936—injustice taking over the world and violence becoming normalized—receives fresh meanings with every generation taking the work on, especially in our galvanizing and unsettled times. The work has been performed often by the Martha Graham dance company, which has been presenting two seasons of work commissioned from female choreographers only, under the title of "The Eve Project" to commemorate a century since women in America received the right to vote (the 19th amendment). Thus, the all-female cast of "Chronicle" has chimed well into the current work of the company. Artistic director of the Graham Company, Janet Eilber, reflects on the performance of the work today:

> I have witnessed many memorable performances of Chronicle! The stage of the Herod Atticus in Athens comes to mind as do several other international venues—Prague, Beijing, Vienna, for example. Although Chronicle offers a universal statement—there is something very American about it—a plain-spokenness—an outspokenness— that stands out more to me when we are overseas and in cultures where one is aware of more restrictions on personal expression.

Because it is an abstract work, this is not because we are representing a specific provocative point of view that might be considered rude to our host country. The total physical commitment of the women is a message that is received kinesthetically as much as—if not more than—intellectually. When we do perform it in the States, it resonates and speaks to the concerns of the moment—from the aftermath of Hurricane Katrina to the #Metoo movement to the current tensions in our election process. Each new cast that becomes Chronicle, brings their own era and experiences to the work. Even casts that are only a few years apart embody the steps in different ways. For our current cast, the rangy discourse on gender, #blacklivesmatter and #Metoo that are so much a part of their lives imbue the piece with a specific energy. The choreography remains the same, but somehow the dancers' own awareness and connection to this moment in time informs how the work is performed and how it is received.[2]

The work is performed differently as different bodies bring their own meaning, their own struggles, and their own solidarities into the work.

Martha Graham in "Spectre—1914" from "Chronicle." Photographer unknown. Courtesy of Martha Graham Resources.

Each dancer tells her own story. One of the truly unique characteristics of the Graham Company, especially when working on the female-only work, is a feminist solidarity across the years that transfers information from one generation to another. "Chronicle" is an exemplar of this intergenerational solidarity through radical dance. A spectre of violence is haunting the world, but so is a spectre of solidarity. This spectre spreads across the globe and goes far and wide, as can be seen in some reflections of Graham alumna and historian Yuting Zhao, currently pursuing a dance degree at Case Western University:

> I first saw Chronicle in Beijing, 2015. I remember I got the ticket last minute and was sitting on the second floor and somewhat one of the last rows. Back then, I knew Martha from books and lectures, but didn't really have an idea of what her work is like in theatre. I'm very glad that my first encounter was via live performance by Graham Company.[3]

Zhao is both a dance practitioner and a dance history specialist:

> As a master student in history, my area was American history in the first half of 20th century, and that is exactly when Chronicle came into being. After all those years of digging into archives, I felt that through Chronicle, I was able to, for the very first time in my life, breath through the era. I could sense the spirit, the human, even the temperature of America in 1930s. I was shocked as well as thrilled. Eventually, that performance brought me to the United States, to Graham School, and to a new life with modern dance.[4]

Zhao feels attracted especially to "Prelude to Action": "My favorite part is Prelude. I love how The *New York Times* called the dance 'a 1936 all-female, who-needs-men Graham juggernaut.'[5] I watch it whenever I deeply doubt myself, or question if the sun will rise tomorrow or whether humanity is still a thing on earth."

And yet all parts resonate for her in different ways, and yet her embodied experience of steps in the street allowed her to understand the fundamentals of the Graham technique:

> I performed Steps in the Street my first semester at Graham School. When we started to learn the choreography, contraction was still an alien concept for me. However, tensing my abs while twisting my body

SPECTRE, HAUNTING **153**

to the extreme trying to learn the entrance walk, the idea of "emotion generated by movement" struck me and a new world just opened up to me. I was amazed of how a simple movement could instantly channel me back into history and fill my cells with sorrow and grief.[6]

"Chronicle" has opened up ways for Zhao's own expressiveness to come into the world: "I'm now working on a group piece inspired by Chronicle for my thesis concert, partly because I don't have the budget to stage the piece, so I was like, how about make your own version. It deals with how the weight of memory drags and disturbs people, while at the same time inspires the rebirth."[7] Many generations of dancers have performed "Chronicle" since its return to the Graham Company. We are coming full circle with the discussion that has spurred the argument of this book. The solidarity that Graham extended toward her cast members in 1936 is expanding and extending nearly a century later. Much revered Graham Company principal dancer Blakeley White-McGuire's life in the company unfolded in parallel to the return of "Chronicle":

> My very first encounter with Sketches from Chronicle was as a student at the Martha Graham Center of Contemporary Dance in the old brownstone on 63rd street. It must have been around 1994 for the Radical Graham performances at BAM. That festival allowed me to see many of Graham's greatest (and modern dance's greatest) works onstage by dancers at the height of their powers and knowledge. I was very fortunate.[8]

Memories of learning a dance are visceral and reflect the time and the place in which the learning unfolds:

> The company rehearsed in Studio 1 with its beautiful wooden floors and doors that opened out into a small garden. It was a dream space. From the inside entrance to the studio, there were double doors that, when closed, still allowed for a sliver of space where students could peek inside to secretly watch the company dancers working. One day I peeked in and saw Terese Capucilli working with Rehearsal Director, Carol Freid on Spectre—1914. I had not yet seen Sketches from Chronicle in performance and was still becoming educated as a student of Graham's technique, philosophy and repertory. But peeking into that studio, I experienced the devotion, passion and precision of Terese and Carol was palpable and intoxicating. Terese looked to me

like a wild creature with her hair down turning in her oversized red shroud. That was my first experience of Chronicle. From that point on, I was able to see the company perform all three reconstructed sections in live performance. It was always a heart-stopper.[9]

Terese Capucilli, whose work in the Graham company enabled "Chronicle" to return to the repertoire, is also an inspiration as a body influencing another body, in solidarity with women working for the love of dance and justice in the world. The stages of White-McGuire's education within the work resonate with the work itself:

> The very first dance I performed as a member of the Martha Graham Dance Company was Steps In The Street which is a common point of entry for new dancers. I was invited into the company by Terese Capucilli and Christine Dakin who were the Co-Artistic Directors at that time in 2002 for the Indisputably Graham performance at City Center. I was cast as a "Pop", the diagonal quartet of women who take the parallel side extension and then drop into fourth position. I loved being a pop, it was intense and difficult—I felt vital and powerful in it.[10]

This memory is never detached from its political and social surroundings, just like Graham's original creation. The social and political landscapes of the Lower East Side in the 1930s may be gone, but New York City's social history provides more layers to the power of this work:

> This was a period not long after the attacks of September 11th, 2001. I had witnessed with my own eyes (along with millions who saw it on television) the World Trade Center collapse to the ground with the understanding that in that moment, thousands of my fellow New Yorkers had been killed just down the street from where I stood. It is still difficult for me to understand the personal impact of my witnessing but I know that that event and the environment of war-mongering, blame, bloodthirsty revenge and feelings of helplessness which followed—led me back to the Martha Graham Center and into my work in her repertory. It was fitting and right that Steps In The Street was my first piece of rep. I had seen people walk uptown like zombies covered in white dust. Homelessness–devastation–exile.[11]

New conditions of alienation unfold; these in turn create new solidarities.

SPECTRE, HAUNTING   **155**

"Chronicle" is a work about witnessing but it is also a work about galvanizing action, as White-McGuire powerfully elucidates:

> My favorite part of the work is towards the end of Prelude To Action when the Leader mounts the drum and the dancers create a circle of airborne turns and sweeping kicks with lifted chests. The music is swelling and the Leader is conjuring a new vision, leading the others into a unified, powerful and resolute conclusion where the dancers show their palms to the audience in a gesture that forces others to bear witness—one cannot look away.[12]

And yet it is the human moments of togetherness off and on stage that allow the work to sustain its power through the ages.

> The most beloved moments of performing Chronicle whether as Chorus or Lead, are those which connected me to my fellow dancers. Working with my dear, dear friend Carrie Ellmore-Tallitsch for years as we were coming into our own as women in the world gave me courage and support to reveal my strength. Witnessing her do the same. Seeing the generations of women step into the dance and discover a different kind of power from sexual power. It would be my wish that every young dancer could perform this masterpiece as a means to understanding the inherent power that waits within them.[13]

And the spirit of inter-generational knowledge transferred as solidarity in radical dance sustains.

The performance of "Chronicle" in 2019 is winning new audiences and opening new vistas into Graham's work—in its context, then, but also here and now. The reviews of the Fall for Dance Festival in 2019, a festival in which the best and greatest of New York City present new and continuing work in short samples, together, commented on "Chronicle":

> The finest event of the season was by the greatest choreographer represented: *Chronicle,* by Martha Graham. Made in 1936 during her political period, it was originally very long. Some years ago, the current Graham company began reconstructing three sections of it, and they were what was on display at the City Center. The resounding music is by Wallingford Riegger, the stark scenery is by Isamu Noguchi, the costumes

156 DANCE AND ACTIVISM

are by Graham herself, one of the most remarkable of her many interactions with fabric. What about that breathtaking dress she wore in the first section—long and full and black, until suddenly it's flaming red.

The review continues to chronicle the next generation taking on the swathe of powerful resistance:

> An amazing dancer, Leslie Andrea Williams, performed the Graham roles in what was not only the finest event of the season but the final one. Williams—tall, mesmerizing—left us gasping at her heroic performance. But everything was heroic: this was dancing on the largest scale, the entire Graham company rising to the occasion, everyone utterly devoted and impassioned, the way it must have been with the dedicated acolytes of the early Graham companies. The Fall for Dance audience, which automatically applauds everything, responded heroically, too; standing, cheering, and I suspect weeping. They didn't want to leave the theater, and neither did I.[14]

The same visceral response to the premiere of the work, noting that the action continues after the curtain falls (and discussed in the second chapter of this book), prevails and sustains throughout the generations that transmitted it and contains the radical power of the work. "Chronicle" is a work that embodies the sequel—Eleanor Marx's perception of history—in its performance, unfolding into the future, calling for action after the dance ends.

Leslie Andrea Williams performed the principal role in "Chronicle" in the 2019 Fall for Dance performance discussed above. She also created history by being the first black woman to perform the principal role in this work. She reflects on her process:

> I first saw Chronicle while I was [a] student at The Juilliard School. For my dance history class, we were assigned to write a review on a piece from the 2014 Fall for Dance show at New York City Center. The Martha Graham Dance Company was performing Chronicle with Blakeley White-McGuire as the lead and Peiju Chien-Pott as the Steps in the Street lead. I was so blown away by the performance, that I chose to write my review on this piece. What really stood out to me was seeing all of these women on stage dancing in a powerful way that I was not used to seeing in my past.[15]

Leslie Andrea Williams in "Spectre—1914" from "Chronicle," performed in 2019. Photograph by Melissa Sherwood. Courtesy of Martha Graham Resources.

At the same time, Terese Capucilli, Williams's teacher at Juilliard, again resonated in the influences in the piece:

> I want to thank Graham legend Terese Capucilli for her reconstruction of the *Spectre—1914* solo. I was extremely lucky to have her as my Graham teacher at Juilliard and to witness her passion and dedication to Martha's work when she restaged *Dark Meadow* during my senior year. Without her, I would not be in the Graham company performing this iconic role. She is the reason I have any sensibility toward the drama and emotion involved in understanding the inner-psyche of Martha's work. And for me, after receiving her approval once she saw me perform the lead, I feel like any other person's approval is secondary. She said that she worked to rebuild *Spectre* using only photographs, a short clip of Martha dancing the solo, and minimal notes on the score. She had to use her instincts to create each section while also staying true to the integrity of Martha's quality and development of her movement in that specific time period. I watched many videos of other dancers performing the solo and through the years it has changed very minimally because the movement is so poignant,

detailed, and speaks to the "premonition of war" so perfectly. I learned from Terese at Juilliard how to study a role and learn from video. How funny is it that after joining the Graham company and being cast in this role, I watched Terese's *Spectre* videos an *infinite* number of times to understand the drama and feeling? I didn't want to copy her, because that's impossible, but instead I used what I saw to try to make the solo work for me, and I'm so happy that she was so pleased with my work.[16]

"Chronicle" lives thanks to the tireless work of women transferring knowledge, power, and solidarity to each other. A work of dance has no ontological weight in the world without bodies. But the Graham legacy, especially, with its placing of the female body center stage, brings its unique lineage of knowledge of power into this unique story of solidarity through movement. Williams reflects on her own process in "Chronicle":

When I first joined the company as an apprentice, my first Graham role I ever learned was the leader of *Steps in the Street*. I felt my talent and strength as a dancer allowed for me to tap into the essence of this role very easily—even as an apprentice. I was studying World War II and the Holocaust because no one ever told me, but I just assumed that the imagery of the piece and the "devastation of war" my directors kept talking about were in reference to that time. But, *Chronicle* focuses mainly on the universal idea of war, which is much more abstract. And in many ways, we as humans are all fighting our own personal wars every day, which I believe is a reason why the piece is so popular with audiences everywhere. I feel that same female strength that I felt when I first saw the piece in 2014. And now that I have danced this piece in the Chorus, as the soloist, and as the Principal, I feel the collective energy of the female presence more than ever. As women, it is so important to come together and stand up for our right to be seen as equals, because we are at times still seen as second-class citizens. We are so powerful. We feel all the emotions of devastation, repression, grief, and trauma, and are able to transform the emotions into love, understanding, and strength. In society, politics, and in the working industries of the world, there still is much room for improvement to allow women to assert their special power.[17]

The dynamics between different parts of the work change as history progresses and as dynamics in the work gain new meanings:

Right now, I really enjoy performing the *Prelude to Action* section. I feel so much energy from the movement, the music, and the other dancers. As the lead, I get to explore what it means to truly be "the light." I am wearing a bright white dress while the chorus dancers are in all black. I stand out by default. But, I am learning how important it is to take myself out of my pride and ego while dancing on stage and think about the greater purpose of the work that is beyond just me alone. I truly enjoy dancing with my fellow female colleagues on stage and "fighting the good fight." I feel a responsibility to convey to the audience what this pure connection I have with the dancers is, because I feel it is relevant to the meaning of the piece. I am a guiding force; therefore, I must remain present and aware of who I am guiding. The choreography for each dancer is extremely challenging. We really do pump each other up while onstage because we are all physically pushed to our limits. If only you could see the dancers in the wings! They are jumping up and down telling me "You can do it!" Now that I stay on stage for the entire section, I try to send that "you can do it" message back to the dancers energetically by using my focus and intention. We are collectively sending power. Sometimes we are communicating so much without words on and off stage. *Prelude to Action* is my favorite part of the work because it is about fighting back and working to achieve something that is greater than yourself. I feel that so strongly when I dance with my colleagues. It's that collective energy that makes this piece resonate. These feelings on stage I will cherish for the rest of my life.[18]

Williams is well aware of the particular weight the work has for her and her audiences.

I am honored to be the first black woman to have ever performed the lead role in *Chronicle*. For the *Spectre* solo, the lead woman wears her hair down and throws it around while she throws her long skirt . . . very dramatic. My hair is naturally a medium length 'fro with tight curls. I am aware that as a black woman, I can wear my hair however I choose. So initially I after thought of getting extensions would be the best option to fit the aesthetic visuals of the solo. But since I was to perform the lead at City Center for Fall for Dance, I decided to not wear hair extensions like I usually do for *Spectre* and just wear my hair in a natural 'fro. The curtain goes up, I'm sitting on the set, it's totally

160 DANCE AND ACTIVISM

quiet ... and all of the sudden I hear someone in the audience go "YESSS!!" I could tell that they were a person of color and already approved of what they were seeing before the piece had even started. It was a really special moment because I really felt like I was doing something special for black dancers out there that never get to embrace their natural hair as classical concert dancers—especially when they are dancing in roles that have been historically danced by white women with long hair. But, I knew that if I was going to perform this role for the New York audience (and a very big audience at that), I wanted to use the opportunity to make something of it. I heard from a friend in the audience that after the show, he had to sit with a black woman who was next to him and comfort her because she was sobbing. He said that she was so overwhelmed by my performance and felt extremely emotional. Hearing things like that made my decision feel that much more important. It's not about me, it's about US! As a black person, I feel that this piece is my own personal way of saying, "Hey world! I am enough!" Through my dancing, I hope to inspire other people of color to take action and make changes in their own lives to be seen and express their power in a predominantly white world. I am honored to be a part of the legacy of women that have performed this role before me and am eternally grateful for the opportunity to learn from the absolute best.[19]

Each dancer tells her own story and so the history of the work changes in performance. In the spirit of continuation, one audience member who came to see Williams dancing the principal as part of Fall for Dance is Graham alumna Megan Curet, who is currently working as an independent choreographer in New York. The themes of "Chronicle"— the dialectic between the individual and the group in dissent, the courage to speak up, and resistance to evil are threads that are crucial for her understanding of the work as well as life:

I first encountered Chronicle during my time at the Martha Graham school when I was training in the professional program. I believe it was 2012 to be exact. I learned Steps in the Streets and remember feeling even then, that I was receiving some piece of dance history in my body. Chronicle then became one of my favorite Graham ballets and stayed with me. 2012 was also the year I founded my dance company while I was a student at the Graham school. I remember feeling the urge to say something dynamic in my work even if I had no idea what it would be.[20]

When thinking of the structure of the work, Curet continues:

Steps in the Street was particularly memorable because it was relevant to any generation of Graham dancers. Women coming together, the marching, the gathering and the call to action. It came to inform my choreographic practice without a doubt. I especially will always remember the deep contractions and arms cupped and the archaic shape of our arms as we entered the space in silence. The entering walks alone could have been a fifteen-minute piece.[21]

The feeling of reverence to generations of past times were part of the learning process: "I mostly remember the nerves and feeling very anxious. It felt like I could do it no justice, some ballets just feel like huge shoes to fill."[22] And yet a sincere love for the work and understanding of its galvanizing force continues its march in the world: "Chronicle is a timeless piece. I saw Chronicle again in September 2019 at the New York City Center during Fall for Dance and I realized, we have yet to arrive at that place and so we must keep marching."[23]

And Curet's own steps keep marching in her own path. Curet brings her training—together with a specific interest in exploring the dynamics of her Puerto Rican heritage as a Bronx native—to her dance work, while never wavering from the political weight of dance. Curet's work "Isla," from 2019, switches gears in response to the one-year anniversary of Hurricane Maria on the Island of Puerto Rico. "Having returned to my family's home to witness the crumbling ceilings and the local shops that have since closed from the storm's damages left a very visceral and raw emotion, which I have tried to translate into the slow movement dynamics of Isla."[24]

A single moving entity enters the stage, wrapped in plastic. As a male dancer, Fernando Moya Delgado, leaves the plastic, angry, folding away his former cocoon. He proclaims: "one year, une anio." The rest of the group, all female, join him on stage. Walking slowly as he repeats "one year, une anio." The steps are slow, measured. Suddenly, the tone shifts; the dancer breaks into a solo: angry, precise, accurate. He exhales loudly, his breath heard over silence. The beginning of music, a Puerto Rican song, pushes the dancers to join in the movement. There is intensity and focus

162   DANCE AND ACTIVISM

in each step, each hand gesture. Curet's choreography shifts between registers of height, registers of movement. Stark movement blends into softer tones; openness of the body into sudden closure. This is not a mournful movement or music. The movement shows consideration of different perspectives of action. Individual and group, line and cluster, bodies are always in motion, reflexive of their own ontological weight as well as their relationship to other bodies. The soundtrack shifts toward narration of American complicity in denying aid to Puerto Rico. One dancer, Kristen Hedberg, moves frantically downstage. The question of complicity in wrongs and our responsibility to create solidarity has accompanied the works discussed in this book, and here, brought to the forefront of the choreography, pushes the audience to think of their own complicity. The soundtrack shifts again, to beat induced electronic music, pushing the movement to another register; repetition of movement seems desperate in this context, almost like an escape that is bound to fail. The steps are measured and contained. The dancers crash on the floor. Shifting between slow, constrained movement and quick yet noticeable frantic breakouts of gesture and despair, alienated bodies stuck within their boundaries are countered by the movement itself. The energy of the angrier movements suddenly bursts into full choreographic sequences, shifting registers suddenly, showing always present movement potential within registers of the body. Even in quiet, subdued and constrained moments there is always the possibility to act. Moving into a line, parallel to the audience, and utilizing hand-gestures invokes a moment from "Steps in the Street," the breadline. Graham walked to her studio and saw breadlines, which then became her angry line of women, protesting alienation. Curet, almost a century later, shows a line of dancers angry at the mistreatment of their fellow countrywomen and men over the sea, in Puerto Rico. Anger from dancing feet that marched in "Steps in the Street" has seeped into "Isla," a little island that is always entrenched in American politics. But both works carry a profound message: one is never inactive as one is always within an active body. One can always be a part in an emerging solidarity that counters alienation. The movement once again shifts in register into a fluid, long stretching of the body, as if exploring its own physical space. Drawing on breath, collapsing and recovering, the dancers shift toward mechanic movement to the soundtrack of counting. Once again drawing into a line, utilizing gesture while kneeling then once again moving upright and shifting in space, the dancers slowly shift into becoming nothing but bodies, collapsing on the floor one by one. The last dancer standing is Megan Curet herself, whose movement shifts from mechanical gesture to finally ending the work by gathering the dancers, now only passive bodies, and covering them with the same plastic cloth that started the work.

The body as material that can perish, is deeply affected by hurricanes and other disasters that are part natural, part man-engineered and managed. But the same body is also able to resist, to join with other bodies, to shift in registers within itself and outside of itself, to protest wrongs and stand up for what is right. Since Martha Graham captured her breadline, many have joined in lines of dissent, raising an angry fist, demanding justice.

The relationship between Washington and Puerto Rico, its unincorporated territory, problematizes the question of responsibilities, inside and outside, belonging and exiled. The hurricane, the deadliest since Mitch in 1998, highlighted the lethal consequences of xenophobia seeping into politics, and creating a humanitarian crisis for 3.4 million people. Silence in the face of evil is complicity, so told us Martha Graham in 1936, so tells us Megan Curet in 2019.[25]

There is more than one possibility for action, and there are those who care for the world, in different ways, whose work has been chronicled in this book, in different ways. Human beings use their bodies to project a vision for a better world for all and have done so for many years. This book has chronicled a century. Women and men have responded to each other, argued with each other, taken to pickets, strikes, marches, outdoor stages, historical ruins, and forbidden spaces to show with their moving bodies that the world can and must become better for all through different forms of solidarity, and that no one is free until everyone is free.

Blakeley White-McGuire, widely acclaimed principal dancer of the Martha Graham Dance Company, has been creating her own work in parallel to holding Graham's work within her body. Her work "Our Only World" is an explicit, outspoken statement about time, agency, and responsibility to the world as a whole. Her program notes elucidate the idea behind the work:

> Our Only World is a movement meditation upon bodily integrity, generational knowledge and personal agency for the occasion of this performance of Dancing Human Rights. Here I present my personal bodily archive of movement ideas, which have been passed to me

164   DANCE AND ACTIVISM

through generations of artists' and teachers' bodies/minds, and witnessed by generations of audiences. For me, ideas of affection and self-care are embedded within the writings of Poet/Ecologist/Activist Wendell Berry, Poet Mary Oliver and the music of Arvo Part. My dance intends to engage audience members' curiosity about the human body in place in order to facilitate better understanding, caring and action towards increasing affection for the environments within which we live, and make and re-make our lives—our only world.[26]

A native of Louisiana, never detached from her histories, the piece carries memory, rupture, and possibility. Starting from a reading of Wendell Berry's "History," placing greed hidden by the façade of freedom opposite the landscapes of the Deep South, White-McGuire's and Berry's hinterlands, the beauty as well as the horror in our only world become unraveled. White-McGuire's movement, alone on stage, is forceful, precise, yet at times, slips into joy—the joy of movement itself, of inhabiting a moving body. For much of the piece the movement occurs during a reading of Berry's text. The text recounts the horrors of greed-infected action destroying the physical as well as the human world, intertwined. There is no dramatization of the text here, no catharsis, no resolution, but raw humanity that is danced; our only possibility in our only world is realizing who we are, the dance articulates. White-McGuire leaves the stage while a film shows opposite a bench, covered in cloth. The film is surreal, out of this world; in it, an image of White-McGuire is broken down into multiple sub-images, against different landscapes. Radicalism does not entail rejection of the body but rather careful consideration of how the body interacts with new media. In order to share our only world and be generous to others in the process of doing so, we must understand all aspects of our world as it is now. We cannot march toward a better future if we do not firmly stand in our present. The film draws the spectator's attention to the bench covered with fabric, invoking many great modern dance works, from Graham's legacy itself (her revolutionary "Lamentation," stretching the body's boundaries within a tube, to "Spectre—1914," the beginning of her anti-fascist work "Chronicle"). The past is always here to haunt us, like a spectre; it is part of our bodies, changing their ontology in the world. We cannot forget the path we have come through, but we can remake the path as it unfolds onward toward a possible new horizon. Memory and action are not antagonistic but rather act in dialectic.[27]

The last part of the dance is performed to a recitation of Mary Oliver's "Wild Geese," read by former principal dancer and reconstructor of "Chronicle," Terese Capucilli. White-McGuire returns to the bench, wrapping herself in the fabric. Invoking countless imageries that had come before her, she is also the only person on stage, able to act in the now. Present, past, and future meld together, open up new possibilities, new horizons. "You do not have to be good," recites Capucilli, and none of the women and men who have acted in the world have tried to be good, but they have tried, in different ways, to do good, for others, for themselves, or just did good by telling their own stories. The fierce movement of White-McGuire's, solo which is in itself an act of solidarity—with women who have shared the stage with her, women who had come before her, and women she opens the door for—is a rallying cry for action, for justice, for consideration of care and openness as a step forward in the sequel. In her unique voice, loud and clear, holding histories from Berry, Graham, and others, but firmly dancing in the present toward a better world, she is bringing her steps onward.[28]

Many spectres are haunting the world. Violence, sexism, racism, white supremacy. These are very present and have been throughout this past century. But many other spectres are haunting the world, empowering people to speak up and stand up. The spectres of solidarity, of integrity, of

Blakeley White-McGuire, "Our Only World". Blakeley White-McGuire dances at Socrates Park, New York City, 2019. Photo by Reiko Yanagi, courtesy of Blakeley White-McGuire.

166 DANCE AND ACTIVISM

courage, and of togetherness. New forms of praxis are creating these new formative, generative, and constructive spectres. The spectres of reverence of knowledge passed through the ages and enabling new worlds to unfold. We have only one world to inhabit, but we have many layers of knowledge aiding us in how we inhabit it. These layers must not be cast away. This is an inconclusive conclusion of a book written in an open-ended dialectic. Every day new presents unravel new futures with countless challenges and many wrongs that mean that human beings' lives in many ways are still lived apart. However, there is an affluence of knowledge to explore and from which to derive strength and inspiration as the work of solidarity countering these many layers of alienation continues. "This is not the end but only the beginning of the struggle," said Eleanor Marx in a speech for the burgeoning British trade movement in 1890.[29] Martha Graham claimed that the goal of dance is to galvanize action. The action indeed continues.

There are new and old challenges for dancer-activists of the twenty-first century. And there are numerous layers of knowledge from past generations as well as present lessons for them to tap into.

As new challenges unfold, we are left to remember that the human spirit prevails, in resistance, in solidarity, in a woman on stage warning against war in "Spectre—1914," but in all women and men who came before her and will come after her, for whom the work of bettering the world through dance is not a choice but a prerogative and a calling. The spectres of solidarity unravel new moments in history and new alliances countering new and old forms of alienation. Every day marvelous new stories are told in dance by dancer-activists. New movements are changing the world. The light goes up. A woman waits on stage, and she is ready for action.

NOTES

1 If We Can't Dance, We Don't Want to Be Part of Your Revolution

1 Emma Goldman, *Living My Life* (New York: Dover, [1931], 1970), 55–56.

2 Alexandra Kolb, *Dance and Politics* (Oxford and Bern: Peter Lang, 2011).

3 Randy Martin, Rebekah J. Kowal, and Gerald Siegmund, *The Oxford Handbook of Dance and Politics* (Oxford and New York: Oxford University Press, 2017).

4 Toni Shapiro-Phim and Naomi Jackson (eds.), *Dance, Human Rights and Social Justice: Dignity in Motion* (Maryland: Scarecrow Press, 2008).

5 Thomas DeFrantz (ed.), *Dancing Many Drums* (Madison, WI: University of Wisconsin Press, 2002).

6 Thomas DeFrantz and Anita Gonzalez (eds.), *Black Performance Theory* (Durham, NC: Duke University Press, 2014).

7 Brenda Dixon Gottschild, *The Black Dancing Body* (New York, Basingstoke: Palgrave, 2003).

8 Jacqueline Shea-Murphy, *The People Have Never Stopped Dancing* (Minneapolis: Minnesota University Press, 2007).

9 See Erin Manning, *The Politics of Touch* (Minneapolis: University of Minnesota Press, 2007), which engaged tango as a case study extensively; Carrie Noland, *Agency and Embodiment: Performing Gesture/ Producing Culture* (Cambridge, MA: Harvard University Press, 2008).

10 Especially *Vibrant Matter: A Political Ecology of Things* (Durham, NC: Duke University Press, 2010).

11 An important intervention in the understanding of politics in political theory came from Katrina Forrester's *In the Shadow of Justice* (Princeton: Princeton University Press, 2019). Chronicling, elucidating, and critically examining the work of John Rawls and its consequences in placing analytical philosophy in its disproportionate position of power in the Anglo-American world, the book also shows the temporal mismatch between the activist movement that Rawls's ideas were initially referring to, and their current prominence in a dramatically different world.

12 Nancy Fraser, Tithi Bhattacharya and Cinzia Arruzza, *Feminism for the 99% : A Manifesto* (London: Verso, 2019); Alison Phipps, *Me, not You: The Trouble with Mainstream Feminism* (Manchester: Manchester University Press, 2020).

13 Lola Olufemi, *Feminism, Interrupted* (London: Pluto, 2019).

14 Jodi Dean, *The Communist Horizon* (London and New York: Verso, 2012). Jodi Dean, *Comrade: An Essay on Political Belonging* (London and New York: Verso, 2019).

15 Martha Graham, quoted in Roger Copeland, *Merce Cunningham, the Modernization of Modern Dance* (New York and London: Routledge, 2005), 117.

16 Karl Marx, "Theses on Feuerbach," in *The German Ideology Parts II & III* (London: Laurence and Wishart, 1949), 198.

17 There have been ample conceptual discussions of what the concept of praxis entails, which also correspond to changing times and differing disciplines. This work attempts to reconfigure the definition of praxis while focusing on dance and drawing the definition from this world in the time span defined in the book.

18 There have been, of course, many discussions from Karl Marx's incipient formulation to Rahel Jaeggi's critical analysis. See, for instance: Dan S. Chiaburu, Tomas Thundiyil, and Jiexin Wang, "Alienation and its Correlates: A Meta-Analysis," *European Management Journal* 32, no. 1 (2014): 24–36; G. A. Cohen, "Marx's Dialectic of Labour," *Philosophy & Public Affairs* 3, no. 3 (1974): 235–61; Ian Everton, *Alienation* (London: Gay Man's Press, 1982); John Bellamy Foster, "Marx's Theory of Metabolic Rift: Classical Foundations for Environmental Sociology," *American Journal of Sociology* 105, no. 2 (1999): 366–405; Dan Jacobson and Timothy O'Keefe, *Alienation* (London: MacGibbon and Timothy, 1960); Herbert Marcuse, *One-Dimensional Man. Studies in the Ideology of Advanced Industrial Society* (New York: Routledge, 2002 [1964]); Peter Railton, "Alienation, Consequentialism, and the Demands of Morality," *Philosophy & Public Affairs* 13, no. 2 (1984): 134–71; Sean Sayers, *Marx and Alienation. Essays on Hegelian Themes* (London: Palgrave Macmillan, 2011); Richard Schacht, *Alienation*, with an introductory essay by Walter Kaufmann (London: Allen & Unwin, 1971); Carlo Scognamiglio, "Alienation," *The European Legacy* 22, no. 1 (2017): 116–18; Carlo Scognamiglio, *The Future of Alienation* (Urbana: University of Illinois Press, 1994); Amy E. Wendling, *Karl Marx on Technology and Alienation* (London: Palgrave Macmillan, 2009).

19 Rahel Jaeggi, *Alienation* (New York: Columbia University Press, 2016), 1.

20 Ibid.

21 Ibid, 3.

22 Ibid, 11.

23 Karl Marx, *Economic and Philosophic Manuscripts* (Lawrence and Wishart, 1970), 108.

24 My reading of Marx relies on Avineri's reading.

25 Rahel Jaeggi, *Alienation*, 16.

26 Ibid.

27 Jean-Paul Sartre, *Notebooks for an Ethics* (Chicago: University of Chicago, 1992), 382.

28 There are also extensive discussions of the concept of alienation in the existentialist tradition. See for instance: Sidney Finkelstein, *Existentialism and Alienation in American Literature* (New York: International publishers, 1965); Jonathan Webber, *Reading Sartre: On Phenomenology and Alienation* (London, New York: Routledge, 2011).

29 Hannah Arendt, *The Human Condition* (Chicago: University of Chicago Press, 1998), 175.

30 Ibid, 184.

31 Ibid, 34.

32 Ibid, 39.

33 Rachel Holmes, *Eleanor Marx: A Life*, (London: Bloomsbury, 2015), xiii.

34 Ibid, 79.

35 Holmes notes that *The Woman Question (from a Socialist Point of View)* and *The Working Class Movement in America*, both published 1886, were ground-breaking texts of socialist-feminism, the first to be written by a woman in the English language. *The Woman Question*, serving as Holmes's epigraph and central to the argument of the book, provides an understanding in her own words, of Eleanor Marx's foci as organizer and theorist as well as those conditions that constrained her own action. Holmes revisits this text in various iterations and readings throughout her own work, calling for its reclaiming as a founding text, worthy to be read alongside better celebrated authors such as Wollstonecraft's *Vindication of the Rights of Woman*, and Woolf's *A Room of One's Own*. Moreover, Holmes asks for the text to be read in the context of the socialist canon in which she intervenes; from Engels and Babel, to Lenin who described this text as "one of the fundamental works of modern socialism." Alongside Engels's *The Origins of the Family, Private Property and the State* (1884), these two texts connect various structures of oppression and theorize the question at the epicenter of her progressive politics: How do we overturn society so that no one is oppressed, and true freedom will prevail for all? The argument therefore moves to a close reading of this text and focus on its position both within Eleanor's praxis and within our own interpretation of activism as solidarity responding to alienation.

36 Eleanor Marx Aveling and Edward Aveling, *The Woman Question (from a Socialist Point of View)* (London: Swan Sonnenchein, Le Bas and Lower, 1886), 3.

37 Ibid., 5.

38 Ibid., 7.

39 Ibid.

40 Ibid., 8.

41 My emphasis.

42 Ibid., 13.

43 Ibid., 10

44 Ibid., 13.

45 Ibid., 12.

46 Ibid., 15

47 Ibid.

48 Ibid., 16.

49 Ibid., 11.

50 Holmes, *Eleanor Marx: A Life*, 254–55.

51 Holmes has recently published a study of the significance of Shakespeare for Eleanor Marx's discovery of drama, feminism and concepts of Englishness in particular, see Rachel Holmes, "Eleanor Marx and Shakespeare," *Shakespeare* 14, no. 2 (2018), Shakespeare and the Karl Marx Bicentennial, 157–66.

52 For instance, Eleanor's work "Shelley and Socialism," originally published in "Shelley and Socialism," by Edward and Eleanor Marx-Aveling, *To-Day*, April 1888, 103–16, available online at www.marxists.org/archive/eleanor-marx/1888/04/shelley-socialism.htm, discussed in Holmes, *Eleanor Marx: A Life*, 310–12; Eleanor's cultural criticism for *Time* is available online at www.marxists.org/archive/eleanor-marx/1890/theatre.htm. Eleanor's own cultural writing, together with that of her friend and comrade Israel Zangwil, can be seen in her lampoon "A Doll's House Repaired" from 1891 available online at www.marxists.org/archive/eleanor-marx/1891/dolls-house-repaired.htm, discussed in Holmes, *Eleanor Marx: A Life*, 338.

53 Marx and Aveling, *The Woman Question (from a Socialist Point of View)*, 34.

54 Ibid., 5.

55 Ibid., 11.

56 Ibid., 6.

57 Ibid., 16.

58 See, in particular, James Baldwin, *The Fire Next Time* (London: Penguin books, 1963).

2 Prelude to Action

1 Library of Congress, Martha Graham Timeline 1894–1949, available at www.loc.gov/item/ihas.200154832/ (accessed August 15, 2019).

2 Ibid. I have written about "Lamentation" in my *Dance and Politics: Moving beyond Boundaries* (Manchester: Manchester University Press, 2016).

3 Quoted in Ellen Graff, *Stepping Left: Dance and Politics in New York City 1928–1942* (Durham, NC, London: Duke University Press, 2007), 120.

4 Edna Ocko noted this was the first of Graham's dances that resonated with the leftist movement. In Hannah Kosstrin, *Honest Bodies: Revolutionary Modernism in the Dances of Anna Sokolow* (Oxford and New York: Oxford University Press, 2017), 2.

5 Library of Congress, Martha Graham timeline.

6 Mark Franko, *The Work of Dance: Labor, Movement and Identity in the 1930s* (Middletown, CN: Wesleyan University Press, 2002), 2.

7 Ibid., 66.

8 Ibid,. 57.

9 Ibid., 67.

10 Tracey Prickett, "From Workers' Dance to New Dance," *Dance Research Journal: The Journal of the Society for Dance Research* 7, no. 1: 47.

11 Ellen Graff, *Stepping Left*, 9.

12 Ibid., 106.

13 Ibid., 113.

14 An elaborate discussion can be found in Ellen Graff, *Stepping Left*, see especially on whiteness, p. 130.

15 Kim Jones, "Transmission as Process and Power in Graham's Chronicle (1936)," in *Transmissions in Dance: Contemporary Staging Practices*, ed. Lesley Main (Cham, Switzerland: Palgrave MacMillan, 2017), 112.

16 Quoted in Jones, "Transmission as Process and Power," 114.

17 Rare footage of early performances of the company including "Chronicle" from 1938 is available online at www.youtube.com/watch?v=Jmo6htlFHVQ.

18 Interview with Janet Eilber, email February 3, 2020.

19 Footage of this section performed by MGDC Principal Peiju Chien Pot is available online at www.youtube.com/watch?v=MW3e6FhfSLs.

20 Jones, "Transmission as Process and Power," 117.

21 Contemporary choreographer Pam Tanowitz referred to it recently as "the most perfect choreography," Netta Yerushalmy in conversation with Pam Tanowitz, Female Trauma, Interdiction, and Agency in "The House of Pelvic Truth" (A response to Martha Graham's Night Journey [1947]), available online at www.youtube.com/watch?v=nzkipxPBcYQ (accessed May 27, 2020).

22 Quoted in Jones, "Transmission as Process and Power," 116.

23 Some footage of this section may be found online at www.youtube.com/watch?v=Xoid5G8j2vY.

24 Burke 1937, quoted in Jones, "Transmission as Process and Power," 112.

25 Quoted in Jones, "Transmission as Process and Power," 118.

26 Some footage of this section performed by MGDC can be seen online at www.youtube.com/watch?v=SUVe-vyNMXQ.

27 Martha Graham, "Graham 1937," in *Martha Graham,* eds. Merle Armitage and John Martin (New York: Dance Horizons, 1966), 83.

28 Ibid., 84.

29 Ibid., 85.

30 Ibid., 84.

31 Ibid., 86.

32 "German Invitation refused by Dancer," *Dance Observer,* March 13, 1936. Music Division, Library of Congress.

33 Jones, "Transmission as Process and Power," 116.

34 Stacey Pricket notes the year 1935 as when Graham and Doris Humphrey found reconciliation with the radical side of left wing dance, including the New Dance Group and new Dance League, see "From Workers Dance to New Dance," *Dance Research: The Journal of Society for Dance Research* 7, no. 1 (1989), 54.

35 Marnie Thomas Wood, interview, February 28, 2020.

36 Ibid.

37 Ibid.

38 Larry Warren, *Anna Sokolow: The Rebellious Spirit* (Amsterdam, the Netherlands: Harwood Academic Publishers, 1998), 2.

39 Ibid., 5.

40 Ibid., 4.

41 Ibid., 7.

42 Ibid.

43 Ibid., 13.

44 Irene Lewisohn, program notes for Neighborhood Playhouse, quoted in Warren, *Anna Sokolow,* 11.

45 E. Sylvia Pankhurst, "A Festival," in *A Suffragette in America: Prisoners, Pickets and Political Change,* ed. Katherine Connelly (London: Pluto, 2019), 92. A new study reveals the significance of arts and dance in particular for Sylvia's life and work. See: Rachel Holmes, *Sylvia Pankhurst: Natural Born Rebel* (London: Bloomsbury, 2020).

46 Warren, *Anna Sokolow,* 12.

47 Ibid., 14.

48 Ibid., 16.

49 Ibid., 21.

50 Ibid., 26.

51 Ibid., 25.

52 Ibid., 26.

53 Quoted in Warren, *Anna Sokolow*, 54.

54 Ibid., 26.

55 Ibid., 31.

56 Ibid., 28.

57 Ibid., 32.

58 Ibid., 51.

59 "Anna Sokolow, the Rebel and the Bourgeoise," in *The Modern Dance: Seven Statements of Belief*, eds. Erick Hawkins and Selma Jean Cohen (Middletown, CN: Wesleyan University Press, 1966), 29.

60 Ibid.

61 Ibid., 31.

62 Ibid., 30.

63 Ibid., 29.

64 Ibid., 31.

65 Ibid., 29.

66 Ibid., 31.

67 Warren, *Anna Sokolow*, 115.

68 Ibid.

69 Hannah Kosstrin reads the work through queer politics lens, showing gay and Jewish peoples' experiences. The work is certainly about themes of loyalty and subversion, yet in my own reading I focus on the temporality of Sokolow's remembrance of her own childhood and then the reception of the work in the twenty-first century, dealing with new challenges of alienation.

70 Some footage of this work performed by DNB may be found online at www.youtube.com/watch?v=JoPLx9EMXz8.

71 Ibid., 116.

72 Another video showing excerpts from "Rooms" can be found online at www.youtube.com/watch?v=s7c9XBgj6F0.

73 Ibid.

74 Anna Sokolow, quoted in James Grisson, *We Must be Ready, Right Now, To Do What We Must* (Beautiful Dreamers, 2014), 14.

75 Walter Terry, *Herald-Tribune*, 1956 , available online at https://sokolowtheatredance.org/rooms-1955/ (accessed May 27, 2018).

76 Interview with Samantha Geracht Myers, February 14, 2020.

77 Former Artistic Director of Sokolow Dance Company.

78 Interview with Jennifer Conley, July 9, 2017.

79 Ibid.

80 Ibid.

81 Ibid.

82 Ibid.

83 Interview with Samantha Geracht-Myers, February 14, 2020.

84 Peggy and Murray Schwartz, *The Dance Claimed Me: A Biography of Pearl Primus*, (New Haven and London: Yale University Press, 2011), 2.

85 Ibid., 3.

86 Ibid.

87 Ibid., 13.

88 Ibid.

89 Farah Jasmine Griffin, *Harlem Nocturne: Women Artists and Progressive Politics during World War II* (New York: Perseus Books, 2013), 7.

90 Schwartz, *The Dance Claimed Me*, 38.

91 Ibid., 3.

92 A video of this work performed by Paul Dennis can be found online at www.youtube.com/watch?v=HKGrHKkkzzE.

93 Ibid., 40.

94 Ibid., 42.

95 Griffin, *Harlem Nocturne*, 30.

96 Ibid., 53.

97 James Baldwin, "As Much Truth as One Could Bear," in *The Cross of Redemption: Uncollected Writings*, ed. Randall Kenan (New York: Pantheon, 2010), 34.

98 Ibid., 69.

99 Schwartz, *The Dance Claimed Me*, 24.

100 Ibid.

101 Ibid., 25.

102 Griffin, *Harlem Nocturne*, 175.

103 Schwartz, *The Dance Claimed Me*, 96.

104 Ibid., 4.

105 Ibid., 3.

106 Griffin, *Harlem Nocturne*, 131.

107 Ibid., 10.

108 Ibid.

109 A version of this dance performed by Nimbus Dance Works at Jacob's Pillow can be seen online at https://danceinteractive.jacobspillow.org/ nimbus-dance-works/strange-fruit/. Another version performed by Dawn Marie Watson can be seen at www.youtube.com/watch?v=aNVRf8okR78.

110 Schwartz, *The Dance Claimed Me*, 64.

111 Anna Kisslegoff, "Pearl Primus Rejoices in the Black Tradition," *New York Times*, June 19, 1988, available online at www.nytimes.com/1988/06/19/arts/dance-view-pearl-primus-rejoices-in-the-black-tradition.html (accessed January 8, 2020).

112 Ibid.

113 Ibid.

114 Epigraph, in Schwartz, *The Dance Claimed Me*.

115 Ibid.

116 Ibid., 95.

117 Ibid., 168.

118 David Gere, "Dances of Sorrow, Dances of Hope: The work of Pearl Primus finds a natural place in a special program of historic modern dances for women. Primus's 1943 work 'Strange Fruit' leaped over the boundaries of what was then considered 'black dance'," *L.A. Times,* April 24, 1994, available online at www.latimes.com/archives/la-xpm-1994-04-24-ca-49822-story.html (accessed January 2, 2020).

119 Schwartz, *The Dance Claimed Me*, 36.

120 Ibid., 234.

121 Kisslegoff, "Pearl Primus Rejoices in the Black Tradition."

122 Kisslegoff, "Pearl Primus Rejoices in the Black Tradition."

123 Schwartz, *The Dance Claimed Me*, 230.

124 From the land of shadows

> Comes a dreadful sight
> Lady with the marble smile
> Spirit of the night
> See the scourge of innocence
> Swinging in her hand
> Hear the silent suffering
> That echoes through the land
> From the tombs of ignorance
> Of hate and greed and lies
> Through the smoke of sacrifice
> Watch her figure rise
> The sick the poor the old
> Basking in her radiance
> Men of blood and gold
> In her bloody footsteps
> Speculators prance
> Men of dreams are praying
> For that second chance

Round her vacant features
Gilded serpents dance
Her tree of evil knowledge
Sprouts a special branch
Madam Medusa
Madam Medusa
Madam Medusa
Knock her right down
And then she bounce right back
Knock her right down
And then she bounce right back
She gone off her head
We've got to shoot her dead
She gone off her head
We've got to shoot her dead
Run for your life before she eat you alive
Run for your life before she eat you alive
Move out of the way 'cause's you're blocking out the day
Move out of the way 'cause's you're blocking out the day.

125 Ibid., 107.

126 Ibid., 235.

127 Ibid., 115.

128 Ibid., 234.

129 Ibid., 199.

3 Ballet beyond Borders

1 Jennifer Homans, *Apollo's Angels, A History of Ballet* (London: Granta, 2010), 10.

2 Ibid., 12.

3 Ibid., 14.

4 Ibid., 15.

5 Nelson Mandela, *Long Walk to Freedom*, (London: Abacus, 1994), 384.

6 Quoted in Michelle LeBaron and Janis Sarra, *Changing our World: Art as Transformative Practice* (Cape Town: African SunPress, 2018), 159.

7 Richard Glasstone, *David Poole: a Life Blighted by Apartheid* (Leicestershire: Book Guild, 2018), 14.

8 Glasstone, *David Poole: a Life Blighted by Apartheid*, p. 15.

9 Ibid., 19.

10 Ibid., 49.

11 Ibid., 66.

12 Audrey King, in a quote from 1977 "Johannesburg Youth Ballet honors founder Audrey King: To celebrate 40th Anniversary the JYB presented A Midsummer Night's Dream and other Ballets at the Mandela," CreativeFeel, available online at https://creativefeel.co.za/2016/10/ballet/ (accessed October 24, 2019).

13 Interview with Kim Segel, JYB alumna, October 20, 2019.

14 Ibid.

15 Address by President Nelson Mandela at the International Day of Solidarity with the Palestinian People, 1997, available online at www.sahistory.org.za/archive/ address-president-nelson-mandela-international-day-solidarity-palestinian-people- pretoria-4- (accessed February 20, 2020).

16 An especially significant intervention in understanding Gaza as an example of state terror came recently from Angela Davis, who shows important connections between state surveillance and terror in the US and Britain (especially G4) and Palestine, see Angela Y. Davis, *Freedom is a Constant Struggle: Ferguson, Palestine and the Foundation of a Movement* (Chicago: Haymarket, 2016), 57.

17 Nidal al Mughrabi, "Gaza's only ballet school a haven of calm for traumatized girls," *Al Arabiya*, December 1, 2015, available online at https://english. alarabiya.net/en/2015/12/01/Gaza-s-only-ballet-school-a-haven-of-calm-for-traumatized-girls.html (accessed October 15, 2018).

18 Nidal al Mughrabi, "Pirouettes and plenty of pink in Gaza's only Ballet school," Reuters, available online at https://uk.reuters.com/article/uk-palestinians-gaza-ballet/pirouettes-and-plenty-of-pink-at-gazas-only-ballet-school-idUKKBN0TJ1FR20151130 (accessed October 1, 2018).

19 Svetlana Alexievich, *The Unwomanly Face of War* (London: Penguin Classics, 2017), xiv.

20 Ibid.

21 Al Mughrabi, "Gaza's only ballet school gives safe haven for traumatized girls."

22 Renate Van der Zeel, "Dance or Die, the Ballet Dancer Forbidden to Perform by Islamic State," *Guardian*, March 13, 2017, available online at www. theguardian.com/global-development-professionals-network/2017/mar/13/its-dance-or-die-the-ballet-dancer-forbidden-to-perform-by-islamic-state (accessed October 25, 2018).

23 Sven Tonigen, "Dance is my passport: Syrian ballet dancer Ahmad Joudeh on dancing as home," available online at www.dw.com/en/dance-is-my-passport-syrian-ballet-dancer-ahmad-joudeh-on-dancing as home/a 48502423 (accessed May 5, 2019).

24 Ahmed Joudeh, quoted in Renate van der Zeel, "Dance or Die."

25 In 2018, Joudeh published his autobiography entitled *Danzo O Muori* (Dance or Die) in Italian. In 2019 a documentary also entitled *Dance or Die* was made about Joudeh.

26 Amy Walker, "All Hail Stormzy for Historic Glastonbury Performance," *Guardian*, June 29, 2019, available online at www.theguardian.com/music/2019/jun/29/stormzy-historic-glastonbury-performance (accessed June 30, 2019).

27 "David Lammy on why there's nothing scary about a black man in a hoodie," *Guardian*, February 13, 2019, available online at www.theguardian.com/world/2019/feb/13/david-lammy-on-why-theres-nothing-scary-about-a-black-man-in-a-hoodie (accessed September 20, 2019).

28 Martha De Ferrer, "Stormzy review: A powerful, stunning Glastonbury Festival headline set," *Somerset Live*, available online at www.somersetlive.co.uk/whats-on/music-nightlife/stormzy-makes-history-powerful-stunning-3033711 (accessed June 29, 2019).

29 Ballet Black tweeted some of this performance, footage of which can be seen online at https://twitter.com/balletblack/status/1144777359519866880?lang=en.

30 Phil Chan and Michele Chase, *Final Bow to Yellowface* (Yellow Peril Press, Ibook), 22.

31 Ibid., 24.

32 Our Vision, on Final Bow for Yellowface, available online at www.yellowface.org/our-vision (accessed December 10, 2019).

33 It is necessary to mention that in December 2017 Martins took a leave of absence after allegations of sexual and physical abuse against him dating from 1983 surfaced and generated an investigation.

34 Phil Chan, interview, December 16, 2019.

35 Ibid.

36 Ibid.

37 Ibid.

38 Ibid.

39 Phil Chan and Michele Chase, *Final Bow to Yellowface*, 28.

40 Ibid., 36.

41 Ibid.

4 Erbil/New York City: Break/Dance

1 Paul Rockower, "The Yes Academy in Iraq," *Huffington Post*, April 8, 2012, available online at www.huffpost.com/entry/yes-academy-iraq_b_1773157?guccounter=1 (accessed April 25, 2016).

2 Ibid.

3 Yasmeen Sami-Alamiri, "Dance Diplomacy: Iraqi break-dancers share message with US audience," *Al Arabiya*, October 22, 2013, available online at

https://english.alarabiya.net/en/life-style/art-and-culture/2013/10/22/
Dance-Diplomacy-Iraqi-break-dancers-share-message-with-U-S-audience.
html (accessed May 4, 2016).

4 Ibid.

5 Ibid.

6 Harriet Agerholm, "Isis Baghdad bombing: Young man who danced in city's parks named as one of the 292 victims of terrorist attack," *The Independent*, August 8, 2016, available online at www.independent.co.uk/news/world/isis-baghdad-bombing-isis-adel-euro-young-dancer-danced-parks-named-292-victims-killed-terrorist-a7126776.html (accessed September 10, 2016).

7 Jonathan Hollander, email interview July 23, 2017.

8 Ibid.

9 Ibid.

10 Project TAG description, email correspondence with Hussein Smko.

11 Email interview with Hussein Smko, July 20, 2017.

12 Ibid.

13 Ibid.

14 Ibid.

15 Ibid.

16 Footage of this work is available online at https://vimeo.com/221912062.

17 Interview with Hussein Smko, July 20, 2017.

18 Ibid.

19 Footage of this work available online at www.youtube.com/watch?v=H9q_nCSeGTc.

20 T. S. Eliot, Burnt Norton, *Four Quartets* (London: Faber, 2001), 5.

21 Antoinette Amantina Jean, email interview, February 9, 2020.

22 Ibid.

23 Ibid.

24 Ibid.

25 Footage of the work can be seen online at www.youtube.com/watch?v=rh96lW8id9c and www.youtube.com/watch?v=BTIZusVeu3Q.

26 Project TAG description, email correspondence with Hussein Smko.

5 Steps in the Street: Revolution DJ

1 On the French Revolution see Jennifer Homans, *Apollo's Angels*, especially pp. 122–23; 322–23.

2 A pioneering conceptualization of the danger of the crowd can be found in Gustave Le Bon, *The Crowd: A Study of the Popular Mind* from 1896, in which he claims that new psychological attributes arise out of sharing a space in the crowd and their danger for the individual's psyche and reason. Further discussions emerged in various guises, including specifically Hannah Arendt's writing on "the Blob" in *The Human Condition*, problematized recently by Hannah Pitkin.

3 A few recent responses to #MeToo can be found in Cinzia Arruzza, Tithi Bhattachrya, and Nancy Fraser, *Feminism for the 99%* (London: Verso, 2019) and especially Allison Phipps, *Me, Not You* (Manchester, Manchester University Press, 2020).

4 Annalisa Mirelli, "Learn the lyrics and dance steps for the Chilean feminist anthem spreading around the world," available online at https://qz.com/1758765/chiles-viral-feminist-flash-mob-is-spreading-around-the-world/ (accessed December 20, 2019).

5 Sandi Bachom, "Flash Mob Performs Viral Chilean Anti-Rape Anthem NYC 1/10/20," available online at www.youtube.com/watch?v=czOQ5ARFFHI (accessed January 17, 2020).

6 AFP News agency, Argentine's women protest for legal abortion, against violence, available at https://www.youtube.com/watch?v=xS1eNYjoayM (accessed May 20, 2020).

7 There has been ample research and writing on the history of tango in a political context, see for instance Marta E. Savigliano, *Tango and the Political Economy of Passion, from Exoticism to Decolonization (Institutional Structures of Feeling)* (Boulder: Westview, 1995); Karoline Gritzner, "Between Commodification and Emancipation: The Tango Encounter," *Dance Research* 35, no. 1 (June 2017) 49–60; Erin Manning, *The Politics of Touch*, (Minnesota: Minnesota University Press, 2006).

8 Charis McGowan, "All female tango festival calls for an end to Machismo," *al Jazeera*, March 12, 2019, available online at www.aljazeera.com/news/2019/03/female-argentina-tango-festival-calls-machismo-190311184858304.html (accessed May 20, 2020).

9 Anonymous, "Gilet Jaune Danse Arabe Autoroute," November 25, 2018, available online at www.youtube.com/watch?v=Uw5fmA9Kq_0 (accessed June 10, 2019).

10 Anonymous, "Best of des Giles Jaunes qui danse!" December 9, 2018, available online at www.youtube.com/watch?v=lr7U-bqc9Ls (accessed on June 20, 2019).

11 And as histories of the transmission of dance on the march progress, men wearing yellow vests broke into dancing at the recent strike of the University and College Union in Bristol, on February 21, 2020.

12 The terms *cissexual* and *cisgender* entered into circulation in 1991 and 1994, respectively, and are defined as "non-transgender." For explanation and

discussion of the concept, see B. Aultman, "Cisgender," *Transgender Studies Quarterly* no. 1–2 (2014), 61–62.

13 Lesley Kernochan, "Transgender day of remembrance flash mob," available online at www.youtube.com/watch?v=r-x8RRaEcYk (accessed January 30, 2020).

14 "Delhi's first LGBT flash mob," available online at www.youtube.com/watch?v=5HUS8EePcoQ (accessed January 30, 2020).

15 See for instance, Jehad Abusalim, "The Great March of Return: An Organizer's Perspective," *Journal of Palestine Studies* 47, no. 4 (2018): 90–100; "Great march of return archives", *972 Mag*, available online at www.972mag.com/topic/great-march-of-return/.

16 The most comprehensive account of the history of Dabke can be found in Nicholas Rowe, *Rising Dust: A Cultural History of Dance in Palestine* (London: I.B. Tauris, 2010). I've written previously on the history of Dabke, see Dana Mills, "The Beat Goes On: The story of Palestine's National Dance," *972 Mag*, September 20, 2017, available online at www.972mag.com/the-beat-goes-on-the-story-of-palestines-national-dance/ (accessed October 15, 2019).

17 "Jewish Voice for Peace, Dabke in Gaza," February 23, 2019, available online at www.facebook.com/watch/?v=561099777730162 (accessed June 15, 2019).

18 This question will be explored further in the next chapter, which hinges on the work of Palestinian writer and activist Edward Said.

19 Lindsey Winship, "Pantsula Revolution! How South Africa's townships dance got political," *The Guardian*, October 8, 2018, available online at www.theguardian.com/stage/2018/oct/08/pantsula-dance-south-africa-via-kanana (accessed May 25, 2020).

20 Anonymous, "How are Lebanese protesters using art to express their views?" *Euronews*, November 29, 2019, available online at www.euronews.com/2019/11/28/how-are-lebanese-protesters-using-art-to-express-their-views (accessed January 20, 2020).

21 BBC News, "Lebanon protests: Protesters sing Baby Shark to toddler," October 22, 2019, available online at www.youtube.com/watch?v=BNd2im6zYno (accessed January 15, 2020).

22 Hamza Hendawi, "Sudan's 'Nubian Queen' protester becomes iconic image of anti- government demonstrations," *The National*, April 10, 2019, available online at www.thenational.ae/world/africa/sudan-s-nubian-queen-protester-becomes-iconic-image-of-anti-government-demonstrations-1.847419 (accessed July 10, 2019).

23 Most memorably, Thunberg was mocked for her public persona by Brendan O'Neill, who referred to her as "weirdo" (referring to her Asperger's syndrome) and critiquing her "cult" in a manner reminiscent of a fear of mobs (or of democracy). See "The Cult of Greta Thunberg," *Spiked*, April 22, 2019, available online at www.spiked-online.com/2019/04/22/the-cult-of-greta-thunberg/ (accessed May 5, 2019).

24 Johnny Armstead, "Extinction Rebellion flash mob Trafalgar Square," October 9, 2019, available online at www.youtube.com/watch?v=MC9d1egcNdA (accessed January 16, 2020).

25 Extinction Rebellion, "XRAussies Having Fun, Getting Fit & Causing Disruption thru DISCObedience!" October 20, 2019, available online at www.youtube.com/watch?v=WGMKumKBZJI (accessed January 17, 2020).

26 For a history of Bella Ciao in its political context see Ilaria Serra, "Teaching Italy through its Music: The Meaning of Music in Italian Cultural History," *Italica* 88, no. 1 (Spring 2011): 94–114; Salome Vogelin, "Reflections on the Politics of Sentiment Score for Performing the Criticality of Sensibility," in *Sensorial Aesthetics in Music Practices*, ed. Kathleen Coessens (Leuven: Leuven University Press, 2019), 158–69; section on "Bella Ciao," protest song of the Italian anti-fascist movement 1943–1945, at pp. 158–59.

27 Maggie Huang, "Extinction Rebellion flash mob 7 Oct Central Station," October 7, 2019, available online at www.youtube.com/watch?v=YEjOarYESow (accessed January 17, 2020).

28 See for instance, Athian Akec, "When I look at extinction rebellion, all I see is white privilege," *The Guardian*, October 19, 2020 available online at www.theguardian.com/commentisfree/2019/oct/19/extinction-rebellion-white-faces-diversity (accessed February 1, 2020); E. Isaksen, "Lay down our differences: An interpretive study of problem representation(s) and inclusion in Extinction Rebellion" (Dissertation, 2020). Available online at http://urn.kb.se/resolve?urn=urn:nbn:se:uu:diva-402470.

29 Kelly Abdou Richman, "Liberating portraits of Ballerinas elegantly dancing in the streets of Cairo," My Modern Met, January 17, 2017, available online at https://mymodernmet.com/ballerinas-of-cairo-mohamed-taher/ (accessed February 2, 2020).

30 France 24, "Paris Opera continues its strike, ballerinas protest over Macron's pension plans," available online at www.france24.com/en/video/20191225-paris-opera-continues-its-strike-ballerinas-protest-over-macron-s-pension-plans (accessed December 26, 2019).

31 France 24, "Ballet dancers down tutus in longest strike ever at Paris Opera," January 3, 2019, available online at www.france24.com/en/20200103-ballet-dancers-down-tutus-in-longest-strike-ever-at-paris-opera (accessed January 1, 2020).

6 Dance as a Home

1 Hannah Arendt, "We, Refugees," in *The Jewish Writings*, eds. Jerome Kohn and Ron Feldman (New York: Shocken Books, 2007), 264.

2 This conceptual and ethical position directly draws on David Owen's *What do we Owe to Refugees?* in which Owen presents an ethical discussion of refugee protection, and the forms of international cooperation required to implement it that are responsive to the claims of both refugees and states. See David Owen, *What do we Owe Refugees?* (London: Polity, 2020).

3 Ibid.

4 Marina Warner, "Living in the Country of Words," in *Others: Writers on Difference*, ed Charles Fernyhough (London: Unbound, 2019), 233.

5 Ibid., 234.

6 Ibid.

7 Ibid., 239.

8 Ibid., 238.

9 Ibid.

10 Ibid.

11 In Italy (DNM).

12 Ibid., 243.

13 Ibid., 236.

14 Ibid., 237.

15 Said, quoted in Lancellot Malliot: "Contrapunctus: Edward Said and Joseph Conrad," *Journal of Conrad Studies* 1 (2005): 179.

16 Edward Said, "Reflections on Exile," in *Altogether Elsewhere: Writers on Exile*, ed. Marc Robinson (Boston: Faber & Faber, 1994), 142.

17 Ibid., 144.

18 R. Radakrishnan, "Edward Said's Literary Humanism," *Cultural Critique* 67 (2007): 15.

19 Said, "Reflections on Exile," 143.

20 Ibid., 146.

21 Ibid., 147.

22 Ibid., 148.

23 Ibid., 149.

24 Ibid.

25 Edward Said, "American Intellectuals and Middle East Politics: An Interview with Edward W. Said, " *Social Text*, no. 19/20 (Autumn, 1988): 50.

26 It is interesting to propose the shift to exilic thinking following Said, rather than tapping into literature in dance studies centralizing kinesthetic empathy. A key interdisciplinary concept in our understanding of social interaction across creative and cultural practices, kinesthetic empathy describes the ability to experience empathy merely by observing the movements of another human being (see Dee Reynolds and Matthew Reason, *Kinesthetic Empathy* [Chicago: University of Chicago Press, 2012]). While popular to an extent, and rooted in the history of dance writing from John Martin, the concept does not manage to disengage inequities of power on stage that are transferred to the audience member. Early critique of Martin's writing on Graham, for instance, sustains this in part; the world on stage still does not represent power relations off it and those who arguably are not presented on stage at all. The move to exilic thinking shifts attention to those unrepresented mostly on the dance stage, rather than reproducing conditions in which an unequal world on stage demands empathy from those not represented in the audience.

27 Ibid., 51.

28 Johannah Fahey and Jane Kenway, "Thinking in a 'Worldly' Way: Mobility, Knowledge, Power and Geography," *Discourse: Studies in the Cultural Politics of Education* 31, no. 5 (December 2010): 630.

29 Ibid.

30 Edward Said, "Intellectual Exile: Expatriates and Marginals," in *Representations of the Intellectual: The 1993 Reith Lectures* (London: Vintage), 35–47, quoted in Fahey, "Thinking in a 'Worldly' Way," 630.

31 Jeanne Morefield, "Said and Political Theory," in *After Said: Postcolonial Literary Studies in the Twenty-First Century*, ed. Bashir Abu-Manneh (Cambridge: Cambridge University Press, 2018), 112–28.

32 Simon Birch, *Shoreline*, accompanying booklet.

33 John Donne, *Nunc lento Sonitu Dicunt, Morieris, Devotions upon Emergent Occasions* (London: Create Space, 2012), 102.

34 Some of the work can be seen online at https://simonbirchdance.com/shoreline-new.

35 The late political theorist Agnes Heller theorized this question in her seminal essay "Where are we at home?" (*Thesis Eleven*, no. 41 [1995]: 1–18).

36 Some of the work can be seen online at: https://vimeo.com/222120707.

37 A snippet of the work can be seen online at: https://vimeo.com/230531066.

7 Spectre, Haunting

1 Paraphrasing Karl Marx, the Eighteenth Brumaire of Napoleon Bonaparte.

2 Interview with Janet Eilber, February 3, 2020.

3 Interview with Yuting Zhao, February 11, 2020.

4 Ibid.

5 Brian Siebert, "Creating for Martha Graham's Company, Competing with the Great Mother," *New York Times*, April 4, 2019, available online at www.nytimes.com/2019/04/04/arts/dance/martha-graham-dance-pam-tanowitz-bobbi-jene-smith.html (accessed February 19, 2020).

6 Ibid.

7 Ibid.

8 Interview with Blakeley White-McGuire, February 11, 2020.

9 Ibid.

10 Ibid.

11 Ibid.

12 Ibid.

13 Ibid.

14 Robert Gottlieb, "The most gratifying fall for dance season in years," *The Observer*, October 22, 2019, available online at https://observer.com/2019/10/2019-fall-for-dance-season-the-most-gratifying-in-years/ (accessed October 25, 2019).

15 Interview with Leslie Andrea Williams, February 14, 2020.

16 Ibid.

17 Ibid.

18 Ibid.

19 Ibid.

20 Interview with Megan Curet, February 14, 2020.

21 Ibid.

22 Ibid.

23 Ibid.

24 Curet Performance Project, Megan Curet, available online at http://megancuret.com/works (accessed January 15, 2020).

25 YouTube clip of the work available online at www.dance.nyc/for-audiences/community-calendar/view/ASPECTOS/2019-11-01/.

26 Program notes, "Dancing Human Rights," Oxford Old Fire Station, January 20, 2020.

27 This work has different iterations depending on the site in which it is performed; this specific analysis focuses on a performance as part of Dancing Human Rights in Oxford, United Kingdom on February 1, 2020.

28 Some footage of the work is available online at https://blakeleyarts.com/works/.

29 Quoted in Rachel Holmes, *Eleanor Marx: A Life*, 333.

BIBLIOGRAPHY

Agerholm, Harriet. "Isis Baghdad Bombing: Young Man Who Danced in City's Parks Named as One of the 292 Victims of Terrorist Attack." *The Independent*, August 8, 2016. www.independent.co.uk/news/world/isis-baghdad-bombing-isis-adel-euro-young-dancer-danced-parks-named-292-victims-killed-terrorist-a7126776.html.

Alexivich, Svetlana. *The Unwomanly Face of War*. London: Penguin, 2017.

Al Mughrabi, Nidal. "Gaza's Only Ballet School a Haven of Calm for Traumatized Girls." *Al Arabiya*. https://english.alarabiya.net/en/2015/12/01/Gaza-s-only-ballet-school-a-haven-of-calm-for-traumatized-girls.html. Accessed October 15, 2018.

Anonymous. "Gilet Jaune Danse Arabe Autoroute," November 25, 2018. www.youtube.com/watch?v=Uw5fmA9Kq_0.

Anonymous. "Best of Des Gilet Jaune Qui Danse!" September 12, 2018. www.youtube.com/watch?v=lr7U-bqc9Ls.

Anonymous. "How Are Lebanese Protesters Using Art to Express Their Views?," November 29, 2019. www.euronews.com/2019/11/28/how-are-lebanese-protesters-using-art-to-express-their-views.

Arendt, Hannah. *The Human Condition*. Chicago: University of Chicago Press, 1975.

Armstead, Jonny. "Extinction Rebellion Flash Mob Trafalgar Square," September 10, 2019. www.youtube.com/watch?v=MC9d1egcNdA.

Bachom, Sandi. "Feminist Flash Mob Performs Viral Chilean Anti-Rape Anthem NYC 1/10/20," October 1, 2020. www.youtube.com/watch?v=czOQ5ARFFHI.

Baldwin, James. "As Much Truth as One Could Bear," In *The Cross of Redemption: Uncollected Writings*, edited by Randall Kenan, 28–34. New York: Parthenon, 2010.

BBC. "Lebanon Protests: Protesters Sing Baby Shark to Toddler." BBC, October 22, 2019. www.youtube.com/watch?v=BNd2im6zYno.

Birch, Simon. *Shoreline*. n.d.

Chan, Phil, and Michele Chase. *Final Bow to Yellowface*. Ibook: Yellow Peril Press, n.d. Accessed May 20, 2020.

Chan, Phil. Interview with author, by email, December 16, 2019.

Conley, Jennifer. Interview with author, by email, September 7, 2017.

Cuesta Camacho, Isabel. Email, December 7, 2017.

Curet, Megan. "Curet Performance Project Website." http://megancuret.com/works. Accessed January 15, 2020.

Curet, Megan. Interview with author, by email, October 2, 2020.

De Ferrer, Martha. "Stormzy Review: A Powerful, Stunning Glastonbury Festival Headline Set," *Somerset Live*, June 28, 2019. www.somersetlive.co.uk/whats-on/music-nightlife/stormzy-makes-history-powerful-stunning-3033711.

"Delhi's First LGBT Flash Mob," July 28, 2015. www.youtube.com/watch?v=5HUS8EePcoQ.

Donne, John. *Nunc Lento Sonitu Dicunt, Morieris, Devotions upon Emergent Occasions*. London: Create Space, 2012.

Eilber, Jane. Interview with author, March 2, 2020.

Extinction Rebellion. "XRAussies Having Fun, Getting Fit & Causing Disruption Thru DISCObedience!" October 20, 2019. www.youtube.com/watch?v=WGMKumKBZJI.

Fahey, Jonathan and Kenway, Jane. "Thinking in a 'Worldly' Way: Mobility, Knowledge, Power and Geography." *Discourse: Studies in the Cultural Politics of Education* 31, no. 5 (December 2010): 627–40.

"Final Bow for YellowFace." www.yellowface.org/our-vision. Accessed October 12, 2019.

France 24. "Ballet Dancers down Tutus in Longest Strike Ever at Paris Opera." France 24, March 1, 2020. www.france24.com/en/20200103-ballet-dancers-down-tutus-in-longest-strike-ever-at-paris-opera.

France 24. "Paris Opera Continues Its Strike, Ballerinas Protest over Macron's Pension Plans." France 24, December 25, 2019. www.france24.com/en/video/20191225-paris-opera-continues-its-strike-ballerinas-protest-over-macron-s-pension-plans.

Franko, Mark. *The Work of Dance: Labor, Movement and Identity in the 1930s*. Middletown, CT: Wesleyan University Press, 2002.

Gere, David. "Dances of Sorrow, Dances of Hope: The Work of Pearl Primus Finds a Natural Place in a Special Program of Historic Modern Dances for Women. Primus' 1943 Work 'Strange Fruit' Leaped over the Boundaries of What Was Then Considered 'Black Dance." *L.A. Times*, April 24, 1994. www.latimes.com/archives/la-xpm-1994-04-24-ca-49822-story.html.

"German Invitation Refused by Dancer." *Dance Observer*, March 13, 1936. Library of Congress, Music Division.

Glasstone, Richard. *David Poole: A Life Blighted by Apartheid*. Leicestershire: Book Guild Limited, 2018.

Goldman, Emma. *Living My Life*. 2nd edn. 2 vols. New York: Dover, 1970.

Graff, Ellen. *Stepping Left: Dance and Politics in New York City 1928–1942*. Durham, London: Duke University Press, 2007.

Griffin, Farah Jasmine. *Harlem Nocturne*. New York: Perseus Books, 2013.

Grisson, James. *Anna Sokolow: We Must Be Ready, Right Now, to Do What We Must*. Beautiful Dreamers, 2014.

Hendawi, Hamza. "Sudan's 'Nubian Queen' Protester Becomes Iconic Image of Anti-Government Demonstrations," *The National*, October 4, 2019. www.thenational.ae/world/africa/sudan-s-nubian-queen-protester-becomes-iconic-image-of-anti-government-demonstrations-1.847419.

Hollander, Jonathan. Email interview on Dancing to Connect. July 23, 2017.

Holmes, Rachel. *Eleanor Marx: A Life*. London: Bloomsbury, 2015.

Homans, Jennifer. *Apollo's Angels: A History of Ballet*. London: Granta, 2010.

Huang, Maggie. "Extinction Rebellion Flash Mob 7 Oct Central Station," July 9, 2019. www.youtube.com/watch?v=YEjOarYESow.

Jean, Antoinette. Interview with author, by email, September 2, 2020.

Jewish Voice for Peace. "Dabke in Gaza," February 23, 2019. www.facebook.com/watch/?v=561099777730162.

"Johannesburg Youth Ballet Honors Founder Audrey King: To Celebrate 40th Anniversary the JYB Presented A Midsummer Night's Dream and Other Ballets at the Mandela." *CreativeFeel*. https://creativefeel.co.za/2016/10/ballet/. Accessed October 24, 2019.

Jones, Kim. "Transmission as Process and Power in Graham's Chronicle (1936)." In *Transmissions in Dance: Contemporary Staging Practices*, edited by Lesley Main. Cham, Switzerland: Palgrave MacMillan, 2017.

Kermochan, Lesley. "Transgender Day of Remembrance Flash Mob." www.youtube.com/watch?v=r-x8RRaEcYk. Accessed January 30, 2020.

Kisslegoff, Anna. "Pearl Primus Rejoices in the Black Tradition." *New York Times*, June 19, 1988. www.nytimes.com/1988/06/19/arts/dance-view-pearl-primus-rejoices-in-the-black-tradition.html.

Kosstrin, Hannah. *Honest Bodies: Revolutionary Modernism in the Dances of Anna Sokolow*. Oxford and New York: Oxford University Press, 2017.

Kultur. "Interview with Anna Sokolow." www.youtube.com/watch?v=LAld_m74bUY. Accessed May 27, 2018.

Lammy, David. "Why There's Nothing Scary about a Black Man in a Hoodie," *The Guardian*, February 13, 2019. www.theguardian.com/world/2019/feb/13/david-lammy-on-why-theres-nothing-scary-about-a-black-man-in-a-hoodie.

LeBaron, Michelle. *Changing Our World: Art as Transformative Practice*. Cape Town: African SunPress, 2018.

Library of Congress. "Martha Graham Timeline 1894–1949," August 15, 2019. www.loc.gov/item/ihas.200154832/.

Mallios, Lancelot. "Contrapunctus: Edward Said and Joseph Conrad." *Journal of Conrad Studies* 1 (2005): 177–93.

Marx, Eleanor and Aveling, Edward. *The Woman Question (from a Socialist Point of View)*. London: Swan Sonnenchein, Le Bas and Lower, 1886.

Marx, Karl. *Economic and Philosophic Manuscripts of 1844*. London: Laurence and Whisart, 1970.

Marx, Karl. *The German Ideology Parts II & III*. London: Laurence and Whisart, 1949.

McGowan, Charis. "All-Women Argentina Tango Festival Calls for End to Machismo." *Al Jazeera*, December 3, 2019. www.aljazeera.com/news/2019/03/female-argentina-tango-festival-calls-machismo-190311184858304.html.

Merelli, Annalisa. "Learn the Lyrics and Dance Steps for the Chilean Feminist Anthem Spreading around the World." *Quarz*, February 12, 2019. https://qz.com/1758765/chiles-viral-feminist-flash-mob-is-spreading-around-the-world/.

Mills, Dana. "The Beat Goes on: The Story of Palestine's National Dance," *972*, September 20, 2017. www.972mag.com/the-beat-goes-on-the-story-of-palestines-national-dance/.

BIBLIOGRAPHY 191

Morefield, Jeanne. "After Said." *Postcolonial Literary Studies in the Twenty-First Century*, December 2018, 112–28.

al-Mughrabi, Nidal. "Pirouettes and Plenty of Pink at Gaza's Only Ballet School." *Reuters*. https://uk.reuters.com/article/uk-palestinians-gaza-ballet/pirouettes-and-plenty-of-pink-at-gazas-only-ballet-school-idUKKBN0TJ1FR20151130. Accessed January 10, 2018.

Myers, Geracht. Interview with Samantha Geracht Myers, email, February 14, 2020.

Pankhurst, Sylvia E. *A Suffragette in America: Reflections on Prisoners, Pickets and Political Change*, edited by Katherine Connelly. London: Pluto, 2019.

Prickett, Stacey. "From Workers' Dance to New Dance." *Dance Research: The Journal of the Society for Dance Research* 7, no. 1 (1989): 47–64.

Radakrishnan, R. "Edward Said's Literary Humanism." *Cultural Critique* 67 (Autumn 2007): 13–42.

Richman Abdou, Kelly. "Liberating Portraits of Ballerinas Elegantly Dancing in the Streets of Cairo," January 17, 2017. https://mymodernmet.com/ballerinas-of-cairo-mohamed-taher/.

Rockower, Paul. "The YES Academy in Iraq." *Huffington Post*. www.huffpost.com/entry/yes-academy-iraq_b_1773157?guccounter=1. Accessed April 25, 2016.

"Rooms (1955)." https://sokolowtheatredance.org/rooms-1955/. Accessed May 27, 2018.

Said, Edward. "Reflections on Exile." In *Altogether Elsewhere: Writers on Exile*, edited by Marc Robinson, 137–49. Boston: Faber & Faber, n.d.

Said, Edward, and Robbins, Bruce. "American Intellectuals and Middle East Politics: An Interview with Edward W. Said." *Social Text* no. 19/20 (Autumn 1988): 37–53.

Sami Alamiri, Yasmeen. "Dance Diplomacy: Iraqi Break-Dancers Share Message with US Audience, Al Arabiya." *Al Arabiya*, October 22, 2013. https://english.alarabiya.net/en/life-style/art-and-culture/2013/10/22/Dance-Diplomacy-Iraqi-break-dancers-share-message-with-U-S-audience.html.

Sartre, Jean-Paul. *Notebooks for an Ethics*. Chicago: University of Chicago Press, 1992.

Schwartz, Peggy and Schwartz, Murray. *The Dance Claimed Me: A Biography of Pearl Primus*. New Haven and London: Yale University Press, 2011.

Siebert, Brian. "Creating for Martha Graham's Company, Competing with the Great Mother," *New York Times*, April 4, 2019. www.nytimes.com/2019/04/04/arts/dance/martha-graham-dance-pam-tanowitz-bobbi-jene-smith.html.

Segel, Kim. Interview with author. Oral interview, October 20, 2019.

Smko, Hussein. "Ballade: Rain Song," February 28, 2018. www.youtube.com/watch?v=H9q_nCSeGTc.

Smko, Hussein. "Echoes of Erbil." Vimeo clip. https://vimeo.com/221912062. Accessed July 5, 2018.

Smko, Hussein. Interview with author, by email, July 20, 2017.

Sokolow, Anna. "The Rebel and the Bourgeouise." In *The Modern Dance: Seven Statements of Belief*, edited by Selma Jean Cohen and Eric Hawkins, 29–37. Middletown, CT: Wesleyan University Press, 1966.

Thomas-Wood, Marnie. Interview with author, by email, January 28, 2020.

Töniges, Sven. "'Dance Is My Passport': Syrian Ballet Dancer Ahmad Joudeh on Dancing as Home." *DW*. www.dw.com/en/dance-is-my-passport-syrian-ballet-dancer-ahmad-joudeh-on-dancing-as-home/a-48502423. Accessed May 5, 2019.

Van der Zeel, Renate. "'It's Dance or Die': The Ballet Dancer Forbidden to Perform by Islamic State." *The Guardian*, March 13, 2017.

Walker, Amy. "All Hail Stormzy for Historic Glastonbury Performance." *The Guardian*, June 29, 2019. www.theguardian.com/music/2019/jun/29/stormzy-historic-glastonbury-performance.

Warner, Marina. "'Living in the Country of Words.'" In *Others: Writers on Difference*, edited by Charles Fernyhough, 233–51. London: Unbound, n.d.

Warren, Larry. *Anna Sokolow: The Rebellious Spirit*. Amsterdam, Netherlands: Harwood Academic Publishers, 1998.

White-McGuire, Blakeley. Interview with author, November 2, 2020.

White-McGuire, Blakeley. *Program Notes: Our Only World*. January 2, 2020.

Williams, Leslie Andrea. Interview with author, February 14, 2020.

Winship, Lindsey. "Pantsula Revolution! How South Africa's Townships Dance Got Political," *Guardian*, August 10, 2018. www.theguardian.com/stage/2018/oct/08/pantsula-dance-south-africa-via-kanana.

Zhao, Yuting. Interview with author, by email, November 2, 2020.

INDEX

Page references in *italic* refer to images.

alienation 7–10, 12, 13, 15, 16–18, 21,
    22, 24, 25, 27, 32, 34–35, 37, 44,
    47–50, 52, 59, 60, 71, 73, 74, 76,
    77, 78. 85, 89, 91, 95, 105, 106,
    107, 110, 111, 115, 116, 120,
    121, 126, 130, 131, 131, 139,
    140, 145, 148, 151, 155, 167,
    170 n.18, 171 n.28, 171 n.35,
    175 n.69
Allan, Lewis 60
Al Qatan ballet school (in Gaza) 72–74
Anbary, Ahuva 62
Angelou, Maya 63
apartheid 21, 24, 68–71, 72, 76, 118–19
Arendt, Hannah 8, 129, 131, 137,
    182 n.2

Baby Shark 121
Baldwin, James 21, 56
Ballerinas of Cairo 124–25
ballet 21, 24, 64, *74*, 65–87, 97, 103,
    109, 117, 118, 124, 125–26
Ballet Black 68, 80–81
ballet class 21, 65, 72, 73, *74*, 79, 86,
    117
barre 65, 87
Battery Dance 92–93, 94, 96, *102*, 106
Berry, Wendell 165
Birch, Simon 140–42
breakdance 24, 89, 90, 90, 91, 92, 97,
    100, 105

Cape Town Performing Arts Board
    69–70

Capucilli, Terese 33, 154–55, 158,
    166
Chan, Phil 81–85
Chile 111–12
civil rights movement 53, 55, 62, 65
Conley, Jennifer 50–52
Connelly, Katherine 43, 174 n.45
contraceptive rights 1, 112
Cuesta Camacho, Isable 142–45
Curet, Megan 162–164
    "Isla" 162–64

dabke 117–18, *119*
Darwish, Mahmoud 129, 134–35
Dean, Jodi 5
dialectics 10, 17, 19, 23–24, 34, 35,
    46, 48, 57, 64, 66, 78, 100, 110,
    110, 112, 122, 130, 133, 141,
    143–44, 146–48, 161, 165, 167,
    170 n.18

Eilber, Janet 151, 32
Erbil 89–107, *95*
Euro, Adel 92–93, 96, 106
Extinction Rebellion (Fridays for
    Future) 122–24

Final Bow for Yellowface 68, 81–85
flash-mob 111–16, 123, 125

Gaza 72–75
    Israeli bombing of 72
Geracht Myers, Samantha 50, 95
Gilets Jaunes 113–15, *114*

Goldman, Emma 1, 5, 7, 14, 20, 27, *28*, 56, 64, 105, 114
Graham, Martha 5, 6, 17, 23, *23*, 25, 28–41, *39*, 42–43, 45, 46, 49, 50, 51, 53, 56, 57, 62, 64, 91, 109, 118, 125, 148, 151–62, *152*, 163, 164, 165, 166, 167, 173 n.4, 173 n.21, 174 n.34, 186 n.26
"Chronicle" 3, *23*, 25, 28–41, *39*, 45, 49, 109, 125, 135, 148, 151–62, *152*, *158*, 164, 165, 166, 173 n.17
"Deep Song" 29, 44
"Heretic" 29, 41, 91
"Imperial Gesture" 29
"Lamentation" 29, 165, 173 n.1
"Panorama" 29, 33
"Prelude to Action" *25*, 31–32, 35, 36, 38, 40, 151, 153, 156, 160
refusal to participate in Berlin Olympics 32, 38
"Spectre—1914" 25, 31–36, 151, *152*, 154, *168*, 158, 165, 167
"Steps in the Street" 25, 31–39, *39*, 40, 109, 148, 153, 155, 159, 161, 162, 163
Great March of Return 117–18

Heidegger, Martin 7–9
historical materialism 6, 9, 18, 66, 77–79, 87, 96, 147–48
hip-hop 87, 89, 90, 91, 92, 93, 94, 97, 100, 113
Holiday, Billie 60, 62
Hollander, Jonathan 92–93, 94, 96, 106, 107
Holmes, Rachel 10, 13, 17, 171 n.35, 172 nn.51, 52, 174 n.45
Homans, Jennifer 67
Humphrey, Doris 33, 174 n.34

Jaeggi, Rahel 7–9, 12, 170 n.18
Jean, Amanita, 101–106, *102*
Johannesburg Youth Ballet 70–71
Jones, Kim 31–32
Joudeh, Ahmed 75–79

King, Audrey 70–71
Kurdistan 90, 93, 94

Lebanon protests 24, 120
Leiwsohn sisters 42–43
Louis XIV 67, 79, 85

Mandela, Nelson 69, 72, 118
Martin, John 29, 55, 174 n.27, 185–86 n.26
Martin, Randy 3, 169 n.3
Marx, Eleanor 10–19, 24, 25, 106, 129, 157, 167, 171 n.35, 172 nn.51, 52
as cultural pioneer 13–14
foundation of Gas Workers Union 12
"Go Ahead" 10, 16, 18, 41, 46
socialist-feminism 11–13, 171 n.35
"The Sequel" (conception of dialectic) 15, 17–18, 20, 25, 106, 112, 157, 166
The Woman Question (from a Socialist Point of View) 11–13
Marx, Karl 6, 10, 12, 25, 129, 170 n.18
#MeToo movement 5, 111–12, 117, 122, 152
Morefiled, Jeanne 135, 139

Neighborhood Playhouse 42–44
New Dance Group 45, 55, 57, 174 n.34
Nubian Queen 121–22

Palestine 86, 117–19, 179 nn.16, 21, 24
Palmyra 75–79
Pankhurst, Sylvia 42, 174 n.45
Paris Opera Ballet 125–26
Pazcoguin, Georgina 81–85
plie 63, 65, 74, 86
Poole, David 69–70
praxis 2, 4, 5, 6–7, 9–10, 13–18, 20, 21, 27, 47, 53, 56, 57, 58, 64, 71, 73, 76, 77, 79, 85, 86, 89, 91, 96, 101, 103, 104, 105, 108–9, 110,

196 INDEX

113, 115, 116, 118, 126–27, 129, 131, 133, 135, 136, 151, 167
Primus, Pearl 22, 23, 53–64, *54*, 65
"Hard Times Blues" 55, 56, 61
and Jim Crow 55, 56, 57
Madison Square Garden rally 22, 55
"Negro Speaks of Rivers" 57
"Strange Fruit" 57, 60–63, 177 n.118
travels to Africa 56
white supremacy in reception of 53, 54, 56, 58, 60

Robbins, Jerome (Jerry), 47
Robinson, Cira 81
Rubinstein, Sivan 145–148

Said, Edward 24, 135–140, 145, 148
counterpoint (countepuntal) thinking 136, 137, 140, 145
exilic thinking 137, 139, 140, 148, 185 n.26
Orientalism 82, 139
Sartre, Jean Paul 8, 171 n.28
Simons, Michelle 62–63
Sokolow, Anna 22, 23, 41–53, *45*, 55, 57, 59, 64, 95, 129, 134, 175 n.69
anti-militarism dances 44
"Dreams" 52, 44
Jewish heritage 41–42, 44
"Kaddish" 44, 129
labour movement 41, 43
"Rooms" 44, 47–53, 95, 175 n.72

solidarity 5, 7, 10, 11, 13, 15–18, 21, 22, 24, 25, 27, 32, 35, 37, 38, 41, 48, 50, 52, 53, 61, 63, 71, 73–75, 77–79, 82–83, 85, 87, 89–91, 93, 96–98, 100, 101, 102, 106–7, 110–13, 115, 117, 120–22, 124, 125, 126–27, 130, 136, 141, 148, 153, 155, 156, 159, 163–64, 166–67, 171 n.35, 179 n.15
Stormzy 80
Smko, Hussein 24, 76, 89–107, *102*, 134
Sudan 121–22
Syria 19, 21, 24, 75–79, 86, 93, 94, 95, 143

tango 112–13, 120, 169 n.9, 172 n.7
tendu 65, 74, 86
Thunberg, Greta 122, 183 n.23
transgender rights 115–17, 182 n.12

Union Square 22, 27, *28*

Warner, Marina 131–35
White-McGuire, Blakeley 154, 156, 157, 164–66, *166*
"Our Only World" 165–66
Williams, Leslie Andrea 157–160, *158*
Wood, Marnie Thomas 40

Zhao, Yuting 153–54
Zuma, Jacob 119–20